Religion in the
American Experience

DOCUMENTARY HISTORY OF THE UNITED STATES

Edited by Richard B. Morris

Chronological Volumes:

David B. Quinn THE DISCOVERY OF AMERICA HR/1505

Alden T. Vaughan: THE PURITAN TRADITION IN AMERICA

Charles Gibson: THE SPANISH TRADITION IN AMERICA HR/1351

Y. F. Zoltvany: THE FRENCH TRADITION IN AMERICA HR/1425

Milton M. Klein: THE DUTCH AND QUAKER TRADITIONS IN AMERICA

Aubrey Land: BASES OF PLANTATION SOCIETY HR/1429

Jack P. Greene: GREAT BRITAIN AND THE AMERICAN COLONIES, 1606-1763 HR/1477

Richard B. Morris: THE AMERICAN REVOLUTION, 1763-1783 HR/1504

Forrest McDonald: CONFEDERATION AND CONSTITUTION HR/1396

Noble E. Cunningham, Jr.: THE EARLY REPUBLIC, 1789-1828 HR/1394

Jack M. Sosin: THE OPENING OF THE WEST HR/1424

Gilbert C. Fite: THE WEST, 1830-1890

Robert V. Remini: THE AGE OF JACKSON

Stanley Elkins & Gerald Mullin: DOCUMENTS IN THE HISTORY OF SLAVERY

Walter Hugins: THE REFORM IMPULSE (1828-1847)

James P. Shenton: THE CIVIL WAR

La Wanda and John Cox: RECONSTRUCTION, THE NEW SOUTH, AND THE NEGRO

John A. Garraty: THE TRANSFORMATION OF AMERICAN SOCIETY, 1870-1890 HR/1395

Richard M. Abrams: THE ISSUES OF THE POPULIST AND PROGRESSIVE ERAS, 1892-1912 HR/1428

Earl Pomeroy: THE FAR WEST IN THE TWENTIETH CENTURY

Stanley Coben: WORLD WAR, REFORM, AND REACTION

William E. Leuchtenburg: THE NEW DEAL: *A Documentary History* HR/1354

Louis Morton: UNITED STATES AND WORLD WAR II

Robert E. Burke: DOMESTIC ISSUES SINCE 1945

Topical Volumes:

Alan F. Westin: THE SHAPING OF THE CONSTITUTION (2 volumes)

Herbert G. Gutman: THE LABOR MOVEMENT (2 volumes)

Robert D. Cross: THE IMMIGRANT IN AMERICAN HISTORY

Douglass C. North & Robert Paul Thomas:
THE GROWTH OF THE AMERICAN ECONOMY TO 1860 HR/1352

William Greenleaf: AMERICAN ECONOMIC DEVELOPMENT SINCE 1860 HR/1353

Hollis R. Lynch: THE AMERICAN NEGRO IN THE TWENTIETH CENTURY

I. B. Cohen: HISTORY OF SCIENCE IN AMERICA

Richard C. Wade: THE CITY IN AMERICAN HISTORY

Robert H. Ferrell: FOUNDATIONS OF AMERICAN DIPLOMACY, 1775-1872,
Volume I HR/1393

Robert H. Ferrell: AMERICA AS A WORLD POWER, Volume II HR/1512

Robert H. Ferrell: AMERICA IN A DIVIDED WORLD, Volume III

Stanley J. Reisor: HISTORY OF MEDICINE

Robert T. Handy: RELIGION IN AMERICA

Religion in the American Experience:

The Pluralistic Style

Edited by

ROBERT T. HANDY

HARPER & ROW, PUBLISHERS
New York, Evanston, and London

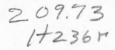

Contents

IV. THE SEARCH FOR UNITY

Introduction

THE HISTORICAL study of religion in the United States grows in both interest and difficulty as the pervasive realities of religious pluralism are recognized for their central importance. Pluralism is an important theme in nearly every aspect of American religious history. As far back as records run, the American religious experience has been a pluralistic one. The religion of the American Indians was pluriform, and remnants of those various patterns continued long after the coming of the white man. Christianity was transplanted from Europe in many forms, to which were added some new, indigenous ones. The faith of Judaism evolved in the United States into three main patterns. In the twentieth century increased mobility has brought representatives of almost every living faith to the North American continent. Therefore, any effort to understand what religion has meant historically on the American scene must assess what influences the pluralistic setting has had on the religious life and thought of individuals and groups— both those involved in organized religion and those not. The pluralistic style of dealing with religion has set its stamp on both the spiritual life and the religious institutions of the American people.

The Christian settlers of the North American continent were very confident of the superiority of their faith over what they understood to be the "pagan superstitions" of the "uncivilized" inhabitants of the land. The story of their efforts to win converts, though it has some heroic chapters, was not marked by signal success. True, the achievements of the Puritan "Apostle to the Indians," John Eliot, for example, proved significant, and the witness of such martyrs as Father Isaac Jogues was impressive. To this day, a network of schools and missions has been maintained among the Indians. But that humanitarian work was soon overshadowed by the displacement of the Indians by land-hungry whites, a tale filled with cruelties, injustices, and broken promises, and marked by savage and hopeless reprisals. The Europeans largely despised the spiritual inheritance of the Indians or condescendingly regarded it as a primitive survival. Yet the American Indian was a religious being, firm in his adherence to ceremonial rights and usages. His life of danger and uncertainty fed the longing for relationship with the unseen world about him. Indian life and religion was and remains notably pluralistic; there are more than fifty linguistic stocks north of Mexico and approximately two hundred Indian languages that are mutually unintelligible. The whole story of religion in America must include the faiths of those who preceded the Western invaders and who continued in those traditions, as well as those who were won to the Christian way.

The Christianity that was destined to become the dominant religion of the United States was transplanted to North American shores *after* the major sixteenth-century divisions of the Western church into Roman Catholic, Lutheran, Reformed, Anglican, Anabaptist, and other communities had taken place. The religious picture was further complicated because these various traditions did not develop homogeneously. Roman Catholic life varied somewhat from country to country, though there were certain similarities and all were under one authority. Differences among Italian, French, Spanish, German, and Irish Catholicism were well known. Lutheran churches in the various states of divided Germany and in the Scandinavian countries developed along somewhat distinctive lines in matters of government and piety, though they all adhered to the Augsburg Confession of 1530. The Reformed or Calvinist churches produced a number of confessions of faith, and showed important differences in their Swiss, French, Hungarian, German, Dutch, Scottish, and English settings. In some places they were established under the law, as were most Catholic and Lutheran churches; in other places they were persecuted minorities. In England, the Reformation had followed a distinctive and somewhat erratic course, but by the time of Queen Elizabeth I (1558–1603) the Church of England had become a broad national church clearly separate from Rome but with strong continuities with the early English Catholic traditions. The term "Anabaptist" was applied to a wide range of small, fluid, quite diverse groups, some with a strong biblical orientation, others mystically inclined. But they all broke with the patterns of the legal establishment of religion and suffered persecution for rejecting the long-accepted traditions of Western Christendom. The pluralization of the Christian tradition along several lines had thus already gone far by the time North

America was settled. This was not so evident in Europe, where in given areas particular churches retained their established position. But it became peculiarly visible when representatives of these many strands encountered one another in the New World.

One other complicating factor should be mentioned: by the early seventeenth century, when the permanent settlements of Europeans in North America began to spread, some of the particular Christian traditions, already diversifying along nationality lines, had begun to interact on one another. Especially significant for the American scene was the effort of the English Puritan Calvinists to push the Church of England closer to the style of the Reformed or Presbyterian churches of the continent. Out of this long struggle, which stimulated the large Puritan migration to New England before it came to its climax in the Puritan Revolution of the 1640's, came the fracturing of the comprehensiveness of the Church of England. Defeated groups of Puritans emerged from the Restoration of 1660 as the "three old denominations" (Presbyterian, Congregational, Baptist) which were thrust out of the Established Church along with a number of more radical sects, such as the Quakers. The dissenting bodies were subjected to sharp persecution, but with the success of the Glorious Revolution of 1688 and the passage of the Toleration Act the following year, they were given grudging toleration. Thus in England by the end of the seventeenth century the denominational system, with its recognized patterns of pluralism, was displacing the territorial system, with its expectancy of religious uniformity. In most places on the continent, the territorial system continued.

Immigration brought representatives of virtually all of these religious groups to North America in the colonial period. To be sure, certain groups came in force into certain areas, intending to maintain the familiar patterns of religious uniformity and establishment. Thus the leaders of the southern colonies of Virginia, Maryland, the Carolinas, and Georgia established the Church of England by law—although they were soon plagued by various minority groups. In four of New York's ten counties, a Ministry Act of 1693 was at times interpreted in favor of the Church of England. The most effective colonial establishments of religion, however, were those formed by the Puritan Congregationalists in Massachusetts (then including Maine), Connecticut, and New Hampshire. The efforts of the Puritans to keep dissenters out of their Zion is a familiar one. Finally, of course, they failed, although the establishments survived in progressively weaker forms until the early nineteenth century. In certain areas, notably in Rhode Island and Pennsylvania, which were devoted to religious freedom, there was extensive religious pluralism from the beginning.

Though most of the immigrants from abroad thought of themselves as Christians, many had only nominal or very slight ties with any church. Some who were numbered among the faithful in Europe did not or could not maintain active connections across the Atlantic. The spiritual life of the unchurched is part of the American experience of religion.

The difficult plight of Jews in Western Christendom has often been described. Some of them came to America seeking freedoms which were denied them elsewhere. Although there were individual Jews in the colonies early in the seventeenth century, the first group to arrive settled in 1654 in what was then still New Amsterdam (soon to become New York). The group comprised Sephardic (Spanish and Portuguese) Jews from Brazil, where the Dutch colony in which they had found freedom had been taken by the Portuguese. Other groups of Jewish refugees, also followers of the Sephardic liturgy, settled in the seaport cities: Newport, Savannah, Philadelphia, Charleston, and Richmond. The total Jewish population was no more than 2,500 by 1776—a very small minority indeed.

The main outlines of American religious pluralism were indelibly set by the end of the colonial period. Immigration not only continued but sharply increased in the nineteenth century, reaching its peak in the early twentieth until it was largely cut off by legislation in 1924. The varieties of American religion further multiplied. Lutheranism, for example, had its German, Finnish, Danish, Swedish, and Norwegian components—often several of each—while the Reformed churches had French, German, Hungarian, Dutch, Scottish, and English branches. The map of Judaism was redrawn several times as a large influx of Ashkenazic (German) Jews entered from about 1820 to 1880, totaling perhaps a quarter of a million. This wave was dwarfed in turn after 1880 by the arrival of several million predominantly Yiddish-speaking Jews from eastern Europe, also grouped as Ashkenazi.

If Indian religion was largely ignored or despised by the whites, the religion the blacks followed in Africa was all but stripped from them through the terrors of the slavery system. How much the African religious past was remembered and continued to influence the spiritual life of the blacks is a matter of scholarly debate, but it does not appear to have been very great. Some efforts to convert the slaves to Christianity were made, after it had been made clear that baptism did not bring freedom. Perhaps one Negro in six had entered church membership by the Civil War. Many slaves did become deeply devout, and found in the biblical stories remarkable vehicles for transmitting faith and aspiration. By the close of the eighteenth century black Christians both slave and free worshiped with whites in many instances. As the freemen encountered the bar of color in white churches, however, they resorted to congregations of their own—the first of which we have record was a Baptist church at Silver Bluff, North Carolina, founded before the Revolution. When, in 1787, Richard Allen, a devout black Methodist, and some fellow worshipers were treated unjustly and discourteously in a Philadelphia church, they withdrew to form an independent movement which later grew into the African Methodist Episcopal Church. The number of black congregations and denominations increased slowly but steadily until just after the Civil War—then the influx of the new freemen was spectacular. The blacks usually did not feel at home in the white churches, nor were they wanted there, while their own churches were institutions under their own control, giving them a sense of belonging. Black Baptist (the National Baptist conventions) and Methodist (African Methodist Episcopal, A.M.E. Zion, and Colored [later Christian] M.E.) bodies predominated, but other independent groups arose. After the Negro thrust into the North during and after World War I a number of black sects, often Pentecostalist in nature, were formed.

In the last great wave of immigration from Europe during the first two decades of the twentieth century the churches of Eastern Orthodox traditions rapidly increased in number and size. Eastern Christianity has many similarities to Roman Catholicism in such things as the emphasis it places on the importance of bishops, the early ecumenical councils, and the seven sacraments. The Eastern and Western traditions had been moving in different directions religiously and culturally before the definitive break in 1054, after which there was no recognition of the primacy of the Pope by the Orthodox. A number of Russian Orthodox Christians entered

American life when Alaska was purchased in 1867; by the turn of the century both Russian and Greek Orthodox churches had become sizable bodies, along with smaller numbers from Orthodox communions in eastern Europe and the Near East. Following World War I these churches were reorganized largely along lines of nationality—Russian, Greek, Rumanian, Ukrainian, Serbian, Syrian, Bulgarian, Armenian, and others. Though accurate statistics are not available, by 1970 these churches together claimed somewhere around 3 million followers, and greatly added to the pluralism of religion in the United States.

Organized religion has been further pluralized by the impact of controversies of various kinds, a number of which have led to schisms. In the eighteenth century, for example, tensions over the theology and practices of the Great Awakenings led to the withdrawal of the Separates from the established churches of New England. At the other extreme, Congregationalists who had been drawn deeply into the thought patterns of the Enlightenment, with its stress on reasonable and natural religion, found themselves in increasing tension with more orthodox Calvinists. In the early nineteenth century the Unitarian schism disrupted many congregations and led to the formation of a new and separate denomination after 1815. At about the same time some became convinced that finally all men were saved, and on this doctrine were the Universalist churches founded. This new denomination developed along very liberal lines, much like the Unitarians, and in 1961 the two bodies finally merged.

Theological differences, notably over the nature of revivalism, contributed to the disruption of Presbyterianism in the middle of the eighteenth century and again in 1837. Both of these divisions were overcome, in each case after several decades, though before the nineteenth-century division was healed, the controversy over slavery further divided each part along sectional lines, thus roughly "quartering" the denomination. After the war the southern bodies formed the Presbyterian Church in the United States and the northern ones the Presbyterian Church in the United States of America. The first major divisions over slavery, however, had been those of the Methodist and Baptist denominations in 1844–1845. The Methodist schism was finally overcome nearly one hundred years later (1939), but the Baptist split goes on. There were a number of other divisions over various issues, some of which have since been overcome.

The religious ferment of nineteenth-century America and the atmosphere of freedom and opportunity combined to create conditions fostering the rise of indigenous religious groups. Best known, perhaps, are the Christian Churches (Disciples of Christ), the Latter-Day Saints (Mormons), the Church of Christ (Scientist), the Seventh-Day Adventists, the Jehovah's Witnesses, and the various Pentecostal groups. The twentieth century has witnessed a vast increase in the total number of denominations. Swelling the total have been groups as differing as those which have drawn their basic direction from the currents of "New Thought" and divine science philosophies to the ultraconservative, pietistic sects.

Pluralistic from the start, American religion has grown steadily more diverse through the centuries. Edwin Scott Gaustad's *Historical Atlas of Religion in America* (New York, 1962) provides useful maps and graphs that give precision to such brief general descriptions as the one given here, while the annual *Yearbook of American Churches* gives the most recent statistical reports as to the size of the various denominations, along with much other information about them. From the 1970 edition, a summary (in millions) of the number of members of the twenty largest American churches is as follows:

Roman Catholic Church	47.9
Southern Baptist Convention	11.3
United Methodist Church	11.0
National Baptist Convention, USA, Inc.	5.5
Episcopal Church	3.4
United Presbyterian Church, USA	3.2
Lutheran Church in America	3.2
Lutheran Church—Missouri Synod	2.8
National Baptist Convention of America	2.7
American Lutheran Church	2.6
Churches of Christ	2.4
Church of Jesus Christ of Latter-Day Saints	2.1
United Church of Christ	2.0
Greek Orthodox Archdiocese of North and South America	1.9
Christian Churches (Disciples of Christ)	1.6
National Primitive Baptist Convention, Inc.	1.4
American Baptist Convention	1.4
Russian Orthodox Greek Catholic Church of America (now the Orthodox Church in America).	1.0

American religious life, thought, and organization have been deeply affected by this pluralistic setting. Pluralism has been accompanied by a train of interrelated consequences which have set their mark on all expressions of religion in the United States. At least four chief characteristics distinguish the pluralistic style of religion in America.

First, there has come about over the centuries virtually unanimous acceptance of religious freedom. Many factors worked together to bring about religious liberty on the American scene, but probably religious multiplicity was the most important single influence, for it meant that no one group could remain strong enough to enforce its will on others. Nor should other factors which contributed to the coming of freedom be overlooked. Some religious groups, especially those stemming from the Anabaptist movement or from the radical wing of Puritanism (Separatists, Baptists, Quakers), had developed biblical and theological arguments for religious liberty, and directly contributed in thought and deed to its coming, on occasion suffering persecution for their beliefs. Others, though accustomed to having their religion supported by law in Old World and New, saw their favored position snatched away from them by the force of circumstances or by the determined opposition of others, and had no choice but to accept their changed status. Some groups which had been clearly committed to the state-church pattern in Europe constituted a minority in America, and soon learned the advantages of freedom. For example, the first Roman Catholic bishop in the United States, John Carroll, sincerely believed that "the great principle of religious freedom" was best for the new nation and best for his church in America. The Episcopal churches quickly came to terms with the lose of the privileged status they had held in the Southern colonies, and rejoiced in the "full and equal liberty" of all religious bodies. Though the last to lose their established status, the Congregational churches of New England were quick to join their voices in praise of freedom, so enthusiastically that some of their followers thought it had always been so.

Once religious freedom was accepted, and the separation of church and state as a means of safeguarding it guaranteed by the First Amendment to the Constitution, no external authority remained to halt or resist the split of an existing church, to prevent

the founding of a new one, or to stop the transplantation of a
religion from abroad. Almost all supporters of religion in America
came to believe sincerely in religious freedom and accepted it as
best both for the churches and for society as a whole. So too, those
little interested in or actively hostile to organized religion, who
have almost axiomatically favored religious freedom.

Second, the voluntary way of winning converts, cultivating constituencies, securing financial support, and attaining mission and
organizational goals began early to characterize religion in America.
In his stimulating book *The Lively Experiment: The Shaping of
Christianity in America* (New York, 1963), Sidney E. Mead has
analyzed the impact on religion of the "voluntaryism" that has
been the corollary of religious liberty. Spiritual leaders have had to
seek and to hold the consent and confidence of the faithful if they
were to be effective. Various organizations have been in competition with each other. At times the conflict has been direct and
bitter; while at other periods, as in the more recent ecumenical era,
the competition has been more indirect and has been moderated
by interdenominational and interreligious cooperation. Not only
have all churches had to assume a voluntary character, but they
have often found that the most effective way to accomplish their
ends was through the proliferation of voluntary societies of various
types.

Third, and intimately related to the voluntaryism of the
churches, has been the stress on activism in American religion.
Given the setting of pluralism, freedom, and voluntaryism, religious bodies soon learned that they could survive only as they faced
with determination the challenges of the American scene with its
great numbers of unchurched people, its vast expanse of territory,
and, by the twentieth century, its formidable urban problems. Such
leaders as the frontier revivalists, the urban missionaries, the social
gospel reformers, and the church bureaucrats learned to become
men of action. Charles Grandison Finney, seminal figure in the
shaping of modern revivalism, once summarized much American
experience in saying that "religion is something to do, not something to wait for." As many observers have noticed, the Catholic
orders that have been concerned with propaganda and good works
have been in the great majority in this nation. American religious
activism has had impressive achievements at home and abroad, but

they have often been at the expense of the virtues of contemplation and meditation, and to the detriment of significant intellectual achievement.

Fourth in this brief characterization of the meaning of the pluralistic style for American religious life is what can be called the internalization of pluralism in the many congregations, denominations, and religious societies and agencies across the land. As religious bodies, ranging from local through regional to national levels, have put their activism to work in order to fulfill their mission, they have reached out and drawn many persons into their network of activities and organizations. In so doing, they have gathered in those who have often been touched, directly or indirectly, by at least one, usually more, of the many religious currents that have flowed in American life. In their haste (and need) to gather supporters, churches have not had or taken the time seriously to educate their new followers, and have in turn been influenced by many streams of life that do not flow out of their own histories. A combination of superficiality and liberality has contributed to the obscuring of differences among the many strands of American religion, a similarity frequently noted, which has been an important factor in the rise of cooperation and ecumenicity. But it has also had as a consequence the fact that given congregations and denominations encompass in their memberships those of quite conflicting feelings and viewpoints about religion, and has been part of the reason why religious bodies find their sense of identity and purpose blurred in the later twentieth century. For in the present century the denominations have ballooned statistically in an impressive way; in 1900 about 35 percent out of a total population of some 25 million were claimed as church members, while seventy years later about 65 percent of a total population exceeding 200 million were at least nominally on church rolls. As the churches and synagogues have taken in members of varying backgrounds and of greatly different spiritual intensities, they have internalized much of the pluralism of the American religious experience. The proliferation of printed materials and of radio and television programs has also contributed a share to the inner diversity of congregations and denominations. Hence, although it is true that the particular histories and doctrinal assertions of the various denominations do continue to have shaping influence and defining force, it is also true that the effects of pluralism have been internalized in the churches. The general spectrum of religious feelings and theological beliefs tends to be reduplicated, with certain distinctive variations, in denomination after denomination. Followers of a certain style of piety or members of a given theological camp often feel more at home with like-minded persons of another denomination than they do with their own fellow denominationalists who belong to an opposition group. Hence the pluralistic style of American religion is not only a matter of religious multiplicity, but has penetrated to the inner citadels of religious institutions.

There have been many efforts to bring the divided churches into some form of larger unity. Somewhat ironically, most efforts toward unity are themselves deeply influenced by the pluralistic style. Efforts toward unity have ranged all the way from the promotion of good will and mutual understanding through institutional cooperation in pursuit of limited goals to actual organizational union. As the largest and most pluralized of the major traditions, Protestantism has seen repeated attempts at various levels to secure greater unity. Thus a "Plan of Union" of 1801 between Congregational and Presbyterian churches brought those sister denominations into virtual union on the frontier for many decades. In 1838 a quite different approach was proposed by a Lutheran pastor, Samuel S. Schmucker. He published a *Fraternal Appeal to the American Churches, with a Plan for Catholic Union on Apostolic Principles*, the first of many such plans for broad Protestant federation or union. So formidable proved to be the obstacles in the path of such plans that various alternates were devised to give channels for cooperation despite the continuation of denominational sovereignty. A whole network of nondenominational voluntary societies for missions, education, publication, dissemination of the Bible, and benevolent and reform enterprises was created in the early nineteenth century.

These nondenominational societies were supported by Christians from many denominations as individuals, yet for the most part the Protestant leadership supported the voluntary undertakings. Committed to religious freedom, evangelical Protestants were nevertheless determined to make America a more Christian (by which they meant a more Protestant) nation. They were convinced it could be done through the voluntary societies by pressure of public opinion. Believing that they were on the side of truth, they assumed that good men would be convinced of the rightness of their efforts, while others could properly be pushed into line.[1] They did not repudiate pluralism—they insisted on religious freedom for themselves, and their denominations remained fully autonomous. But they qualified pluralism by seeking to advance evangelical Protestantism by vigorous use of voluntary means and public opinion while vehemently opposing certain other options, such as Roman Catholicism and Unitarianism. They believed that through the voluntary approach a nation with genuine religious freedom could become a Christian nation and were baffled and annoyed when those who did not share their premises declared they were being persecuted. For the evangelical leaders believed that they represented the best part of an advancing Christian civilization soon to be triumphant in the land and across the world. They did not feel deeply the need for the official coordination of their evangelical churches and agencies, for the Christian civilization of which they were all a part provided sufficient unity for their purposes.

During the latter decades of the nineteenth century and the opening years of the twentieth, however, new and difficult situations confronted the Protestant forces. The great tide of immigrants in those years brought many non-Protestants into the country. The Roman Catholic church gained especially, but sizable numbers of Jews, Eastern Orthodox, and persons only nominally related to any religion or openly secular in orientation arrived. At the same time, the industrialization and urbanization of the country proceeded rapidly. Currents of naturalistic and scientific thinking that were often hostile to organized religion were attracting attention. Under these changing conditions, the task of affirming the Protestant character of American life was proving more formidable, and the individualistic, voluntary way of attempting to deal with the problems of pluralism appeared quite inadequate. Hence, a number of Protestant churches began to reach out to form official agencies of cooperation in order to deal more effectively with the situation. At the national level, conspicuous associations that en-

1. On this point, see John R. Bodo, *The Protestant Clergy and Public Issues, 1812–1848* (Princeton, 1954); Robert T. Handy, *A Christian America: Protestant Hopes and Historical Realities* (New York, 1971); Martin E. Marty, *Righteous Empire: The Protestant Experience in America* (New York, 1970).

joyed the official support of a number of churches were the Foreign
Missions Conference of North America, which traced its origins
back to 1893, the Missionary Education Movement (1902), the
Home Missions Council (1908), and especially the Federal Council of the Churches of Christ in America (1908).[2] Such agencies
were at first almost wholly Protestant in makeup. The Federal
Council and the allied agencies accepted the realities of pluralism
and were devoted to religious freedom, but they sought by official
denominational cooperation to maintain the Protestant character
of American life in a time of change.

Many events led to the recognition and (in many cases reluc-
tant) acceptance by Protestants of the fact that twentieth-century
America was no longer a Protestant nation, and that the prevailing
trend in the culture was in a secular direction. The shock of World
War I, the disillusionments of the 1920's, the Depression, the rise
of the dictators, World War II, the liberating papacy of Pope John
XXIII and the Second Vatican Council, and especially the "coming of age" as fully American of Catholicism, Judaism, and Orthodoxy have all played a role in ending the "Protestant era" of
American history. By mid-twentieth century it had become generally clear that American religious pluralism could no longer be
thought of in primarily Protestant terms with some tolerated
"minority" groups on the fringes, but it had to be seen as a
complex, radical, and unqualified pluralism involving Roman Catholicism, several types of Judaism and Mormonism, a score of
Eastern Orthodox communions, many denominations of Protestants, and a wide range of smaller movements, some of which are
related to historic Christianity, while others are of quite different
background. The "coming of age" of the black Protestant
churches, which had customarily been overlooked as significant
partners by white Protestants, further highlighted the complex
nature of American religious pluralism.

In this changing context, the earlier Protestant cooperative
agencies began to take on broader ecumenical aspects, and to
include Orthodox churches and, to some extent, Catholics. The

2. These developments are explained fully in two books by Samuel McCrea
Cavert, *The American Churches in the Ecumenical Movement, 1900–1968*
(New York, 1968), and *Church Cooperation and Unity in America: A
Historical Review: 1900–1970* (New York, 1970).

National Council of the Churches of Christ in the United States of America, which replaced the Federal Council and a number of other cooperative agencies in 1950, had the much greater support of Orthodox churches, and by the late 1960's was securing increasing cooperation from Roman Catholicism. The National Council has been broadly liberal in theological tone and has been receptive to the contributions of those who stress the social role of religious organizations. A number of smaller conservative Protestant churches and agencies, critical of this stance, organized the National Association of Evangelicals in 1942.

A quite different road toward larger unity has been marked out by the union of denominations. Some of these approaches have been achieved within a given denominational family, as when the Presbyterian church in the United States of America joined with the United Presbyterian Church (a smaller group of Scottish background) to form the United Presbyterian Church in the United States of America in 1958. Several major events of Lutheran unification occurred in the early 1960's, when what had been eight churches became two, the Lutheran Church in America and the American Lutheran Church (see Document 28). The Methodist church joined with the Evangelical United Brethren Church (of German background) to form the United Methodist Church in 1968. One of the successful unions was across denominational lines, for in 1957 the formation of the United Church of Christ brought together churches of Congregational, Reformed, Lutheran, and Christian (a body which had originated in the frontier revivalism of the early nineteenth century) backgrounds. In 1962 a Consultation on Church Union was begun; by the end of the decade it had developed a Plan of Union for the nine denominations in its membership.[3]

Alongside the efforts of the denominations to find larger areas of cooperation and to explore possibilities of union, the latter part of the twentieth century has seen significant fresh interest in religious dialogue across the boundaries of religious traditions in all categories. Not only have there been notable increases in Catholic-

3. African Methodist Episcopal Church, African Methodist Episcopal Zion Church, Christian Churches (Disciples of Christ), Christian Methodist Episcopal Church, Episcopal Church, Presbyterian Church in the United States, United Church of Christ, United Methodist Church, United Presbyterian Church.

Protestant and Christian-Jewish dialogues, but new exchanges between Eastern and Western religions have been opened. True, many persons have remained quite untouched by these developments, and older attitudes rejecting such encounters have persisted. The various ecumenical and interreligious endeavors themselves illustrate the pluralistic style, for they take many forms, are devoted to religious liberty, use voluntary means, tend to be activistic, and themselves internalize much of the pluralism with which they seek to deal.

Within and beyond the various forms of organized religion in the United States, many Americans have found a rich and satisfying religious life. Many have found that the view of ultimate reality they glimpsed from their exposure to religious teachings was fundamentally true and that the spiritual comfort they found was genuine. At the same time, many of the faithful as well as those indifferent or hostile to organized religion have felt that much in American church life has been superficial if not commercialized, and that the patterns of race, nationality, and class have not been sufficiently overcome. Critics from both inside and outside the denominations have suggested that organized religion has too easily sanctified the American style of life, and has provided a halo for what is essentially a civil religion.[4] The devout have often advanced such criticism in the hope that the core of truth in their tradition could be separated from the husks that have grown around it, while the indifferent have more often sought to reduce the influence of institutions that do not seem to them to have solid foundations.

To document with any fullness the American experience of religion in a single small volume is manifestly impossible. Something of the vastness of the literature of American religion can be glimpsed in such a fine work as A Critical Bibliography of Religion in America, by Nelson R. Burr (Princeton, 1961). This selective, narrative bibliography covers some 1,200 pages and gives some indication of the vast field of available materials for a documentary history. The selections for this collection have been made with an eye to providing sample illustrations of the pluralism of American

4. See H. Richard Niebuhr, The Kingdom of God in America (New York, 1937), which has become something of a classic. For a discussion of civil religion, see Elwyn A. Smith (ed.), The Religion of the Republic (Philadelphia, 1971).

religious life and its meaning for the American people. Because one of the volumes in this series deals with Puritanism—Alden T. Vaughan's *The Puritan Tradition in America*—that subject has been accorded limited documentation in this collection. The emphasis has been placed on institutional life rather than on theological thought.[5] The organization is more topical than chronological. The first part focuses on the roots of religious pluralism by attention to some of the forms in which Christianity and Judaism were transplanted from Europe. Part II illustrates tensions within Protestantism that often led to further divisions. The third part considers certain religious patterns that were indigenously developed, while the last part furnishes some examples of the quest for unity in American religion.

Though I am indebted to many teachers, colleagues, and students for countless ideas and suggestions in connection with this and other writings, special thanks go to four persons. Winthrop S. Hudson's friendship, conversations, and books have been helpful in many ways, especially his one-volume treatment of American religious history, *Religion in America* (New York, 1965). H. Shelton Smith and Lefferts A. Loetscher were my colleagues in the preparation of a two-volume work, *American Christianity: An Historical Interpretation with Representative Documents* (New York, 1960–1963). To their insights and wisdom I owe much; fuller treatments of some things so briefly mentioned here can be found in that work. The encouragement and suggestions of the general editor, Richard B. Morris, who has the ability to say much in few words, are especially appreciated.

5. See Sydney E. Ahlstrom (ed.), *Theology in America: The Major Protestant Voices from Puritanism to Neo-Orthodoxy* (Indianapolis, 1967).

I

Transplanting European
Religious Traditions to America

1. Puritan Bulwarks against Pluralism

THE LEADERS of the Puritan settlements of New England set out to build a commonwealth based on what they understood to be the plain law of the Bible. The governments of both state and church were based on the teachings of the Scriptures as they interpreted them. Those conducting the experiments in holy living thought of themselves "as lights upon a Hill more obvious than the highest Mountaine in the World" to reflect the glory of Christ to all. An early effort to recount the history of the new colonies in the wilderness was made by Captain Edward Johnson of Woburn, Massachusetts. Apparently he intended to name his work The Wonder-working Providence of Sion's Saviour in New England, but the London publisher gave it a long title beginning with A History of New England (1654).

An important lay member of the orthodox party in Massachusetts Bay, Johnson summed up the original hopes for New England as held by the Puritan leadership by the literary device of having "the Heralds of a King" give instructions to the colonists before they left England. The great hopes and plaguing fears of the leading Puritans (as remembered after several decades of experience in America) were eloquently expressed. The Puritans were especially afraid of religious pluralism. Convinced that theirs was the best interpretation of God's word, they did not intend to allow others to follow variant paths. In the passage that follows, the "Heralds" instruct the civil leaders to apply all of the Ten Commandments in their governing, both those of the "first table" dealing with duties to God and also those of the "second table," involving duties to man. They were enjoined not to make league with any of seven particular groups of "sectaries." These groups were ones with which Puritan leaders did have trouble in the early years; they presaged the religious pluralism that later triumphed. Some of the groups listed, such as the Gortonists, found refuge in Rhode Island. The Seekers were an English Puritan sect whose members were not convinced that the True Church was to be found amid the warring churches of the day; Roger Williams had moved from Puritan Congregationalism through Separatist and Baptist positions to Seekerism soon after he founded Rhode Island. The principal Antinomian was Anne Hutchinson, who like Williams had been banned from Massachusetts. (She is also referred to in Chapter IV of this document as one of the "silly Women.") Significantly, Roman Catholics and Anglican prelates are also listed among the sectarians. The passage makes clear that religious pluralism was threatening the most rigorous of the American establishments of religion from the beginning, although minority groups were not openly tolerated there until later in the century.

SOURCE: J. Franklin Jameson (ed.), Johnson's Wonder Working Providence, 1628–1651 (Original Narratives of Early American History; New York, 1910), pp. 28–32.

CHAP. IV. *How the People in Christs Churches*
are to behave themselves.

Now you his People, who are pickt out by his provide[nce] to
passe this Westerne Ocean for this honourable service, beware you
call not weake ones to Office in this honourable Army, nor Nov-
ices, lest they be lifted up with pride. You see how full you are
furnished for the worke, give no eare to any Braggadociaes, who to
extoll themselves will weaken the hands of those whom Christ
hath made strong for himselfe. Yea, such will be the phantasticall
madnesse of some (if you take not heed) that silly Women laden
with diverse lusts, will be had in higher esteeme with them, than
those honoured of Christ, indued with power and authority from
him to Preach; Abuse not the free and full liberty Christ hath
given you in making choyce of your own Officers, and consent in
admitting into his Churches, and casting out such Members as
walke disorderly; you are to walke in all humility, lest in injoyment
of such freedoms as you formerly have not exercised, you exceede
the bounds of modesty, and instead of having your moderation
knowne to all, your imbecility, and selfe-exaltation bee discovered
by many. In admission of others into Church society, remember
your selves were once Aliens from the Covenant of Grace, and in
Excommunication, consider how your selves have been also
tempted: in sincerity and singleness of heart, let your words be few,
do nothing [to] be had in high esteeme among men; And think it
no imputation of a weake discerning to be followers of those
[who] are set over you in the Lord as they follow Christ; Let your
Profession outstrip your Confession, for seeing you are to be set as
lights upon a Hill more obvious than the highest Mountaine in the
World, keepe close to Christ that you may shine full of his glory,
who imployes you, and grub not continually in the Earth, like
blind Moles, but by your amiable Conversation seeke the winning
of many to your Masters service. Beware of a proud censorious
spirit, make it no part of your Christian communication to be in
continuall discourse of others faults; Let all things be done in love,
and looke not for more smoothnesse in stones as yet unplaced in
Christs building than is in thy selfe, who has been long layd
therein: wait with patience and cast not off as Reprobates such as

cannot presently joyne with you in every poynt of Discipline, and yet hold fast to sound and wholesome Doctrine. If you will be a people to his prayse, who hath called you, seeke the turning of many to Righteousnesse, purge out all the sowre Leven of unsound Doctrine, for the minde of Christ is to build up his Churches, and breake them down no more; And therefore be sure there be none to hurt or destroy in all his holy Mountaine, and as he hath pressed you for his service, that by passing through the Flouds of Persecution you should be set at liberty, and have power put into your hands, Then let none wrest it from you under pretence of liberty of Conscience. Men of perverse judgements will draw disciples after them, but let your consciences be pure, and Christs Churches free from all Doctrines that deceive. . . .

CHAP. V. What Civill Government the People of Christ ought to set up, and submit unto in New England.

Fayle not in prosecution of the Worke, for your Lord Christ hath furnished you with able Pilots, to steere the Helme in a godly peaceable, Civill Government also, then see you make choyce of such as are sound both in Profession and Confession, men fearing God and hating bribes; whose Commission is not onely limitted with the commands of the second Table, but they are to looke to the Rules of the first also, and let them be sure to put on Joshuas resolution, and courage, never to make League with any of these seven Sectaries.

First, the Gortonists, who deny the Humanity of Christ, and most blasphemously and proudly professe themselves to be personally Christ.

Secondly, the Papist, who with (almost) equall blasphemy and pride prefer their own Merits and Workes of Supererogation as equall with Christs unvaluable Death, and Sufferings.

Thirdly, the Familist, who depend upon rare Revelations, and forsake the sure revealed Word of Christ.

Fourthly, Seekers, who deny the Churches and Ordinances of Christ.

Fifthly, Antinomians, who deny the Morrall Law to be the Rule of Christ.

Sixtly, Anabaptists, who deny Civill Government to be proved of Christ.

Seventhly, The Prelacy, who will have their own Injunctions submitted unto in the Churches of Christ. These and the like your Civill Censors shall reach unto, that the people of and under your Government, may live a quiet and peaceable life in all godlinesse and honesty, and to the end that you may provoke Kings, Princes, and all that are in authority to cast downe their Crownes at the Feet of Christ, and take them up againe at his command to serve under his Standard as nursing Fathers, and nursing Mothers to the Churches and people of Christ; when your feete are once safely set on the shores of America, you shall set up and establish civill Government, and pray for the prosperity thereof, as you love the peace of his Churches, who hath called you to this service, he hath for that end shipped among you, some learned in the Law of God, and practised in rules of good reason or common Lawes proper to our English Nation. Be sure you make choyce of the right, that all people, Nations and Languages, who are soonly to submit to Christs Kingdome, may be followers of you herein, as you follow the Rule of Christ; your Magistrates shall not put open the Gates for all sorts. But know, they are Eyes of Restraint set up for Walles and Bulworks, to surround the Sion of God; Oh for Jerusalem her peace, see that you mind it altogether, you know right well that the Churches of Christ have not thrived under the tolerating Government of Holland, from whence the Lord hath translated one Church [Plymouth] already to the place whither you are now to goe; and further it is well known, loose liberty cannot indure to looke Majesticall authority in the face. . . .

2. Problems of Southern Establishments

SOME OF the many difficulties faced by the establishments of the Church of England in the southern colonies are disclosed in this frank letter by Nicholas Moreau, pastor of St. Peter's Parish in New Kent County, Virginia, to the Lord Bishop of Lichfield and Coventry in England in 1697. The political overtones that mark any established church are evident: Moreau obviously was a strong supporter of the controversial Sir Francis Nicholson, a former governor of the colony who was soon to be reinstated. He was also strongly opposed to James Blair, who served as commissary (assistant) for the Bishop of London in Virginia for more than half a century. The difficulties for the Anglican parishes caused by disease, the low quality of many of the clergy, the tension between nationalities, the infiltration of the Quakers and other dissenters, and the lack of a resident bishop are explained in this as in hundreds of other letters sent back to England. The formation in 1701 of the Society for the Propagation of the Gospel helped some, but it was not possible to secure a bishop for the Episcopal churches in America until after the Revolution.

SOURCE: William Stevens Perry (ed.), *Historical Collections Relating to the American Colonial Church*, Vol. I (Hartford, 1870–1878), pp. 29–32.

VIRGINIA, 12th April, 1697.

MY LORD,

After my dutiful respects presented unto your Lordship, I make bold to acquaint you that being landed in these parts of Virginia in August last, and being ready to go for Maryland, wherein your charity had vouchsafed to recommend me to his Excellency Nicholson, I heard such great talk among the Gentlemen of this Country that the said Governor was to come here to be Governor, that I did resolve to settle here if I could. And his Excellency Nicholson being here, would say nothing of the contrary. His Grace of Canterbury has recommended me to Mr. Blair, Commissary, but to no purpose, because the said Commissary has cast an odium upon himself by his great worldly concerns, so that I was forced to make use of the commander of the fleet who did recommend me to this Parish wherein I live now.

Though I think your Lordship is acquainted somewhat with this Country methinks you shall be glad if I give you some account of our Indians, who indeed, though illiterate & ignorant, have the best secrets any Physician in Europe might have. They have taught me how to cure any intermittent fever in three days time, and did try it effectual; the whole business is, to dip a parcel of root in a glass of wine for four and twenty hours, and the wine so drunk in the morning, fasting, for 3 days, cureth the fever without return. I have learned several other things of them of a very great moment, but it would be too tedious an account for your Lordship. If it pleaseth God to send me over again in England, I shall be heartily willing to communicate these secrets to your Lady, unto whom I make bold to send a small quantity of snake root, the best sudorific, indeed, and counter poison that nature and arts can afford. I don't like this Country at all, my Lord, there are so many inconveniences in it with which I can not well agree. Your clergy in these parts are of a very ill example, no discipline nor Canons of the Church are observed. This Clergy is composed for the most part of Scotchmen, people indeed so basely educated and so little acquainted with the excellency of their charge and duty, that their lives and conversations are fitter to make Heathens than Christians. Several Ministers have caused such high scandals of late, and have raised such prejudices amongst the people against the Clergy, that hardly they can be persuaded to take a minister in their parish. As to me, my Lord, I have got in the very worst parish of Virginia and most troublesome. Nevertheless, I must tell you that I find abundance of good people who are very willing to serve God, but they want good Ministers; ministers that be very pious, not wedded to this world, as the best of them are. God has blessed my endeavors so far already that, with his assistance, I have brought to church again two families, who had gone to the Quakers' meeting for three years past, and have baptized one of their Children three years old. This child being christened took my hand and told me: "You are a naughty man, Mr. Minister, you hurt the child with cold water." His father and mother come to church constantly, and were persuaded by me to receive the Holy Communion at Easter day: which they did perform accordingly with great piety and respect. I have another old Quaker 70 years of age who left the Church these 29 years ago, and hope to bring him to church again within few weeks. *Lucere et non ardere parvum: ardere et non lucere, hoc Imperfectum est: lucere et ardere, hoc perfectum est:*[1] saith St.

1. To enlighten and not to encourage is trifling; to encourage and not to enlighten is faulty; to illumine and to kindle is ideal.

Bernard. If ministers were such as they ought to be, I dare say there would be no Quakers nor Dissenters. A learned sermon signifies next to nothing without good examples. *Longum Iter per prae-cepta, Breve autem per Exempla;*[2] I wish God would put in your mind, my Lord, to send here an eminent Bishop, who by his Piety, charity, and severity in keeping the canons of the Church, might quicken these base ministers, and force them to mind the duty of their charge. Though the whole country of Virginia hath a great respect for my Lord Bishop of London, they do resent an high affront made to their nation, because his Lordship has sent here Mr. Blair a Scotchman, to be commissary, a counsellor, and President of the College. I was once in a great company of Gentlemen, some of them were Counsellors, and they did ask me, "Don't you think there may be in England amongst the English, a clergyman fit to be Commissary and Counsellor and President of our College?" I have wrote all these things, my Lord, freely, but have said nothing by myself. It was only to acquaint your Lordship how the things are here. The Governor is very well beloved by the whole country, but because his time is over they think of another Governor and do desire earnestly to have his Excellency Nicholson, who indeed is a most eminent Governor; and as fit (as said to me, once, your Lordship), to be a Bishop as to be a Governor. If his Excellency was Governor here, and your Lordship would send here a good Bishop, with a severe observation of the Canons of the Church, and eager for the salvation of Souls, there would be a great alteration in the Church. Religion and piety, should flourish presently, and we should be mighty glad and contented. When I do think with myself of Governor Nicholson, I do call him the Right hand of God, the father of the Church, and more, a father of the poor. An eminent Bishop of that same character being sent over here with him, will make Hell tremble and settle the church of England in these parts forever. This work, my Lord, is God's work and if it doth happen that I see a Bishop come over here I will say as St. Bernard said in his Epistle to Eugenius Tertius, *hic digitur Dei est.*[3] I have been very tedious to your Lordship, but God's concerns have brought me to that great boldness. . . .

---

2. The lesson is tedious by giving rules, but short through examples.
3. This is the finger of God.

3. A Presbyterian Accepts Pluralism

CONGREGATIONAL AND Presbyterian churches in the colonial period both adhered to the Westminster Confession, but outside of New England the Presbyterian churches grew rapidly in the eighteenth century, gathering settlers from the British Isles but also from New England. Two main parties were discernible in Presbyterianism, one composed of Puritan Presbyterian groups from England and New England, the other drawn from Scottish and Scotch-Irish elements which tended to be doctrinally strict. Though the Presbyterian Church was established in Scotland, many Presbyterians in the middle colonies had not been treated kindly by the Anglican establishments in Ireland or by the Congregational establishments of New England, and there was growing sentiment for religious freedom. In the following paragraphs from a letter of October 14, 1730, to Thomas Prince of Boston, the Reverend Jedediah Andrews, a Presbyterian pastor in Pennsylvania, described the religious situation in his province, commenting on how well the many religious groups got along together.

SOURCE: Samuel Hazard (ed.), Register of Pennsylvania, 15, 200–202.

Such a multitude of people coming in, from Ireland, of late years, our Congregations are multiplied, in this Province, to the number of 15 or 16, which are all, but 2 or 3, furnished with ministers. All Scotch and Irish, but 3 or 4. Besides divers new Congregations that are forming by these new comers, we all call ourselves Presbyterians, none pretending to be called Congregational, in this Province. In the Jersies there are some Congregat'l assemblies, that is, some of the people are inclined that way, being originally of N. Eng'd, yet they all submit to our Presbytrys readily eno,' and the ministers are all Presbyt'n, tho' mostly from N. E. There is indeed, one Congreg'n in the back pt of Newark, that don't join with us, neither ministers nor People; besides that, all the rest do. There is, in the Jersies, about a dozen Congreg'ns, but not all constantly supplied with preaching; tho' most of 'em are, and the rest getting into a settled way, as fast as they can, and some new Congreg'ns growing up there also. There is, besides, in this Province, a vast number of Palatines, and they come in still, every year. Those that have come of late years, are, mostly, Presbyt'n, or, as they call themselves, Reformed, the Palatinate, being about three-fifths of that sort of people; they did use to come to me, for baptism for their children, and many have joined with us, in the other sacram't. They never had a minister, 'till about 9 years ago, who is a bright young man, and a fine scholar. He is, at present, absent, being gone to Holland, to get money to build a Ch'h, in this City; but they are scattered all over the country; those that live in Town, are mostly a kind of Gibeonites, hewers of wood, &c. They are diligent, sober, frugal people, rarely charged with any misdemeanour. Many of 'em, that live in the country and have farms, by their industry and frugal way of living, grow rich, for they can underlive the Britons, &c. The first comers of 'em, tho' called Palatines, because they came lastly from the country, are mostly Switzers, being drove from the Canton of Bern, for they are Baptists [Anabaptists], and won't fight or swear. They don't shave their heads, and are many of 'em wealthy men, having got the best land in the Province. They live 60 or 70 miles off, but come frequently to Town with their waggons, laden with skins, (which belong to the Indian traders) butter, flour, &c. There are many Lutherans, and some Reformed, mixed among 'em. In other parts of the country they are, chiefly, Reformed; so that I suppose, the Presbyt'n party are as numerous as the Quakers, or near it. There is lately come over a Palatine candidate of the ministry, who having applied to us at the Synod, for Ordin'n, 'tis left to 3 minist'rs to do it. He is an extraordinary person for sense and learning. We gave him a question to discuss about Justification, and he has answered it, in a whole sheet of paper, in a very notable manner. His name is John Peter Miller, and speaks Latin as readily as we do our vernacular tongue, and so does the other, Mr. Weis. The Ch'h [of England] party will not grow much, except in the Town, where there is a great Congreg'n of 'em. There are some few small congreg'ns of 'em in the country.—Tho' there be so many sorts of Religions going on, we don't quarrel about it. We not only live peaceable, but seem to love one another. . . .

The first European Inhabitants here, were low Dutch and Swedes, who got titles from the D. of York, which were confirmed by the Propr'r Mr. Penn. There are in this Province and the Jersies, Swedish assemblies, Lutherans. The ministers come from Sweden, and when they have been here 11 or 12 years, they are sent for home, and others sent in their room, for they think it a kind of hardship to be here, and so they call 'em home and advance 'em.

These Swedish Mission's are usually men of good learning, and good behav'r. They soon learn English, and often preach among Ch'h people in vacant places. I have been well acquainted with some of them, and wrote a certificate, lately, for one, that is going home.

4. Methodist Growth under Asbury's Guidance

THOUGH John Wesley had served as an Anglican missionary in Georgia in the 1730's before he returned to England to become the central figure in Methodism, the beginnings of Methodist work in America date from the 1760's. Several Wesleyan lay preachers then came as immigrants, to be followed by eight lay missionaries named by Wesley. The only one of these to remain active in the work through the American Revolution (and on into the nineteenth century) was Francis Asbury (1745–1816). Born in England of humble circumstances, the devout young man volunteered to serve in America, arriving in 1771. Until his death, he was to travel almost continually, preaching, organizing, and guiding Methodist work. American Wesleyanism was a movement of religious societies in nominal relationship to the Church of England until 1784. When the Revolution ended, Wesley arranged for the American societies to become an independent church, with Dr. Thomas Coke (1747–1814) and Asbury as superintendents. (To Wesley's dismay, they soon adopted the title of bishop.) At the Christmas Conference in Baltimore, the lay leaders of American Methodism accepted the plan, and a number of preachers were ordained. The selections that follow, from early in Asbury's massive Journal, describe his coming to North America and refer to the historic events of 1784.

SOURCE: *Journal of Rev. Francis Asbury, Bishop of the Methodist Episcopal Church*, Vol. I (New York, n.d.), pp. 11–16, 25–26, 486–487.

On the 7th of August, 1771, the Conference began at Bristol, in England. Before this, I had felt for half a year strong intimations in my mind that I should visit America; which I laid before the Lord, being unwilling to do my own will, or to run before I was sent. During this time my trials were very great, which the Lord, I believe, permitted to prove and try me, in order to prepare me for future usefulness. At the Conference it was proposed that some preachers should go over to the American continent. I spoke my mind, and made an offer of myself. It was accepted by Mr. Wesley and others, who judged I had a call. From Bristol I went home to acquaint my parents with my great undertaking, which I opened in as gentle a manner as possible. Though it was grievous to flesh and blood, they consented to let me go. My mother is one of the tenderest parents in the world; but, I believe, she was blessed in the present instance with Divine assistance to part with me. I visited most of my friends in Staffordshire, Warwickshire, and Gloucestershire, and felt much life and power among them. Several of our meetings were indeed held in the spirit and life of God. Many of my friends were struck with wonder, when they heard of my going; but none opened their mouths against it, hoping it was of God. Some wished that their situation would allow them to go with me.

I returned to Bristol in the latter end of August, where Richard Wright was waiting for me, to sail in a few days for Philadelphia. When I came to Bristol I had not one penny of money; but the Lord soon opened the hearts of friends, who supplied me with clothes, and ten pounds: thus I found, by experience, that the Lord will provide for those who trust in him.

On *Wednesday, September* 4, we set sail from a port near Bristol; and having a good wind, soon passed the channel. For three days I was very ill with the sea-sickness; and no sickness I ever knew was equal to it. The captain behaved well to us. On the *Lord's day, September* 8, brother W. preached a sermon on deck, and all the crew gave attention.

Thursday, 12th. I will set down a few things that lie on my mind. Whither am I going? To the New World. What to do? To gain honour? No, if I know my own heart. To get money? No: I am going to live to God, and to bring others so to do. In America there has been a work of God: some moving first amongst the Friends, but in time it declined; likewise by the Presbyterians, but amongst them also it declined. The people God owns in England, are the Methodists. The doctrines they preach, and the discipline they enforce, are, I believe, the purest of any people now in the world. The Lord has greatly blessed these doctrines and this discipline in the three kingdoms: they must therefore be pleasing to him. If God does not acknowledge me in America, I will soon return to England. I know my views are upright now: may they never be otherwise!

On the *Lord's day, September* 15, I preached on Acts xvii, 30: "But God now commandeth all men everywhere to repent." The sailors behaved with decency. My heart's desire and prayer for them was, and is, that they may be saved: but O! the deep ignorance and insensibility of the human heart!

The wind blowing a gale, the ship turned up and down, and

from side to side, in a manner very painful to one that was not accustomed to sailing: but when Jesus is in the ship all is well. O what would not one do, what would he not suffer, to be useful to souls, and to the will of his great Master! Lord, help me to give thee my heart now and forever.

Our friends had forgotten our beds, or else did not know we should want such things; so I had two blankets for mine. I found it hard to lodge on little more than boards. I want faith, courage, patience, meekness, love. When others suffer so much for their temporal interests, surely I may suffer a little for the glory of God, and the good of souls. May my Lord preserve me in an upright intention! I find I talk more than is profitable. Surely my soul is among lions. I feel my spirit bound to the New World, and my heart united to the people, though unknown; and have great cause to believe that I am not running before I am sent. The more troubles I meet with, the more convinced I am that I am doing the will of God.

In the course of my passage I read Sellon's Answer to Elisha Cole, on the Sovereignty of God; and I think, no one that reads it deliberately can afterward be a Calvinist.

On the Lord's day, September 22, I preached to the ship's company on John iii, 23: but alas! they were insensible creatures. My heart has been much pained on their account. I spent my tine chiefly in retirement, in prayer, and in reading the Appeals, Mr. De Renty's life, part of Mr. Norris's Works, Mr. Edwards on the Work of God in New-England, the Pilgrim's Progress, the Bible, and Mr. Wesley's Sermons. I feel a strong desire to be given up to God—body, soul, time, and talents; far more than heretofore.

September 29. I preached to the ship's company again, on these words, "To you is the word of this salvation sent." I felt some drawings of soul towards them, but saw no fruit. Yet still I must go on. Whilst they will hear, I will preach, as I have opportunity. My judgment is with the Lord. I must keep in the path of duty.

On the 6th of October, though it was very rough, I preached on deck to all our ship's company, from Heb. ii, 3: "How shall we escape, if we neglect so great salvation?" The Lord enabled me to speak plainly, and I had some hopes that the interesting truths of the Gospel did enter into their minds. I remember the words of the wise man, "In the morning sow thy seed, and in the evening withhold not thy hand." As to my own mind, I long and pray, that I may be more spiritual. But in this I comfort myself that my intention is upright, and that I have the cause of God at heart. But I want to stand complete in all the will of God, "holy as he that hath called me is holy, in all manner of conversation." At times I can retire and pour out my soul to God, and feel some meltings of heart. My spirit mourns, and hungers, and thirsts, after entire devotion.

October 13. Though it was very windy, I fixed my back against the mizen-mast, and preached freely on those well-known words, 2 Cor. v, 20: "Now then we are ambassadors for Christ, as though God did beseech you by us: we pray you in Christ's stead, be ye reconciled to God." I felt the power of truth on my own soul, but still, alas! saw no visible fruit: but my witness is in heaven, that I have not shunned to declare to them all the counsel of God. Many have been my trials in the course of this voyage; from the want of a proper bed, and proper provisions, from sickness, and from being surrounded with men and women ignorant of God, and very wicked. But all this is nothing. If I cannot bear this, what have I learned? O, I have reason to be much ashamed of many things, which I speak and do before God and man. Lord, pardon my manifold defects and failures in duty.

October 27. This day we landed in Philadelphia, where we were directed to the house of one Mr. Francis Harris, who kindly entertained us in the evening, and brought us to a large church, where we met with a considerable congregation. Brother Pilmore preached. The people looked on us with pleasure, hardly knowing how to show their love sufficiently, bidding us welcome with fervent affection, and receiving us as angels of God. O that we may always walk worthy of the vocation wherewith we are called! When I came near the American shore, my very heart melted within me, to think from whence I came, where I was going, and what I was going about. But I felt my mind open to the people, and my tongue loosed to speak. I feel that God is here; and find plenty of all we need.

November 3. I find my mind drawn heavenward. The Lord hath helped me by his power, and my soul is in a paradise. May God Almighty keep me as the apple of his eye, till all the storms of life are past! Whatever I do, wherever I go, may I never sin against God, but always do those things that please him!

Philadelphia, November 4. We held a watch-night. It began at eight o'clock. Brother P. preached, and the people attended with great seriousness. Very few left the solemn place till the conclusion. Towards the end, a plain man spoke, who came out of the country, and his words went with great power to the souls of the people; so that we may say, "Who hath despised the day of small things?" Not the Lord our God: then why should self-important man?

November 5. I was sent for to visit two persons who were under conviction for sin. I spoke a word of consolation to them, and have hopes that God will set their souls at liberty. My own mind is fixed on God: he hath helped me. Glory be to him that liveth and abideth forever!

Tuesday, November 6. I preached at Philadelphia my last sermon, before I set out for New-York, on Romans viii, 32: "He that spared not his own Son, but delivered him up for us all, how shall he not with him freely give us all things?" This also was a night of power to my own and many other souls.

November 7. I went to Burlington on my way to York, and preached in the court-house to a large, serious congregation. Here also I felt my heart much opened. In the way from thence to York I met with one P. Van Pelt, who had heard me preach at Philadelphia. After some conversation, he invited me to his house on Staten Island; and as I was not engaged to be at York on any particular day, I went with him and preached in his house. Still I believe God hath sent me to this country. All I seek is to be more spiritual, and given up entirely to God—to be all devoted to him whom I love.

On the Lord's day, in the morning, November 11, I preached again to a large company of people, with some enlargement of mind, at the house of my worthy friend Mr. P.; in the afternoon preached to a still larger congregation; and was invited to preach in the evening at the house of Justice Wright, where I had a large company to hear me. Still, evidence grows upon me, and I trust I am in the order of God, and that there will be a willing people here. My soul has been much affected with them. My heart and mouth are open; only I am still sensible of my deep insufficiency, and that mostly with regard to holiness. It is true, God has given me some gifts; but what are they to holiness? It is for holiness my spirit mourns. I want to walk constantly before God without reproof.

On Monday I set out for New-York, and found Richard Boardman there in peace, but weak in body. Now I must apply myself to my old work—to watch, and fight, and pray. Lord, help!

Tuesday, 13. I preached at York to a large congregation on 1 Cor. ii, 2: "I determined not to know anything among you, save Jesus Christ, and him crucified," with some degree of freedom in my own mind. I approved much of the spirit of the people: they were loving and serious; there appeared also, in some, a love of discipline. Though I was unwilling to go to York so soon, I believe it is all well, and I still hope I am in the order of God. My friend B. is a kind, loving, worthy man, truly amiable and entertaining, and of a child-like temper. I purpose to be given up to God more and more, day by day. But O! I come short. . . .

Thursday, the 27th [1772]. We arrived in York. I found brother P. had set off for Philadelphia in the morning. In the evening I met the society, and felt myself assisted and enlarged. At night I slept with holy thoughts of God, and awoke with the same: thanks be to God!

After having preached in a large upper room, at Mr. T.'s in Amboy, where many came to hear, and I was much favoured in my own soul, an innkeeper invited me to his house, and kindly desired that I would call on him when I came again.

Friday, 27. I set off on a rough-gaited horse, for Burlington; and after being much shaken, breakfasted at Spotswood; fed my horse again at Crosswick's, and then thought to push on to Burlington; but the roads being bad, and myself and horse weary, I lodged with a Quaker, on whom I called to inquire the way. He not only invited me to tarry all night, but also treated me with great kindness. The next day I rode to town very weary; and on the Lord's day preached in the court-house to many hearers.

Monday, 30. After riding to New-mills, in company with some friends, in a wagon, I preached in a Baptist meeting-house, and was kindly received.

Tuesday, 31. Finding the people were divided among themselves, I preached from these words: "This is his commandment, that we should believe on the name of his Son Jesus Christ, and love one another;" and humbly hope my labour was not in vain. The same night we came to Burlington. . . .

Saturday, December 4 [1784]. Rode to Baltimore, and preached on Mark xiv, 29, 30, with freedom. I spent some time in town, and was greatly grieved at the barrenness of the people; they appear to be swallowed up with the cares of the world.

Sunday, 12. At the Point my heart was made to feel for the people, while I enlarged on, "Blessed are the pure in heart," &c. I was close and fervent in town at four o'clock. A young man pushed the door open while we were meeting the society; he was carried before a justice of the peace, and committed to jail, but he was bailed out.

Tuesday, 14. I met Dr. Coke at Abingdon, Mr. Richard Dallam kindly taking him there in his coach; he preached on, "He that hath the Son hath life." We talked of our concerns in great love.

Wednesday, 15. My soul was much blest at the communion, where I believe all were more or less engaged with God. I feel it necessary daily to give up my own will. The Dr. preached a great sermon on, "He that loveth father or mother more than me," &c.

Saturday, 18. Spent the day at Perry-Hall, partly in preparing for conference. My intervals of time I passed in reading the third volume of the British Arminian Magazine. Continued at Perry-Hall until *Friday*, the twenty-fourth. We then rode to Baltimore, where we met a few preachers: it was agreed to form ourselves into an Episcopal Church, and to have superintendents, elders, and deacons. When the conference was seated, Dr. Coke and myself were unanimously elected to the superintendency of the Church, and my ordination followed, after being previously ordained deacon and elder, as by the following certificate may be seen.

Know all men by these presents, That I, Thomas Coke, Doctor of Civil Law; late of Jesus College, in the University of Oxford, Presbyter of the Church of England, and Superintendent of the Methodist Episcopal Church in America; under the protection of Almighty God, and with a single eye to his glory; by the imposition of my hands, and prayer, (being assisted by two ordained elders,) did on the twenty-fifth day of this month, December, set apart Francis Asbury for the office of a deacon in the aforesaid Methodist Episcopal Church. And also on the twenty-sixth day of the said month, did by the imposition of my hands, and prayer, (being assisted by the said elders,) set apart the said Francis Asbury for the office of elder in the said Methodist Episcopal Church. And on thie twenty-seventh day of the said month, being the day of the date hereof, have, by the imposition of my hands, and prayer, (being assisted by the said elders,) set apart the said Francis Asbury for the office of a superintendent in the said Methodist Episcopal Church, a man whom I judge to be well qualified for that great work. And I do hereby recommend him to all whom it may concern, as a fit person to preside over the flock of Christ. In testimony whereof I have hereunto set my hand and seal this twenty-seventh day of December, in the year of our Lord 1784.

THOMAS COKE

Twelve elders were elected, and solemnly set apart to serve our societies in the United States, one for Antigua, and two for Nova-Scotia. We spent the whole week in conference, debating freely, and determining all things by a majority of votes. The Doctor preached every day at noon, and some one of the other preachers morning and evening. We were in great haste, and did much business in a little time.

Monday, January 3, 1785. The conference is risen, and I have now a little time for rest. In the evening I preached on Ephes. iii, 8, being the first sermon after my ordination: my mind was unsettled, and I was but low in my own testimony.

Tuesday, 4. I was engaged preparing for my journey southward. Rode fifty miles through frost and snow to Fairfax, Virginia, and got in about seven o'clock.

5. A Catholic Minority in a Protestant Society

As an aftermath of the stormy course of the Reformation in England and of the quarrels of that nation with France and Spain, there was intense anti-Catholic feeling in English society at the time of the settlement of the colonies in the New World. Prejudice against Catholics manifested itself in many ways, as in penal legislation against Catholics in eighteenth-century Maryland (although that colony had been founded originally as a Catholic refuge). The number of Catholic communicants remained small throughout the colonial period; an unknown number of immigrants of Catholic background were lost to the faith in the uncongenial Protestant atmosphere. What Catholics there were fell under the general care of the vicar apostolic of the London district. Bishop Richard Challoner (1691–1781), who had been born a Protestant but reared under Catholic auspices and educated at the émigré college at Douai, was named coadjutor vicar apostolic in 1740. In 1756 he prepared a letter on Catholicism in America, summarizing the overall situation as best he could. The letter was later expanded; for the later version see Smith, Handy, Loetscher, American Christianity, Vol. I, pp. 300–305. The letter illustrates how colonial Catholic life was centered in Maryland and Pennsylvania, and highlights the importance of the Jesuits.

SOURCE: Edwin H. Burton, The Life and Times of Bishop Challoner 1691–1781, Vol. II (London, 1909), pp. 125–127.

As to the state of religion in our American settlements; the best account I can give is:—

1. There are no missioners in any of our colonies upon the continent, excepting Mariland and Pensilvania; in which the exercise of the Catholic religion is in some measure tolerated. I have had different accounts as to their numbers in Mariland where they are the most numerous. By one account they were about 5,000 communicants: another makes them amount to about 7,000: but perhaps the latter might design to include those in Pensilvania; where I believe there may be about 2,000. There are about twelve missioners in Mariland, and four in Pensilvania, all of them of the Society [of Jesus]. These also assist some few Catholics in Virginia, upon the borders of Mariland, and in N. Jersey bordering upon Pensilvania. As to the rest of the provinces upon the continent, N. England, N. York, etc., if there be any straggling Catholics, they can have no exercise of their religion, as no priests ever

come near them: nor, to judge by what appears to be the present disposition of the inhabitants, are ever like to be admitted amongst them.

2. As to the islands, the state of religion is much worse than on the continent. The Catholics we have there are chiefly Irish; and neither priests nor people are half so regular as the Marilandians and Pensilvanians are. In Jamaica there are many Catholics; and two priests in our time have made some attempt to settle there, but could not succeed. The inhabitants are looked upon to be generally almost abandoned wicked people. In Barbadoes there was an Irish Augustinian who apostatized. The few Catholics there have sometimes been helped from Montserrat. This latter, which is one of the least of our Islands, has the greatest number of Catholics, such as they are, under the care of two Irish missioners: but little or nothing is done by them with relation to the care of their negroes who are numerous. There are also some Irish Catholics in the Islands of Antegoa, under the care of a Dominican, who happens to be now in town, and gives us a very indifferent account of the practice of religion among his countrymen there. There are also a few Catholics in the island of St. Christopher's, who are helped sometimes from Montserrat. And not long ago an Irish Augustinian took out faculties here to go and settle in Newfoundland, for the help of a number of his countrymen that were drawn thither by the fishing trade. I take no notice of the neutral French and Indians in Acadia who had their priests from Canada, but have been lately translated hither upon occasion of this present war.

3. All our settlements in America have been deemed subject in spirituals to the ecclesiastical Superiors here, and this has been time out of mind, even, I believe, from the time of the Archpriests. I know not the origin of this, nor have ever met with the original grant. I suppose they were looked upon as appurtenances or appendixes of the English Mission. And, after the division of this kingdom into four districts, the jurisdiction over the Catholicks in those settlements has followed the London district (as they are all reputed by the English as part of the London diocese); I suppose because London is the capital of the British Empire; and from hence are the most frequent opportunities of a proper correspondence with all those settlements. Whether the Holy See has ordered anything in this regard, I cannot learn. But all the missioners in those settlements do now, and have, time out of mind,

applied to the Vicar Apostolic here for their faculties which is true of the *padri* also [the Jesuits] in Mariland and Pennsilvania; at least from the time of the Breve of Innocent XII in 1696, only that they used rather to ask for approbation, but now also for faculties.

4. Some have wished, considering the number of the faithful, especially in those two provinces, destitute of the sacrament of confirmation, and lying at so great a distance from us, that a bishop or vicar should be appointed for them. But how far this may be judged practicable by our superiors I know not: especially as perhaps it may not be relished, by those who have engrossed that best part of the mission to themselves, and who may, not without show of probability, object that a novelty of this kind might give offence to the governing part there; who have been a little hard upon them of late years.

6. The Manifold Transplantations of Lutheranism

LUTHERAN BEGINNINGS in North America go back to the early seventeenth century. The Dutch and Swedish groups were overshadowed by the extensive German immigration of the eighteenth century, which in turn was dwarfed by the vast human tides from the various states of Germany and the Scandinavian countries and Finland in the nineteenth. The Lutherans were divided not only along national but also along theological lines. Lutheran organization developed largely through the formation of state and regional synods. The first significant attempt at an overall organization was the formation of the General Synod in 1820, but it was not all-inclusive. A number of immigrant groups which arrived after it had been founded felt it was too Americanized, and the formation of a rival General Council in 1867 weakened it. Meanwhile, other "old Lutherans" from Germany formed independent organizations of their own, such as the Missouri, Buffalo, Iowa, and Wisconsin Synods. Hence there were more than twenty independent Lutheran churches by the end of the nineteenth century. Because of both language barriers and their distinctive confessional positions, Lutherans remained largely isolated from other Protestant churches until the twentieth century. The following brief interpretation of American Lutheran history gives a glimpse of some of its complexities.

SOURCE: O. M. Norlie and G. L. Kieffer (eds.), *The Lutheran World Almanac and Annual Encyclopedia for 1921*, pp. 66–68.

The Lutheran Synods in America

Shortly after the Reformation there were Lutheran settlements in Florida and South America. But as far as we know, the first Lutheran pastor to come to America and the first to die here was Rasmus Jensen, of Aarhus, Denmark. Pastor Jensen was the ship pastor on the ill-fated Jens Munk expedition to discover a northwest passage. King Christian IV had equipped two ships for this expedition and had placed Munk in charge of it. Munk had 65 men under him, including a pastor and a doctor. He set sail on May 16, 1619, came to Hudson Bay about July 1, and sailed back and forth in this bay until September 7, when he went into winter quarters. Munk has written a diary, which is still to be seen at the University of Copenhagen, in which he tells of the horrible sufferings, from pestilence, hunger, cold and lonesomeness during the next nine months. All died except four, of whom he was one. He tells of his pastor and their Christmas celebration:

"The holy Christmas Day," says he, "we all celebrated and kept, as a Christian should. We had a sermon and chanting, and after the sermon we gave the pastor a Christmas offering according to the good old custom, each one according to his means. Even though money was not plentiful among us, each gave what he had. In lieu of money one man gave a white fox skin, so that the pastor could line his coat, but, alas, after that he was not permitted to wear it out." Munk tells later of the plague attacking both the doctor and the pastor. On January 23 he tells of the pastor's having sat up in his cabin and preached his last sermon to his parish. On February 23 he died. Thus there had been regular Lutheran services in America from September, 1619, until January, 1620, almost a year before the Mayflower pilgrims came to our shores. The Lutherans are not newcomers in this land.

History. The earliest Lutherans to settle in North America came from Holland to Manhattan Island in 1623 with the first Dutch colony. For some years they had great difficulty in establishing worship of their own, the Dutch authorities, ecclesiastical and civil, having received instructions "to encourage no other Doctrine in the New Netherland than the true Reformed." A Lutheran pastor, the Rev. John Ernest Goetwater, was sent to this country in 1657 by the Lutheran consistory of Amsterdam to minister to two Lutheran congregations in New York and Albany, but he was not allowed to enter upon his ministrations, and after a few months was sent back to Holland by representatives of the Reformed faith. When the English took possession of New York, in 1674, the Lutherans were allowed full liberty of worship.

The first independent colony of Lutherans was established on the Delaware by Swedes who were sent over in 1638 by the prime minister of King Gustavus Adolphus. Reorus Torkillus, the first Lutheran minister to settle in the territory of the United States, arrived in 1639. He held Lutheran services in Fort Christina, and the first Lutheran church, a blockhouse, was built soon afterwards.

In 1643 the Rev. John Campanus, another Swedish Lutheran minister, arrived, and in 1646 built a Lutheran church at Tinicum, Pennsylvania, 9 miles southwest of Philadelphia. He also translated Luther's Catechism into the Indian language, antedating Eliot's

Bible, though the latter was published first. In 1669 a block church was erected by the Swedes at Wicaco, now a part of Philadelphia, and about 1694 the first English Lutheran services were held in Germantown and in Philadelphia by Heinrich Bernhard Koester. The block church at Wicaco was superseded in 1700 by the Gloria Dei church at Wilmington, Delaware, the cornerstone of which was laid in 1698. The first German Lutheran church in Pennsylvania, that at Falckner's Swamp, Montgomery County, is thought to date from 1703, and the Rev. Daniel Falckner was its first pastor. In 1710 a large number of exiles from the Palatinate settled in New York and Pennsylvania, and in 1734 a colony of Salzburgers planted the Lutheran church in Georgia. In 1728 the missionary, John Caspar Stoever, traveled from Germantown and the banks of the Delaware to the Susquehanna at York, and finally to Maryland, and organized German Lutheran congregations in the interior of Pennsylvania. But it was left to the Rev. Henry Melchior Muhlenberg, who arrived in Philadelphia in 1742, and became the patriarch of the Lutheran church in America, to bring these primitive congregations into order, to infuse into them a sound piety and a true church life, to provide them with good pastors, and to introduce schools for the education of the children. The sphere of Muhlenberg's activities included New York, New Jersey, and Maryland.

By the middle of the eighteenth century Pennsylvania contained about 30,000 Lutherans of whom four-fifths were Germans and one-fifth Swedes. In 1748 Muhlenberg, with six other ministers and with lay delegates from congregations, organized the Synod, or Ministerium, of Pennsylvania, the first Lutheran Synod in this country. In 1786 the second Synod, the Ministerium of New York, was formed, and in 1803 the Synod of North Carolina; but it was not until 1818, with the organization of the Synod of Ohio, that the growth of the denomination became rapid.

The extraordinary growth of the Lutheran communion in this country is due primarily to immigration from Lutheran countries, a large proportion of American Lutherans being either German immigrants or the offspring of German immigrants. There are also large bodies from Sweden, Norway, Denmark, and Finland, and some from other European countries.

As Lutheran immigration increased there was a corresponding development of activity on the part of different Synods in their efforts to reach all newcomers, the lead being taken by the Pittsburgh Synod, organized in 1843. As a result a number of independent Synods were formed, each adapted to the peculiar condition of language, previous ecclesiastical relation, or geographic location. As, however, the churches came into closer fellowship, the distinctive features in many cases faded out of view and there were evident marked tendencies toward the elimination of the dividing lines. In some instances especially among the smaller Synods, the churches gradually became absorbed in the other Synods. This has been the case in the Texas Synod, the Synod of Michigan, and the Immanuel Synod, while the Slovak Synod joined the Synodical Conference as a body. These movements for unions have resulted in the organization of the Norwegian Lutheran Church of America and in plans for the United Lutheran Church in America. . . .

Doctrine. The system of faith held by Lutherans is set forth in the Augsburg Confession. A number of other symbols, known as "Luther's Catechisms, Larger and Smaller," the "Apology of the Augsburg Confession," the "Smalcald Articles," and the "Formula of Concord," are regarded as setting forth more or less fully the doctrinal system in the Augsburg Confession, and the differences between the various bodies, so far as they are doctrinal in character, as based chiefly upon deductions made from these other symbols; all alike accept the Augsburg Confession. The special features of each body are given in the statement for that body.

The cardinal doctrine of the system is that of justification by faith alone. The doctrine second in importance is that the Word of God is the only rule and source of faith and life. The Word of God reaches the mind and soul through the preaching of the Law and the Gospel, which begets daily repentance and faith, the two true marks of a Christian life. The sacraments of baptism and the Lord's Supper are not regarded as mere signs or memorials, but as the channels through which God offers His grace. The Lutheran system does not center in the doctrine of the sovereignty of God or in the doctrine of the church, but it centers in the gospel of Christ for fallen man. It is conservative in spirit, and holds to all the teachings and customs of the ancient Church that do not appear to it to be in conflict with the Scriptures. Its unity is a unity of doctrine, and its independence is an independence of government. Unity of government in the Lutheran church as a whole on earth, is a secondary matter to Lutherans, since the true unity is that of the invisible Church, to which belong all in every land and Church who are true believers, and these are known to God alone. The visible Church exists in its work and office, and for the defense of the truth, but not as an object in itself. Lutherans believe in the real presence of the Lord's body in the sacrament, but they reject both transubstantiation, as held by the Roman Catholic church, and consubstantiation, as attributed to them by some writers. They believe that the real body and blood of the Lord Jesus Christ are present in, with, and under the earthly elements in the Lord's Supper, and that these are received sacramentally and supernaturally. Infant baptism is practiced, and baptized persons are regarded as having received from the Holy Spirit the potential gift of regeneration, and as members of the church, though full membership follows confirmation. The mode of baptism is considered of secondary importance.

In this connection it should be stated that as it is the custom of the Lutheran church to receive into full membership only those who have been confirmed, and as confirmation is after arrival at the age of thirteen years, no members under that age are reported for the Lutheran bodies.

Polity. The polity of the Lutheran church is congregational in so far as the authority of ecclesiastical bodies over the local church is concerned; on the other hand, in its general organization, particularly for administrative or consultative purposes, it is rather representative, and any lay member of the congregation is eligible to election as a delegate to the Synod to which the congregation belongs.

The organization of the local church includes primarily the congregation and a church council, consisting of the pastor and the church officers who are usually elders and deacons, though in some case they are deacons and trustees. The church officers are laymen and are elected for a term of years, varying according to state laws. The pastor is elected by the male voting members of the congregation, can be dismissed by the congregation without reference to general ecclesiastical authority, and frequently does not even have a vote except by virtue of his position in the congregation. Where there are elders and deacons, the elders care for the spiritual concerns of the congregation, while the deacons have charge of temporal affairs. Where there are deacons and trustees, the deacons have the care of spiritual matters, and the trustees of temporal affairs. In certain cases a board of trustees, aside from the elders and deacons, has charge of the property. Each church governs its own secular affairs according to its constitution.

Above the local church are conferences and Synods of varying constitution and form, according to the different bodies. Some have no ecclesiastical authority, and are simply gatherings of churches for mutual consultation. Others have legislative authority committed to them, and their action is ordinarily recognized and approved by the churches. In general, however, each church retains its right of approval or disapproval, but in case of disapproval the higher body is at liberty to drop the church or the pastor, or both, from the rolls, or at least to advise this course.

Ordination to the Lutheran ministry is in general conducted by district Synods at their annual meetings, although in exceptional cases it may be at another time and place by a committee appointed for the purpose. It follows examination of the candidate by a committee of the Synod, which covers his scholastic attainments, his fitness for the office and his loyalty to the Lutheran Confessions, particularly the Augsburg Confession. Each minister is a member of the Synod which ordained him, or of the Synod in which he is a pastor, and is subject to its discipline.

The Lutheran churches have a liturgical form of worship and observe the various general festivals of the Christian church year.

7. The Growth of the Catholic Church in the Nineteenth Century

TINY AT the birth of the nation, the Roman Catholic Church in the United States expanded numerically and geographically with great rapidity in the nineteenth century, largely because of immigration. By mid-century it was already the largest single denomination, although it was plagued by inner tensions among the various nationality groups. At the time of the Third Plenary Council of the American episcopate at Baltimore in 1884, Catholics were becoming conscious of their growing strength. In a sermon at that council, Bishop Bernard J. McQuaid (1823–1909) of Rochester, New York, an American-born son of an Irish factory worker, interpreted the course of American Catholic history since 1784. Commenting not only on the spectacular increase in membership but also on the extensive network of Catholic institutions, McQuaid emphasized especially the importance of parochial schools. Troubled by the Protestant tone of the culture and its schools, and disturbed by the failure to get tax monies for church schools, the Third Plenary Council had decreed that schools should be founded within every parish within two years, unless unusual circumstances prevented.

SOURCE: *The Memorial Volume: A History of the Third Plenary Council of Baltimore, November 9–December 7, 1884* (Baltimore, 1885), pp. 161–176.

The growth of the United States within the century of their existence as an independent sovereignty, in population, in commerce and manufactures, in extension and development of territory, in literature and fine arts, in diffusion of elementary knowledge among the masses of the people, in successful trial of government of the people by the people, is unparalleled in the history of the world.

Scarcely had peace between the mother country and the thirteen revolted colonies been declared, after a trying and bloody struggle of seven years, than the emancipated colonists resolutely set to work to construct a form of government that should keep in view the best and largest interest of the people while strongly upholding law and order. These colonies threw wide open their vast domain and invited the oppressed and downtrodden of European countries to enter into possession. There were forests to be felled and fields to be broken up and cultivated. There was no room for the idler, the drone or the dreamer. It was a new country of immense resources for the hardy sons of toil. It offered the freedom and dignity of self-respecting manhood to lovers of liberty and independence.

The readiness with which the invitation was accepted is known to all. From every country and from every class of life the bravest and most venturesome, longing for escape from the thraldom of the old countries of Europe, flocked to the shores of the young republic. The narrow strip of seaboard running from Massachusetts to Georgia rapidly widened westward to the Mississippi, and then, without more than a temporary break, reached to the Pacific. It is a mighty empire bounded by the two oceans, the Great Lakes on the north and the Gulf on the south. The three millions of revolutionary days have increased to the fifty-five millions of today. The thirteen colonies are replaced by thirty-eight States. The experiment of government by the people has withstood successfully rude shocks, serious defects, conflicts of material interests, even a civil war. All avenues of advancement to wealth and honor have been thronged with the children of intellect and industry. The home, the freedom and the prosperity promised in the invitation have been found by millions. The dire forebodings of eventual disruption and ruin have come to naught. The predictions of anarchy to befall a government so largely entrusted to the people have not been verified. The old country first pitied us, then fought us, and again defeated, feared us. It is now compelled, most reluctantly, it is true, to learn from us the advantage and necessity of entrusting to the people a larger share in the direction and control of political affairs. Ours is a government of the people by the people, in the largest sense consistent with the maintenance of good order and the equal rights of its citizens.

It is assigned to me to speak of the growth of the Catholic church in a country such as the one here described.

In no better way can I place before you the growth of the church than by grouping the statistics of church work, such as we have them, at three periods of the century just ended.

1. The condition of the Catholic church in 1784.
2. Her progress after fifty years, in 1834.
3. The church as she is today, in 1884.

In 1783 the number of Catholics, according to Bishop Carroll's calculation, as quoted by Shea, might amount in Maryland to sixteen thousand souls; in Pennsylvania, to seven thousand; and in the other States, to fifteen hundred; not as many all told as may be counted today in a single parish in some of our large cities. Mass was commonly celebrated in private houses. There were few or no churches. There was no bishop, and in the judgment of the eighteen or twenty missionaries who ministered to the spiritual wants of these scattered members, as expressed in a letter to Rome, there was no need of a bishop, inasmuch as a vicar apostolic, in spiritualibus, would suffice. There was no college, school, asylum or hospital. Of religious communities of men or women there was not one. It is a bare picture on a large canvas that is here presented to our view.

The See of Baltimore was erected by Pius VI on the 6th day of November, 1789, and in 1790 its first Bishop, Rev. John Carroll, was consecrated. The establishment of a hierarchy placed the church in America in line with her sister churches in other parts of the world, and gave her officials a rule to work by. In a diocese the bishop is the recognized conservator of Catholic faith and morals, in unity and harmony with the head Bishop of the Universal Church. With this first bishop began the regulation of discipline and the founding of institutions needed for the growth and stability of the church as an organized body.

Bishop Carroll, and others after him, planned to place bishops in every extended geographical district. It was rightly judged that these bishops would give a start and direction to the church's work from the beginning. In this sense Bishop Connolly, of New York, wrote to the Cardinal Prefect of the Propaganda on the 28th of February, 1818: "Bishops ought to be granted to whatever State here is willing to build a cathedral, and petition for a bishop as Norfolk has done." On the 31st of October, 1818, he wrote to Archbishop Maréchal: "I approve of erecting Charleston into a bishopric, and wish that every one of the seventeen United States had each a bishop." Indeed there was no delay in carving up the country with episcopal sees; bishops sometimes preceded the priests. There were only four priests in New York when Bishop Connolly came to his diocese; two in that of Charleston, comprising the States of North and South Carolina and Georgia, when Bishop England took possession of his allotted district; the same number preceded Bishop Bruté's arrival at Vincennes. At a later date, Bishops Loras and Miles prepared the way for the coming of the first priest into the Dioceses of Dubuque and Nashville.

Vast territory, slow and tedious modes of traveling, few helpers in the work, the poverty of the Gospel fell to the lot of our American pioneer-bishops. That they were apostolic men of God no one can doubt. They were eminently far-seeing and hopeful laborers in an unbroken and rough field—in a wilderness of spiritual destitution.

Six prelates met for the holding of the first Provincial Council of Baltimore in 1829, and ten for the second in October, 1833. Their work, as seen in the decrees of these councils, gave evidence of wisdom, prudence and learning, in adapting discipline to the peculiar circumstances in which they, their priests and the faithful under their care were placed. From the first their thoughts and efforts were directed towards the education of the young. Colleges and academies sprang into existence; Christian free schools, such as are known today, for want of religious communities, devoted to the education of the people's children, languished when set agoing and were few in number. The duty of providing churches, ever so small and poor—mere shanties and log-cabins oftentimes—engrossed the time and means of bishops.

From the beginning of the century until 1834, Catholics who had known suffering and persecution in Maryland and Europe, moved among their fellow-citizens quietly and with exceeding humility and meekness. They were specially careful not to offend their separated brethren, and received in return becoming pity and tolerance. No one feared them; they were so few in number, so inconsequential and so anxious not to offend. The condition of tolerance was accepted as a boon rather than demand the right of equality before the law to which they were born.

About this time, however, the steady influx of immigrants from all the countries of Europe, but chiefly of Catholics from Ireland, the building of large and costly churches in important cities, as here in Baltimore and in New York, the opening of colleges and convents, the multiplying of bishops and priests, turned pity into fear. The Fathers of the second Council refer to this change of feeling and treatment in their pastoral letter. "We notice with regret," they write, "a spirit exhibited by some of the conductors of the press engaged in the interests of those brethren separated from our communion which has within a few years become more unkind and unjust in our regard. Not only do they assail us and our institutions in a style of vituperation and offence, misrepresent our tenets, vilify our practices, repeat the hundred-times-refuted calumnies of days of angry and bitter contention in other lands, but they have even denounced you and us as enemies to the republic, and have openly proclaimed the fancied necessity of not only obstructing our progress, but of using their best efforts to extirpate our religion." This is a mild arraignment of an exhibition of fanatical bigotry that suddenly burst on the church. Secular and religious press alike, and all the pulpits from Maine to Louisiana, weekly and oftener poured out torrents of rancorous abuse and calumny, and left unused no art or device with which to fan the flame of religious hate and passion in the minds and hearts of their readers and hearers. In the August of 1834 the answer to this temperate rebuke of the bishops was the setting fire to the convent of the Ursuline Nuns of Charlestown by citizens of Boston town and vicinity. Gallant men burned over the heads of defenseless women and schoolgirls their rightful home, even as less than a century before savage Indians, wrought to rage by many wrongs, had set ablaze the huts and cabins of the early settlers in Massachusetts.

While noting this phase of intolerance as a hindrance to the growth of the church within the first half of the century, it will not be out of place to refer to the continuance of the same spirit of opposition, amounting to persecution, which furiously manifested itself in 1844 and in 1854. This malevolent spirit deepened and grew bolder among our non-Catholic fellow-citizens as soon as our numbers, wealth and activity arrested attention by the building of churches, convents and schools. These outbursts of malignant hate and fear were like to the upheavings of volcanoes; slumbering for years, suddenly masses of fire and burning stones shoot into the air, and, falling, roll in hot streams down the side of the mountain, carrying devastation in their path.

The angry passions engendered by persistent onslaughts in press and pulpit, outrageous calumnies, unmanly insinuations, fearful forebodings and warnings of evil to come upon the country at a time when it was struggling into existence, prepared the minds of bigots for barbarous deeds. Maria Monk's "Disclosures," as the utterances of an abandoned woman were called, the stock in trade of venal book publishers and fanatical parsons, deceived and led astray many who honestly desired to live at peace with their neighbors. The riots and burnings of 1834 were the outcome of years of guilty misrepresentation. In 1844 politicians, always dragging their nets in foul waters, thought they saw political capital in the still seething religious ignorance and prejudice prevalent among the people. The bad elements already existing among our own population had been considerably augmented by recent arrivals from Europe, too ready to revive in America the religious wars in which they had been engaged at home. The Philadelphia riots, church burnings and murders followed as a consequence. Disturbances in other parts of the country broke out at the same time and from similar causes. The riots and murders of 1854 were akin in character and cause to those of 1844; they had their source in religious rancor and political scheming trading on the passions of ignorant bigots. There were no riots in 1864. The civil war, just ending, had put a stop to the diabolical machinations of bigots and politicians. Men who had stood shoulder to shoulder in the hour of danger, who had rested side by side under the shelter-tent, had learned forbearance and mutual respect, and to treat with contempt the old-time calumnies and all who uttered them. The politician's objection to Catholics because they were foreigners was valid as against Columbus in the mind of the aboriginal natives, and will end only when America forgets the hospitality she owes to the downtrodden of the world, and which the progenitors of her citizens of today had received in their turn. The reign of insults and wrongs that lasted from 1830 to 1860 proved a formidable hindrance to the advance of the Church. The timid, the ill-instructed, the ambitious, the vain, feared to belong to a body of so little esteem in the world's eye, and fell away. Fanaticism and proselytism worked hand in hand. Money was lavishly spent in perverting the minds of the young. The spenders of it thought that they were doing God's work. Because the enemies of the church are not working on the same lines today, it is not to be inferred that the battle is over, and that all danger has passed.

But the main cause of defections must be looked for in the years from 1784 to 1834, and be attributed to the scarcity of priests and churches. Bishop England, of Charleston, in a letter to the Society of the Propagation of the Faith in France, estimated these losses at three million and a half at the time of his writing, in 1839. He gives, however, no trustworthy data on which to base such a conclusion, and I cannot but consider it as greatly exaggerated. Yet it must be confessed that the number of those that lost the faith, or, that having no means of hearing the Word of God and of receiving the helping graces of the sacraments, lapsed into indifference, is startlingly great. Even when parents never apostatized, their children succumbed to the influence of their surroundings, and learned to despise and deny the belief and practices of their parents' religion through the adverse and malignant pressure of companionship and daily intercourse with revilers of Catholic doctrines. Social seductions and fashions overmaster the young and lead them captive. When mixed marriages in such conditions of society intervened to increase the danger, the children had no hope and were invariably lost. Without Catholic lessons at home, with neither church nor priest to teach and support them, they fell an easy prey to the vigilant and zealous labors of the enemies of the Catholic church. In spite of all disadvantages and losses from peculiar and unavoidable evils, the church made headway. The French emigrant priests driven to our shores by the revolution of 1789 were men of learning and piety. They had passed through the fires that try men's souls. Their zeal was unbounded, and their success was marked in holding many Catholics to the practice of religion and in winning the esteem and good will of non-Catholics whose antagonism they disarmed. Chevereux and Matignon, Dubois and Bruté, Flaget and his companions in the West, Dubourg in the South, and the Sulpicians who chose Baltimore for their field of labor, performed noble work and laid broad and solid foundations. Nor should we forget to speak a word of praise of the Society of the Propagation of the Faith, established in Lyons, whose generous and unfailing pecuniary help came to the assistance of the American church in her days of struggling infancy. It was this help which set a-going dioceses and institutions and enabled bishops and priests to live while seeking after the wandering sheep of a widely scattered flock.

By 1834, after fifty years of faithful perseverance under most trying difficulties, the Church of the United States was able to show an archbishop, eleven bishops, two hundred and fifty priests, about thirty colleges and academies, but not a dozen parochial schools for the half-million Catholics who comprised our population at that time. This exhibit may not strike one as very remarkable, but its merits should be judged by the greatness of the sacrifices, the zeal of the laborers, their small number and limited resources.

Between 1830 and 1850 the tide of immigration began to set in strongly. Poverty, famine and revolutions swelled the crowds of fleeing emigrants. Disasters at sea and long voyages could not hold back men and women whose hearts were turned toward the promised land. The first immigrants coming in large numbers were from Ireland. Of all the peoples of Europe they were the best fitted to open the way for religion in a new country. Brave by nature, inured to poverty and hardship, just released from a struggle unto death for the faith, accustomed to the practice of religion in its simplest forms, cherishing dearly their priests whom they had learned to support directly, actively engaged in building humble chapels on the sites of ruined churches and in replacing altars, they were not appalled by the wretchedness of religious equipments and surroundings in their new homes on this side of the Atlantic. The priest was always the priest, no matter where they found him, or from what country he had come; the Mass was always the Mass, no matter where it was offered up. They had lived among the bitterest of foes and had never quailed or flinched; misrepresentations and calumnies, sneers and scorn, made no impression on their faithful hearts. Men who prefer death to denial of Christ are not cowards or traitors. In such a school of discipline they had been trained to do missionary work. They and their descendants have not in a new hemisphere unlearned the lessons taught at home.

Quickly following the Irish came the Germans from all parts of the fatherland. They, too, were a sturdy race, able to hold their own. Many of them had also known persecution for religion's sake; most of them remembered the stories of bloody times which had come down to them among the traditions of their hearths. They were prompt to rival their Irish brethren in building up the church. At home they had their old parish churches, with the chants and ceremonial, which lend to religion much that is consoling and instructive. The religious traditions and glories of the old land they have sought to emulate in this. Better than all, they have stood fast by the duty of maintaining Christian schools for Christian children. There is much that they can copy from the Irish, and much that the Irish can learn from the Germans. Both have bravely led the way to the church's march. All the other nationalities of Europe can kneel at their feet and imbibe salutary and profitable lessons.

Before proceeding to account for losses to the church, even during this favorable period from 1834 to 1884, a brief summary of statistics, as found in Sadlier's Directory, will show at a glance what has been accomplished in church work.

A Cardinal of the Holy Roman Church, the Most Eminent and Illustrious Archbishop of New York; an Apostolic Delegate, the Most Reverend and Illustrious Metropolitan of this See of Baltimore; thirteen other archbishops, and coadjutor archbishops, and sixty-one bishops and vicars apostolic rule over God's church in this republic; 6,835 priests, under the leadership of these successors of the Apostles, in 7,763 churches and chapels, feed their flocks with the bread of life and devotedly care for their souls. In 708 seminaries, colleges and academies, the higher education of clerics and of the youth of both sexes is carried forward by learned professors and accomplished nuns. Many thousands of brothers and sisters, of all the teaching orders and communities, assist these priests and perform a part that, without their services, would be left undone. Our orphans, the aged, the abandoned, are sheltered in 294 asylums, and our sick are nursed in 139 hospitals. The crowning glory of the church's work, however, is derived from her success in providing, not for the exceptional members of her household, the few who are bereaved, sick and helpless, but for the many who constitute her army of able, active and self-maintaining members. For the children of the Catholic community, for the offspring of the parents who build churches, asylums and hospitals, she has within these fifty years built and she now sustains 2,532 Christian schools, in which secular learning is imparted without sacrificing instruction in the belief and observances which the Lord commanded His Apostles and their successors to preach to the end of time. During the year 1883, 481,834 pupils frequented these Christian schools, built, fostered lovingly and supported for the people's children without aid from the state. The charity which comes to the relief of the sick and the fatherless is beautiful indeed, and the blessing of heaven falls hourly on those who tend and those who help; but the duty of instructing the many, the hope of the future, cannot be omitted without punishment in this world and the next.

The Directory estimates the Catholic population at 6,623,176. It is easy to see that these figures are not based on correct information. The editor fulfills his task in accurately counting up the numbers sent to him. But estimates of population, year after year the same, in rapidly growing dioceses, must be at fault, for they are clearly wide of the mark. An estimate that would place our Catholic population at eight million, would, in my judgment, not be far from the truth. A few years hence, with priests in abundance, having parishes restricted within territorial limits, so that a pastor may be able to know his parishioners, and when baptisms, marriages and deaths are faithfully recorded and reported, it may be possible to reckon our numbers without guessing.

The dry figures here submitted for consideration give no adequate idea of the amount of work performed during these fifty years. They do not tell of the sacrifices of the poor people who furnished the money, often drawing out of purses all but empty; they do not tell that the stone church of today, monumental in size and beauty of architecture, replaced an humbler one of brick, which in its turn had displaced the first modest wooden structure; they do not tell that driven by state monopoly in schoolteaching, upheld in unlimited expenditures of money from the public treasury, Catholics are forced to make their school buildings and furniture unnecessarily expensive and grand; that needless costliness is forced upon them to maintain the honor and good name of their schools in the face of state extravagance; they do not tell that the burden and the cost of these churches and schools have for the most part fallen on poor people and poor priests; they do not tell of the many priests that, broken in health and spirit, sank into untimely graves, victims of toil of body and anxiety of mind more than nature could endure.

Again, the bald figures summing up the number of cathedrals, churches, colleges, convents, etc., do not convey an idea of the character of these edifices. There are among them edifices which Europe of modern days cannot equal in size, grandeur and completeness. What has Europe to place by the side of the New York cathedral as her contribution to church building in the nineteenth century? Look at the seminary buildings at Overbrook, Baltimore, Boston; at our collegiate buildings in the East and in the West; at convents and monasteries innumerable; at our charitable institutions. These are not state buildings erected with money from the state treasury. The people's pence and the personal sacrifices and savings of priests, brothers and nuns have built them. Not much help has come from our rich members. They testify what can be accomplished by a believing flock when untrammeled by governmental interference. Free and unhampered, upheld by the fidelity and generosity of the masses of her children in Christ, growth and prosperity have marked the course of the church along every line of work—in every agency and force. If material and intellectual America can point with exultation of soul to its marvelous accomplishments, so can spiritual and intellectual Catholic America hold up its head as not unworthy of its predecessors in the faith in any country and in any age. If non-Catholic America can with just pride call attention to its colleges and universities, the noblest of modern times in wealth of endowments, the gifts to learning of its millionaire friends and patrons, so can Catholic America bespeak consideration for what zeal, devotion and the generosity of the poor have brought into existence. In this study of successful work we must ever keep in mind who were the workers and what was the treasury from which the required millions were drawn.

With the proof here presented of large and substantial growth, giving well-founded hope of continuance and permanence, the Catholics of the United States can face their brethren in any quarter of the world and bid those whose surroundings are at all like ours to compare work with work, success with success, loss with loss. We frankly admit that we have not always held our own. But we in America do not take reproof from our brethren in Europe with amiability and good grace. Many of the Christians they have turned out on our shores have not been models of piety and holiness; nor does the light of faith burn brightly in their souls. They accept the services of religion as a compliment to the priest rather than as a necessary fulfillment of duty. They must be helped rather than be a help. Thousands already perverted by the soul-destroying influences of secret societies and the demoralizing notions of socialism, so prevalent in Europe, impede our onward course. Our humble Catholics are amazed at the looseness of principles in the hearts of many who come to us, and are disedified. We cannot but ask: Are there no losses to the church on the other side of the ocean? Corrupted in faith and morals before they leave home, they bring corruption with them.

The hindrances to our growth in the first half of the century were not unknown in the second half. The one which came from the low social standing of Catholics in most parts of the country, little by little yielded to claims that could not be ignored. Wealth, education and refinement asserted their rights. Political, commercial and professional preeminence, in many quarters, told in our favor. Members of our church were of marked distinction in every walk of life—on the bench, at the bar, in the medical profession, in the army and navy—wherever brightness of intellect and capacity for work are needed they are to be found. Even in the political arena, while their religious connection does not advance their interests, it is ceasing to be an actual impediment, and it is discovered that political punishment for religious belief is becoming a dangerous experiment.

While all admit that the social status of our numbers has changed for the better in cities and towns, it is highly satisfactory to know that in rural and agricultural districts, where so many of our body are found today and where their homes will be greatly multiplied in the future, our farmers and their families win the respect due to their worth and useful citizenship. They cannot be, nor are they, despised. When known, they advance in the esteem of their neighbors.

Misrepresentations and evil reports still are heard, but newspapers that care for their reputation do not repeat false charges that will not be believed by their readers. Fair play and a love for the truth on the part of non-Catholics have put a stop to low abuse of their neighbors and associates in business, whom they know to be honorable and upright men, and whose wives and daughters they know are pure, gentle and amiable. The people's good sense reformed pulpits and newspapers.

Church contentions and squabbles, having their origin in a faulty understanding of the rights and duties of the clergy and laity in the management of temporalities and money transactions, have led to heavy losses. When the century began men's minds were warped by non-Catholic ideas with regard to the tenure of ecclesiastical property. It was thought that the freedom and independence in political affairs, common in the country, should extend to church matters. Good Christians were easily led astray by one or two cunning and infidel minds in a congregation. An occasional mistake or blunder on the part of an ecclesiastic served as an excuse for fault-finding. But in what other profession or in what other line of commercial and monetary transactions have the mistakes been so few and the failures so infrequent? And when ecclesiastics have blundered in business concerns, has it not been because other responsibilities than those rightly within the sphere of their work have been assumed by them? The better to understand the cogency of this argument, it is no more than just to remember that hundreds of millions have passed under the control and use of priests within the half century. It is simply a marvel that in the handling and disbursing of these large sums of money so little has been lost and so seldom have pastors forfeited the confidence of their flocks. Pastors can do nothing without the cooperation of their parishioners, and soon learn that a wise appreciation of the rights of those who freely open their purses at the call of religion or charity best secures a generous response. Both then work hand in hand for God's glory; the frictions incidental to human nature are little noted, and the few in a congregation who are ill-disposed find no encouragement from the majority. This well-ordered and happy condition of church management, based on the proper consideration of the rights and duties of priests and people, is a gratifying note of stable growth.

It is often remarked that a country which does not furnish a supply of priests for its altars will lose the faith. This saying cannot be predicated of a new land into which thousands and hundreds of thousands are year by year flowing. These immigrants must bring their priests with them. But when the newly arrived families have had time to settle down in their new homes the developing of vocation begins. No one fosters piety and zeal for God's honor in a child's soul like a devout, God-fearing mother. You cannot have homes in which the Christian virtues are cultivated without vocations to the priesthood and the religious life. In our young republic vocations abound. Our preparatory and theological seminaries are filled with promising aspirants to the work of the sanctuary; our convents are thronged with holy virgins bringing to the service of religion whatever of bodily strength, intellectual capacity and devotion of soul they have to offer and that can be used. Our schools would be empty buildings but for the armies of teaching Brothers and Sisters who fill so well the office of instructors. Here, too, is evidence of faith and stability.

Christian families demand Christian schools. The father and mother most exact in the religious education of their children are the most earnest in providing Christian schools. Their own efforts to teach their young ones convince them of the necessity of the everyday school to supplement and enforce their words and lessons. Parents who rarely give a lesson to their children are the loudest in protesting against schools strictly Catholic. They do not know the value of a child's soul, often as they may have heard that Christ died to save it.

Scarcely had the work of building churches for our rapidly increasing population been taken in hand by priests and people than a yet heavier task was imposed on them. Churches might suffice for the elders of the flock, who, trained to religion in a Catholic atmosphere at home, could neither be cajoled nor deterred from its practices; but what was to become of children growing up in an atmosphere not simply innocuous, but positively dangerous and hurtful? Bishops and priests were most unwilling to add to the burden already weighing down their congregations. They sought, as well in justice they might, that a portion of their own money paid to the state might come back to them. Unkindly, rudely, contemptuously, their reasonable request was spurned. Politicians and parsons were our fiercest antagonists. When passions are aroused it is useless to argue. The passions of a nation cool slowly. There were some Catholics who hoped that an education purely secular might be made to answer. No doubt it will give to the children of secularists the husks of education—all they ask. They wonder that Catholics seek for more. They cannot comprehend our doctrine that the school for the child is as necessary as the church for the parent. Without further argument or dispute, but, nevertheless, grieving and groaning under the wrong put upon us by process of law and the vote of the majority, Catholics gathered their children into their own schools, that therein they might breathe a Catholic atmosphere while acquiring secular knowledge. Without these schools, in a few generations our magnificent cathedrals and churches would remain as samples of monumental folly —of the unwisdom of a capitalist who consumes his fortune year by year without putting it out at interest or allowing it to increase. The church has lost more in the past from the want of Catholic schools than from any other cause named by me this evening. The 2,500 schools, with a half million of scholars, which now bless our country, tell Catholics and non-Catholics that the question of religious education is settled, so far as we are concerned. The good work so well advanced will not halt until all over the land the children of the Church are sheltered under her protecting care. The establishment of these schools and their improvement in management and instruction is our surest guarantee of future growth and fixedness.

The gross exaggerations of writers who substitute imaginings for facts, in asserting that millions upon millions of our Catholic people have lost their faith, are not deserving of much notice. The immigrant who landed on our shores faced two dangers which affrighted him. If, in the early days of our history, he sought a home out in the agricultural districts, there was neither church nor priest; if, deterred by dangers to his faith from settling on farm-land, he clung to cities and factory towns, he lived without a home and his children perished in infancy, victims to the miseries of tenement life. The immigrants of today can find healthful homes in all parts of the United States near to churches, schools and priests. They have no excuse for settling far from a church or from a neighborhood that will soon be blessed with one.

I bring to a close my allotted task. No one more than myself feels how inadequately it has been executed. Compressing so extensive a subject into a small compass has been difficult. Memory goes back to early days in our history. My first lessons in religion came from some who were among the pioneers of the church in our country. My first years of priesthood were spent as a missionary in New Jersey. While journeying through this district, hunting up the stray sheep of the fold, the experience was acquired that without churches and schools our children, and especially those of mixed marriages, would be lost. No doubt every missionary's experience has been the same.

But what a change since those days! There were among the first bishops and priests men who conceived and planned great things for the church's welfare; their plans when enunciated seemed visionary, the speculations of dreamers, of impracticable workers. A few years demonstrated that their plans were insufficient and too restricted for the wants of the country. We plan today with the light of the past to guide us. Another generation may smile at our narrowness of vision and weakness of heart.

A noble duty, worthy of a man's labor and life, the building up of Christ's church in a great, growing and free republic, falls to our lot. God and country, most dear to us, claim love and service. It is for us to help say to the world that government of a free people by the people, whose conceptions of morality are based on God's law, can safely be entrusted to the people, and that this largeness of trust gives ample scope to the Christian's ambition in furthering a sacred cause. No man's help is beneath consideration. The humblest layman, the very child in the school, their capable and devoted teachers, they who pray in cloisters, missionaries who live in the saddle, priests who minister in crowded cities, professors in our seminaries, bishops who rule, have each and every one a part to take. What glowing words of praise may justly be spoken in commendation of our predecessors! They fought the good fight, they laid a solid foundation, they showed the way, they illustrated their teachings by their lives. Let us not prove unworthy of them and their examples.

8. Jews in America:
A Mid-Nineteenth-Century Summary

Isaac Leeser (1806–1868) came as an immigrant from Germany to Richmond, Virginia, in 1824. Deeply devoted to the Jewish religious tradition, he volunteered to assist in the Sephardic synagogue in Richmond. He studied what Judaica was available, and wrote newspaper articles in defense of Jewish thought. In 1829 he was called to serve as minister of the Hebrew Portuguese Congregation in Philadelphia. He labored to build a strong, enduring Jewish tradition in America and was active in educating, translating, publishing, and institution building. When a massive History of All the Religious Denominations in the United States was projected, he prepared a long article on the "History of the Jews and Their Religion." The latter part of the article is reprinted here, beginning with a list of "thirteen cardinal principles which are the key of our theological views," and concluding with a summary of Jewish history in America.

source: History of All the Religious Denominations in the United States: Containing Authentic Accounts of the Rise and Progress, Faith and Practice, Localities and Statistics, of the Different Persuasions: Written Expressly for the Work, by Fifty-Three Eminent Authors, Belonging to the Respective Denominations (2d ed.; Harrisburg, 1849), pp. 316–319.

1. The belief in an almighty Creator, who alone has called all things into being, and still continues to govern the world which He has made.

2. The belief in the absolute and perfect unity of the Creator, that He is therefore indivisible in every sense of the word, always the same, who was, is, and ever will be, unchanged as from the beginning.

3. The belief in the incorporeality of the Creator, that He is not a material being, and cannot be affected by accidents which affect material things.

4. The belief in the absolute and perfect eternity of the Creator.

5. The belief that the Creator is the sole being to whom we should pray, since there is no one who shares his powers, that we should address our prayers to him.

6. The belief in the truth of all the words of the prophets.

7. The belief in the truth of the prophecy of Moses, and that he was the greatest of all the prophets and wise men who have lived before him or will come after him.

8. The belief in the identity of the law which we now have, and that it is unchanged, and the very one which was given to Moses.

9. The belief in the permanency of the law, and that there has not been, nor will there ever be, another law promulgated by the Creator.

10. The belief in the omniscience of the Creator.

11. The belief that the Creator will reward those who keep his commandments, and punish those who transgress them.

12. The belief in the coming of the King Messiah, who is to accomplish for the world and Israel all that the prophets have foretold concerning him. And

13. The belief in the resurrection of the dead, when it may please the Almighty to send his spirit to revive those who sleep in the dust.

It were easy enough to prove all the above from scripture passages; but it is deemed unnecessary in this mere summary of our faith, nothing doubting but that the inquirer will look for further light in works treating especially on this important subject. It will be seen that a distinctive feature in our belief is "the permanency of the law revealed on Sinai through Moses the father of the prophets," which precludes the admission of any new revelation, or the abrogation of the old covenant. Another, "the belief in the absolute unity of God," with the addition that "there is no being but the Creator to whom we should pray," precludes the admissibility of a mediator, or the mediating power between God and us mortal sinners of any being whose existence the imagination can by any possibility conceive as possible. We think and maintain that these principles are legitimate deductions of the text of Holy Writ; and we must therefore, if even on no other grounds, reject the principles and doctrines of Christianity which teach, first, that a new covenant has been made between God and mankind other than the revelation at Horeb; and, secondly, that there is a mediator, an emanation of the Deity, through whose merits only man can be absolved from sin, and through whose intercession prayers will be accepted. All this is foreign to our view of scriptural truth, and as such we reject it, and hold fast to the doctrines which we have received from our fathers.

The Messiah whom we expect is not to be a god, nor a part of the godhead, nor a son of god in any sense of the word; but simply a man eminently endowed, like Moses and the prophets in the days of the Bible, to work out the will of God on earth in all that the prophets have predicted of him. His coming, we believe, will be the signal for universal peace, universal freedom, universal knowledge, universal worship of the One Eternal; objects all of high import, and well worthy to be attested by the visible display of the divine glory before the eyes of all flesh, just as was the presence of the Lord manifested at Sinai, when the Israelites stood assembled to receive the law which was surrendered to their keeping. In the days of this august ruler the law, which was at first given as "an inheritance of the congregation of Jacob," will become the only standard of righteousness, of salvation, for all mankind, when will be fulfilled to its fullest extent the blessings conferred upon Abraham, Isaac, and Jacob, that "in their seed all the families of the earth should be blessed." We believe, further, that the time of this great event is hidden from our knowledge, and is only known to the Creator, who in his own good time will regenerate the earth, remove the worship of idols, banish all erroneous beliefs, and establish his kingdom firmly and immovably over the hearts of all sons of man, when all will invoke Him in truth, and call him God, King, Redeemer, the One who was, is, and will be, for ever and ever. We believe that the time may be distant, thousands of years removed; but we confidently look forward to its coming, in the full confidence that He who has so miraculously preserved his people among so many trials and dangers, is able and willing to fulfill all He has promised, and that his power will surely accomplish what his goodness has foretold; and that He will not rest in the fulfillment of his word, till all the world shall acknowledge his power, and ceaseless incense ascend to his holy Name from the rising of the sun even unto his setting; when the altars of falsehood shall crumble and the dominion of unbelief be swept from the face of the earth.

The Jews in the United States

From the smallness of the numbers of our people, compared with the rest of mankind, it will be readily understood that, comparatively speaking, but few Jews will be found in America. Still despite of this fact, they are found in every portion of the Union, with the exception almost (for there are a few even there) in the northern range of states. Probably the first settlement of Jews took place in New Amsterdam, when it was under the Dutch government, about 1660. They no doubt were Spaniards and Portuguese who, like their brethren who were settled in Holland, fled from the bloody Inquisition to seek refuge under the equitable protection of the laws of the Batavian republic. The writer of this has learnt that a correspondence is yet in existence which took place between the Israelites and the Dutch authorities in New Amsterdam; but he has never seen it, wherefore he is unable to say anything with precision further than he has stated above. This much, however, he believes certain, that the number of our people did not increase rapidly, since we are not friendly to making proselytes, and owing to the great difficulties emigrants of our persuasion must be exposed to in new communities on account of the duties of our religion. Be this as it may, but one synagogue was needed in New York, till about 1817, when a second one was established in the central part of the city. Since that period four other congregations have been organized, and all the places of worship, though so rapidly multiplied, are frequently over full, so as to require temporary meeting places. The number of Jews in the city of New York is said to be about 10,000, and rapidly increasing by emigration from Europe, owing to the oppressive laws enforced against us in many countries as stated in a preceding part of this article. There are two congregations in Albany, and one or more in the country, of which, however, I have too vague information to say any thing with certainty.

A few years before the American revolution a congregation assembled in Newport, Rhode Island; but with the falling off of the business of that place, after the conclusion of the peace of 1783, the Jewish population left it by degrees, some going to New York, some to Richmond, and others to different other towns. There are a synagogue and burying ground, both said to be in good order—a legacy having been left by the son of the former minister, Touro, to keep them from falling into decay.

In Pennsylvania Israelites were settled long before the revolution in various places. But, I believe, that no regular congregation was organized till about 1780, when the occupation of New York by the British induced many from that place to come hither with their minister, Gershom Mendes Seixas; and a synagogue was erected upon the site of the present building, and consecrated about the fall of 1781. There are now three congregations in Philadelphia, numbering about from 1,500 to 1,800 souls; one congregation is at Easton, one in Hanover, and considerable settlements in Franklin county, Bucks, and elsewhere, which will no doubt be organized as congregations before long.

In Maryland the Jews were, until lately, excluded from a participation of equal rights; but soon after the repeal of their disabilities, many Europeans joined the former few settlers, and there is now a considerable congregation of about 1,500 souls in Baltimore, where there is a synagogue. There are also a few families in Frederick, Hagerstown, &c.

In Virginia the Jews settled about 1780, or even earlier; but their number is small in that state; and there are but two congregations in the whole state, and both at Richmond. Others dwell at Petersburg, Norfolk, Lynchburg, Wheeling, but they amount in the whole state to scarcely more than 600.

In North Carolina, where the constitution excludes us from the rights of citizens, there are but a few families.

But in South Carolina we are much more numerous, and Israelites are found in all parts of the state; still there is but one regular congregation, at Charleston, where there is a handsome synagogue; the congregation was organized in 1750.

In Georgia there is a synagogue in Savannah. The first Jews came over soon after General Oglethorpe, in 1733; but they have never been very numerous; though it appears from present indications that many European emigrants, and persons from the north will, it is likely, soon seek a home in that state.

In the southern and western states the arrival of Israelites is but recent; still there is a congregation at Mobile; another, numbering about 125 families, in New Orleans; another at Louisville; two at Cincinnati; one or two in Cleveland, and one at St. Louis. There are probably others, but they have not become generally known. A small congregation also has recently been formed at New Haven, in Connecticut, probably the only one in the New England states, unless Boston be an exception.

We have no ecclesiastical authorities in America, other than the congregations themselves. Each congregation makes its own rules for its government, and elects its own minister, who is appointed without any ordination, induction in office being made through his election, which is made for a term of years or during good behavior, as it may meet the wish of the majority. As yet we have no colleges or public schools of any kind, with the exception of one in New York, under the direction of the Rev. Samuel M. Isaacs, one in Baltimore, and another in Cincinnati, and Sunday schools for religious instruction in New York, Philadelphia, Richmond, Charleston, Columbia, South Carolina, Savannah, and Cincinnati. There can be no doubt that something will be done for education, as soon as we have become more numerous. The American Jews have but one religious periodical, and this is printed in Philadelphia; it is called "The Occident and American Jewish Advocate," and appears monthly.

In all our congregations where the necessity demands it, there are ample provisions made for the support of the poor, and we endeavor to prevent, if possible, any Israelite from being sent to the poor house, or to sink into crime for want of the means of subsistence.

Upon the whole, we have increased in every respect within the last five years; and we invoke the blessing of Heaven that He may prosper our undertakings, and give us the means to grow in grace and piety, that we may be able to show the world the true effects of the law of God upon the life of a sincere Israelite, which must render him acceptable to his neighbors of every creed, and a worthy servant in the mansion of his heavenly Father.

9. Judaism Transformed by Later Immigration

WHEN Isaac Leeser wrote at mid-century, the Ashkenazic Jews from Germany had become by far the largest element in American Jewry, greatly outnumbering the Sephardic Jews from Spain and Portugal. By 1880 there were perhaps a quarter of a million Jews in the United States, and Reform Judaism had become very conspicuous. Then began an immigration of Jews from eastern Europe in unprecedented numbers, leading to the resurgence of Orthodox Jewry and the development of a "middle position" in Conservative or Historical Judaism. In 1965, Rabbi Manheim S. Shapiro summarized the impact of this great influx on Jewish life and thought in an article on "The American Jewish Community," reproduced in part.

SOURCE: Benjamin Efron (ed.), Currents and Trends in Contemporary Jewish Thought (New York, 1965), pp. 162–169. Reprinted by permission of Ktav Publishing House, Inc.

Jewish Immigration from Eastern Europe

During the nineteenth century the strong democratic spirit that had arisen in the West and the Industrial Revolution stimulated social and economic unrest in the East European countries. Their monarchs and rulers began to impose severe restrictive measures to stamp out any liberal sentiments and movements among their peoples. One method that they used for distracting the aroused peasantry and city workmen was to turn their general feelings of anger toward the Jews.

Life was hard for the common people in general of Eastern Europe, but it became increasingly intolerable for the Jews of that area. The restrictions upon where they could live, upon the occupations they could enter and upon the kinds of education they could obtain, made making a living difficult for the vast majority. In addition, they were often in actual danger of their lives from pogroms, organized attacks upon Jewish residents by bands of peasants or by official military contingents, in which Jews were killed and their homes and property pillaged or set afire.

A massive migration of Jews took place from Eastern (and Southern) Europe. Substantial numbers settled in Germany, France, the Netherlands and England, but for the great majority the goal was America, the land of freedom and opportunity.

But these were a different kind of immigrant from the earlier Jews who had arrived here. First of all, they came in much larger numbers. In the years from 1880 to 1920, as many as 100,000 to 150,000 would arrive in a single year. Most were poor (on the average, they arrived here with about $9.00 each), and had always been poor. In the countries they came from they had lived their lives almost totally isolated from the surrounding population. They had grown up accustomed to living among other Jews, speaking Yiddish as their mother tongue, and maintaining their own communal life and institutions. Furthermore, their customs and habits, formed by Orthodox religious practice over centuries and by the conditions imposed upon them by a hostile environment, made them feel and seem strange in their new country.

They tended, therefore, to settle in the major cities along the Eastern seaboard, such as New York, Boston, Philadelphia and Baltimore, clustered together in crowded neighborhoods, like the East Side of New York, where rents were cheap. Many of them found employment in the factories and sweatshops of the ready-to-wear garment industry that was beginning to spring up in America. And they began to establish communal institutions that would continue some of the important religious and cultural elements of their old way of life.

One of the important organizations the new immigrants started was the landsmanschaft (association of fellow-countrymen), composed of people from the same region or town. Thus there were societies of people who came from the city of Bialystok or Minsk; from Latvia or Bessarabia. These groupings enabled the newcomers to come into contact with others who spoke the same language, knew the same people, followed the same customs. Many of them established mutual-assistance societies to provide loans to members who needed help, and burial societies to provide for the costs of a funeral and a cemetery plot for a member who had died.

In the same way, groups of people who had come from the same place formed Orthodox synagogues of their own; the older American temples and synagogues seemed to them different and alien. The synagogue, too, enabled them to maintain what was familiar: the same order of prayer, the same pronunciation, the familiar melody of the prayers and hymns, the same pattern of organization. They also established talmud torahs, schools in which their children could be taught Hebrew, Tanach (Bible), Talmud, and worship. Sometimes the synagogue provided education for children, but often the schooling was provided by independent *rebbes* (teachers) who established small afternoon schools in their homes or in a rented room. Many of the *talmud torahs* were established independently by people who banded together for this purpose and who secured funds from the parents of the pupils and from voluntary contributions.

A large part of the East European immigrants had been influenced by a movement called the *Haskalah* (scholarship), which had sought to modernize Jewish life in Eastern Europe by reviving Hebrew as a language for communication and literature, and by encouraging Jews to study all that had been developed in Western culture including science, literature and mathematics. They centered attention also upon the scientific study of Jewish history and thought, and the use of Yiddish as a literary and cultural language.

One result of this intellectual activity was the development among the immigrants of a whole network of cultural undertakings: Yiddish daily newspapers, a substantial number of Yiddish theaters presenting plays and musicals, many literary and dramatic societies, discussion and study groups, journals and research publications and societies and associations of writers, actors and musicians.

Another organized movement that was brought to America by the East Europeans was Zionism. This development had come about as a result of many influences: the eternal commitment of Judaism to the "return to Zion" as ordained by God's covenant with the Jews, the nationalist spirit of the times which moved Jews also to want to establish a nation of their own, and the reaction to the active anti-Semitism Jews had experienced in various European countries. For these and other reasons Zionism had stirred the feelings of many East European Jews, but they differed as to how the Zionist goals could be achieved. Each point of view, whether general Zionist, labor Zionist or cultural Zionist, usually had its own organization with its own activities, journals and leaders.

Again, many East European Jews had been influenced by the labor and radical movements of the late nineteenth century and were therefore often antireligious. However, they felt themselves deeply Jewish and organized socialist-minded societies like the Workmen's Circle (which also provided insurance, death benefits, and Yiddish, nonreligious, Jewish schools for children). Largely workers, the early East European Jews organized Jewish trade unions, or set up Jewish locals in the craft unions of industries where Jews were working in substantial numbers.

The Reaction of the Older Jewish Community

The reaction and feeling of the older-established American Jews to these new immigrants was mixed. In part, they were apprehensive. In the period of the large-scale immigration from Eastern and Southern Europe, there was a rising antiforeign movement in America, directed against both Jews and non-Jews. Almost all of the immigrants coming from that part of the world were poor and strange in their dress and ways, and different in their language and customs. For the Jews there was hostility not only because of the general antiforeign sentiment, they encountered also a rise in anti-Semitism which flared among some American groups at this time. This made the older established Jews fearful lest Americans develop an intense anti-Jewish feeling, which would endanger all Jews, including the many already Americanized Jewish families.

On the other hand, many of the older Jewish families were also moved by sympathy for these East European Jews, who were after all their coreligionists, and who had suffered such fearful disabilities in their countries of origin. They wanted to help them over the difficulties they were having in making their way in the new land.

The net result of these feelings was a multiplication of efforts to assist Jews in need, and to help them in the process of adjustment to America. Old charitable institutions and welfare programs were expanded, and new ones were created. Jewish hospitals, free loan societies, orphanages, homes for the aged, educational aid societies and free schools grew and multiplied. In addition, classes in English and citizenship were instituted. Family aid agencies were developed. YMHA's were established to provide wholesome recreation for the children and young people from the immigrant families and to make available health, civic, recreational and cultural training for the older people.

Each of these activities required drives for funds to support them. At the same time, the East European immigrants themselves were also raising funds for similar programs that they wanted to conduct under their own auspices. There were so many fund drives and charity collections in the Jewish communities that the leaders began to develop united or federated campaigns for entire cities.

In this process, too, there were mixed forces at work. For some, the important factor was that a single annual fund-raising campaign for all the various charities would make it simpler for the giver to make a decision about how and where his philanthropic contributions should be made. For others, the important element was that it would make the work of fund raising easier and its administration less expensive. For still others, the significant point was that the use of charity funds could be planned better.

For some years, there was a conflict between the federations established by the "uptown" Jews (the older residents), and the organizations of the "downtown" Jews, those from the more recent immigrants. In some cities, there were actually two separate federations operating simultaneously for as much as fifteen years. Ultimately, however, as these two groups became more similar in outlook and activity, the federations merged. Now, in almost every American city where there are substantial numbers of Jews, there is a single Jewish federation, or its equivalent.

The large stream of Jewish immigration slowed down to a virtual standstill in 1924, when, after World War I, the United States adopted restrictive immigration laws. Over the years since then, with the exception of such groups as the Chassidim, who prefer like the Amish and Mennonites to cling to "old world" ways, the vast majority of American Jews have adapted to American life, language and ways of living. In 1964, it is estimated that around 85 percent of all American Jews were born and educated in this country.

In this period there were many historic events, each of which had its effect upon the feelings of Jews and on the programs of Jewish organizations. The need to help Jews overseas in the early years of the twentieth century led to the creation of organizations like the American Jewish Committee and the Joint Distribution Committee. The discrimination in different fields in America led to programs to combat restrictions against Jews in employment, education, housing and other areas. The rise of Hitler and Nazi propaganda, which seemed to encourage anti-Semitic activity in the United States, led to organizations and movements to combat such teachings.

At the same time, as it became apparent that the Jews of Germany and indeed of all Europe would need assistance and a place of refuge, American Jews began to work vigorously for the establishment of a homeland for Jews in Palestine. This was intensified after World War II, when the remaining Jews who had survived Hitler's attempts to destroy all the Jews were without any means of subsistence and had almost no place to go, for the doors to many countries were closed. Nor did the eventual establishment in 1948 of the state of Israel put an end to assistance to Israel by American Jews, since Israel continued to be threatened by its Arab neighbors. Also, the vast problem of providing for the immigration and settlement of Jews in Israel required massive financial resources.

This was, in short, a period of vast and important change, in which the ways of expressing Jewish identification and interest in America have taken on new forms.

Categories of Jewish Organizations

A look at the current patterns of Jewish activity and organization, and their development from the beginnings described above, presents the following picture. Jewish institutions in America fall into these categories: religious; civic and community relations; Zionist and Israel-related; educational, recreational and cultural; health, welfare and social service; coordinating and servicing; and professional associations. Sometimes these overlap; for example, a religious body may also act in community relations; a Zionist body or a community relations organization may also conduct educational and cultural activities, etc.

For the most part, each of these types of activity has its own particular supporters, generally members of an organization which emphasizes a particular outlook or interest. The funds for most of the activities of these various groups come from federated campaigns in all the various communities where Jews live, from their own members or from unorganized contributors.

The religious bodies consist of the various congregations, Orthodox, Conservative and Reform, with their affiliated groups: boards of directors and trustees; brotherhoods and sisterhoods; religious school committees and parent-teacher associations; and youth groups. For each branch of Judaism, the congregations are usually banded together in national associations to provide for exchange of information and experience, and to perform services which would be too difficult or costly for any single congregation to conduct alone. Examples are the publication of prayerbooks or religious-school textbooks, the development of school curricula, or the planning of adult education or social action activities. The principal national bodies of this kind are the Union of Orthodox Jewish Congregations, the United Synagogue of America (Conservative) and the Union of American Hebrew Congregations (Reform).

Each of the branches of Judaism has institutions for the training of rabbis and of other religious and educational personnel. There are numerous Orthodox institutions of this kind, but perhaps the most prominent of them are the Rabbinical Seminary and Teacher's Seminary of Yeshiva University. The central Conservative institution of this kind is the Jewish Theological Seminary. The Reform seminary is the Hebrew Union College-Jewish Institute of Religion.

10. Eastern Orthodoxy in a Western Land

SEPARATED FORMALLY from Western Christendom in 1054, Eastern Orthodox Christianity was little known in North America, except in Alaska where Russian Orthodox missions had been established, until late in the nineteenth century. In the first quarter of the present century, large numbers of immigrants from Russia, Greece, and other eastern European lands brought about twenty Orthodox communions to America. The largest was the Green Orthodox Church, which became a member of the National and the World Councils of Churches. The following descriptive account makes very clear that the transplantation of European religious traditions to America did not stop with the colonial period, but continued through the first quarter of the twentieth century.

SOURCE: Greek Archdiocese of North and South America, *HMEPO-ΛΟΓΙΟΝ*, 1964 Year Book (New York, 1964), pp. 93–97.

The Greek Orthodox Church in America

The Greek Archdiocese of North and South America represents the Greek Orthodox church also known as the One Holy Catholic Apostolic church, the original Eastern Church which is "Christianity's oldest church," that has had a venerable unbroken existence and history dating from the first century A.D.

The first Orthodox church in America was founded almost a century ago, in 1864, by a small colony of Greek merchants in New Orleans, Louisiana. However, the firmer establishment of Greek Orthodoxy in America began later, towards the end of the last and the beginning of this century, coinciding with the acceleration of immigrants from Greece, which continued thereafter into the 1920's.

The New York Community, for example, was founded in 1892, the same year that the first Greek Orthodox church was opened in Chicago. The industrial city of Lowell, Massachusetts, for years a great center of Greek immigration, had its first Greek church in 1894. With the turn of the century, Greek Orthodox churches were established throughout the length and breadth of the United States, and in Canada; Philadelphia in 1901; Birmingham in 1902; Boston in 1904; Atlanta and Savannah in 1905; and Montreal in 1906. The pioneering of Greek Orthodoxy in America continued at an intensified rate throughout the first two decades of the twentieth century, and by 1920 60 percent of the present-day Greek Communities and their houses of worship were firmly founded.

In spite of this rapid growth during the early years of this century, Greek Orthodoxy remained a small and minor religion of the land, little known and little recognized. This was inevitably so because the Greek immigrants in this country, though large in number in proportion to the total population of their Motherland, were a small minority group when compared with the large influx of other nationalities that had emigrated to the United States much earlier. The Greeks, moreover, were newcomers to this country, totally unversed in the English language, without background, influence or financial means. They thought of themselves as temporary residents grateful to be here, but convinced that their sojourn was not permanent and that they would eventually return to Greece. But as their first generation of children grew up as Americans and inevitably espoused new ways as their own, their parents began to realize that their role on the American scene was more than transitory and they slowly turned their energies, that had been entirely occupied with making a living for themselves and their families, to conforming with their destiny of establishing themselves as good Americans proud to be of Greek descent and of the Greek Orthodox faith. While they prospered as hardworking and law-abiding citizens of the United States they retained pride and belief in their illustrious Hellenic traditions of the past, and in the Christian Greek Orthodox faith of their church, which they perpetuated in these early years with fervor and dedication, but without effective organization and centralized authority.

The first Greek Orthodox churches in the United States were under the jurisdiction of the Ecumenical Patriarchate of Constantinople (Istanbul), which assigned to them their priests. In 1908, however, the jurisdiction was transferred to the Holy Synod of the Church of Greece. This arrangement was maintained until 1918, unfortunately to the detriment of the Communities of America, which during this period remained without the necessary organization and without a responsible and authorized religious leader they so greatly needed.

A constructive step towards solving the administrative problems of Greek Orthodoxy in America was the arrival here in 1918 of Metropolitan Meletios, an emissary of the Ecumenical Patriarchate, who on October 20 of that year established the "Synodiki Epitropeia" (Synodical Council), which set the pattern for a church deriving authority from a centralized source.

This was in effect the first step towards the establishment of the Greek Archdiocese of North and South America, which was incorporated in 1921, and officially recognized by the State of New York in 1922.

When Metropolitan Meletios was elected Ecumenical Patriarch Meletios IV in January of 1922, one of his first official decrees on March 1st of that year was to revoke the dependence of Greek Orthodoxy in America on the Holy Synod of Greece, and to restore the ecclesiastical jurisdiction to the Ecumenical Patriarchate. This was formalized on May 11, 1922, when Patriarch Meletios declared the Church of America an Archdiocese, appointing the Rt. Rev. Alexander, Titular Bishop of Rodostolou, as his Patriarchal Exarch here.

It is regrettable that from 1922 to 1930 turbulent political events in Greece divided the Greeks in America, and this division also manifested itself here ecclesiastically. Fortunately, the necessity for religious unison and concord was quickly realized by the Greeks in this country, and this need was also understood by the newly elected Ecumenical Patriarch Photios II, who after sending Metropolitan Damaskinos to America in May 1930 to govern the Greek Communities temporarily, appointed Metropolitan Athenagoras of Kerkyra (Corfu) as Archbishop of North and South America on August 30, 1930. Archbishop Athenagoras arrived in New York on February 24, 1931, and began a long tenure here as head of the Greek Orthodox Church in America, which did not end until he was elected Ecumenical Patriarch of Constantinople on November 1, 1948.

It may truly be said that the modern organized period of the Greek Orthodox church in the new world dates from the beginning of Archbishop Athenagoras' administration. A remarkable ecclesiast with a great dedication, dynamic energy, magnetic personality, far-sighted statesmanship and visionary enthusiasm, Archbishop Athenagoras initiated an authoritative administration that went far towards uniting the Greek Orthodox Communities in America under a centralized Archdiocese, and laid a sure ground work for the future of Greek Orthodoxy in America. In addition to serving so well his communants here, before he assumed the spiritual leadership of the world's 250,000,000 Greek Orthodox as Ecumenical Patriarch in 1949, Athenagoras attained a high degree of influence among Americans, who respected and admired him. Most indicative of this is the fact that when he left America to take up his high duties at the Ecumenical Patriarchate, he traveled on an official airplane of the government, personally assigned for his use by the President of the United States.

Archbishop Michael, who succeeded the present Patriarch, and remained as Archbishop until his death on July 13, 1958, most effectively furthered the consolidating work of his illustrious predecessors, and greatly strengthened the Greek Orthodox church in America, which during this period, with added resources and efforts, may be said to have entered the stage of maturity.

Archbishop Michael, a brilliant scholar and linguist, enhanced the prestige of Orthodoxy among Americans, and strengthened the Greek Archdiocese. He established the Dekadollarion, a ten-dollar subscription to the Archdiocese by every member of the church; he founded the Greek Orthodox Youth of America; he promoted vigorously the campaign for national recognition of Eastern Orthodoxy as a major faith in America; he created an Archdiocese Office of Information and Public Relations; he brought about the acceptance of the Regulations and Uniform Parish By-Laws of the Archdiocese by almost all the Greek Orthodox Communities under its jurisdiction and he gained membership for the Greek Orthodox church of America in the National Council of the Churches of Christ in the United States of America and in the United States Conference for the World Council of Churches. His efforts for widespread recognition of the church were appropriately acknowledged and rewarded when he was invited by the President of the United States to deliver an invocation as the official representative and leader of the Greek Orthodox church in America, at the Presidential Inauguration in January, 1957.

The enthronement of Archbishop Iakovos on April 1, 1959, in a most impressive ceremony at the Holy Trinity Cathedral in New York City, ushered in the dawn of a new era for Greek Orthodoxy in America. The new spiritual and administrative leader of 1,500,000 Greek Orthodox communicants in the New World is eminently fitted to guide and inspire the faithful in the lasting perpetuation of the Greek Orthodox Church as a permanent and vital American institution. A young man (he was fifty years old on

July 29, 1961), the former Metropolitan James of Melita, who served as the representative of the Ecumenical and the other Greek Orthodox Patriarchates in the headquarters of the World Council of Churches in Geneva from 1955 until his election as Archbishop, is an American citizen who had served the church in this country as a dedicated and progressive clergyman of exceptional qualities since his arrival here in 1939.

II

Tensions within Protestantism

11. The Great Awakening

THE Great Awakening, which reached its dramatic peak in New England in the early 1740's, was a major event in American history. Indeed, the Awakening can be seen as a whole series of events, beginning with revival movements in Reformed and Presbyterian churches of the middle colonies in the 1720's and 1730's, becoming most conspicuous with the preaching of Whitefield and Edwards in the northern provinces, and then continuing in a series of southern phases into the Revolutionary era. George Whitefield (1714–1770), Anglican revivalist of torrential eloquence, was active in all of these stages. Jonathan Edwards (1703–1758), a Calvinist, who was probably the greatest theological mind America has produced, became famous not only for his Awakening preaching but also for his carefully reasoned psychological and theological defenses of what he defined as true revivalism. Although the Great Awakening was highly controversial, it left a permanent stamp both on religion and on society. It represented a shift from the traditional, catechetical ways of winning converts to the faith to emotionally based appeals for personal decision. It affected preaching and worship, and provided much of the dynamic which enabled the churches to extend their mission across a vast continent and then to foreign lands. It further broadened the growing pluralism of American church life, and contributed to the decline of the patterns of uniformity and establishment and to the rise of religious freedom. In its vision of the coming millennium, it helped to shape a strong sense of American destiny. As an intercolonial movement which saw the movement of leaders across sectional lines, the Great Awakening helped to form a national consciousness and a democratic spirit, so important in the Revolutionary epoch.

The Awakening continues to be an object of fascination in the effort to understand American history; a spate of sourcebooks have made its materials readily available, especially The Great Awakening: Documents Illustrating the Crisis and Its Consequences, edited by Alan Heimert and Perry Miller (Indianapolis, 1967), and The Great Awakening: Event and Exegesis, edited by Darrett B. Rutman (New York, 1970). No single document can give an adequate sense of the sweep and depth of this major turning point in American social and religious history. The private Journals of the Reverend Ebenezer Parkman, one of the supporters of the Awakening, does give the reader something of an inside look into the Awakening at its peak in Massachusetts. Some of the leading figures of the Awakening march through its pages—Jonathan Edwards and the remarkable Mrs. Edwards; Charles Chauncy, soon to become the most uncompromising opponent of the Awakening and a representative of the liberalizing drive within Congregationalism; James Davenport, who was bringing disrepute to the Awakening by his emotional extremes. Here too are named many of the common people, both those who were won to faith through the Awakening and those, like poor Sarah Sparhawk, who were driven over the edge of sanity by its excesses.

SOURCE: Joseph Tracy, *The Great Awakening: A History of the Revival of Religion in the Time of Edwards and Whitefield* (Boston, 1842), pp. 204–212.

Extracts from the Private Journal of the Rev. Ebenezer Parkman, of Westborough, Massachusetts

January 7, 1742. Cold day; but I rode over to the private meeting at deacon Forbush's, and preached on John 3:36; after which I had a brief exercise of prayer and exhortation to the society of young women. It is agreeable to see how readily and gladly many receive the word.

26. Catechetical exercise to young women.

28. There being at Leicester very considerable awakenings among some of the people, they set apart this day for fasting and prayer, for obtaining a plentiful effusion of the Holy Spirit upon them; and they having sent for me to assist on that occasion, I went up. Mr. Edwards, of Northampton, was there, and preached a very awakening sermon on Rom. 9:22—"Vessels of wrath." I preached in the afternoon on Zech. 12:10. In the evening, Mr. Hall preached on Isa. 54:13 N.B. Some stirrings.

29. Mr. Edwards preached on John 12:23, a peculiarly moving and useful sermon. May God bless it to me, to draw my heart effectually to Jesus Christ, by his love, by his bitter and ignominious sufferings on the cross for me! I prevailed on Mr. Edwards, before we went out of the pulpit, to come by divine leave next week to Westborough.

31. I cannot help remarking what a wonderful time was now appearing; for there are great movings upon the hearts of the people of the country, in one part thereof and another. O! that I and mine might be stirred up earnestly and seasonably to put in for a share! The Lord grant us this mercy, and let us not be left behind!

February 1. It was a rainy day, but I rode to Grafton and Sutton. Mr. Edwards was come from Leicester. Mr. Edwards preached to a large assembly on Ps. 18:25. At evening, in a very rainy, stormy time, I preached to a considerable assembly on Ps. 68:8. Religion has of late been very much revived in Sutton, and there is a general concern about their souls.

2. A rainy morning. Mr. Edwards put on resolution and came with me to Westborough. Mr. Edwards preached to a great congregation on John 12:32, and at eve at my house on Gen. 19:17. N.B. Mr. James Fay was greatly wrought on by the sermon on John 12:32. So were Samuel Allen and Ezekiel Dodge, who manifested it to me; and doubtless multitudes besides were so. *Deo Opt. Max. Gloria.*[1]

6. Mr. James Fay, who thinks he sees things in a new light, and that he is now converted, was here to see me and discourse with me.

9. Mr. James Fay came for me to go and see Isaiah Pratt, who lay in a strange condition at his house, not having spoke nor been sensible since nine o'clock last night. I went to him, and seeing him lie so insensible, and his pulse *exceeding slow*, I advised them to send for Dr. Gott, to bleed him; but sitting by him and rousing him, by degrees he came to. Many were present, and were astonished. When he regained his senses, he said he had not been asleep, had seen hell, and seen Christ; and said Christ told him his name was in the book of life, &c. When he had taken some slender food, he yet further revived, and spake more freely. We gave thanks and prayed, and I gave some exhortation. N.B. One of the deacons of the church was there, who took me aside to lament to me his dullness and backwardness in the things of the kingdom of God. These things are now (blessed be God) more frequent, which heretofore were very rare. May God increase them, and furnish me abundantly for his work, in every part of it!

10. By agreement with Mr. Cushing, this day was kept in a religious manner at my house, as a time of humiliation and supplication, but as privately as we could. And I sent a letter last week to the neighboring ministers to join with us, in that we might unitedly implore divine direction in such an extraordinary day as this is, and that we might obtain the outpouring of God's Spirit upon us and our respective charges; but none came but Mr. Cushing.

11. Mrs. Pratt with her son were here according to my appointment, to acquaint me further with what he had seen, or appre-

1. Glory to God, highest and greatest.

hended he saw, in the time of his trance or reverie the other night. He having informed me of his seeing (as he thought) the devil, who met him as he seemed to be in the way towards heaven, and told him that there was no room for him there; of his seeing hell, and hearing the most dreadful noise of roaring and crying; his seeing heaven, so wondrously happy a place as nobody could tell but those that were there; and Christ, who looked more pleasant than ever he had seen any man, and who had a great book before him, and in turning over the leaves of it, told him that his name was there, and showed it him; and that he had seen a great many more things, which were such great things that he could not speak of them;—I told him that these things were not to be depended upon, but that the apostle Peter has cautioned us, saying, that we have a more sure word of prophecy, to which we should do well to take heed, &c. I endeavored further to instruct, direct, and comfort him, and lay the charges of God upon him. P.M. I preached at Mr. James Fay's, on Luke 19:9, to a great multitude, and it pleased God to give it some success. As soon as the exercise was over, Deacon Fay broke forth with a loud voice, with tears of joy, and blessed God that he saw this day, &c.; desiring that I would in due time have an exercise at his house; and bore a message from his brother, old Mr. Samuel Fay, that I would have one at his also—which it was a cheerful thing to hear, considering his temper and conduct for some years past. The rest of the people seemed so inclined to religious matters, that they did not freely go away. Many tarried to discourse of the affairs of their souls, and hear of the experiences of one another.

12. At eve, Mr. Stephen Fay was here in great distress concerning his spiritual state, fearing that all he had done in religion was only to still conscience. I directed him to read what was most awakening still, and most searching; and particularly Mr. Alliene's Alarm and Mead's Almost Christian.

March 9. N.B. Mr. Pattershall informs me of Mr. Croswell's irregular zeal at Charlestown.

11. Fast in this place, on account of the extraordinary dispensations of God's grace in the land; that we might on the one hand implore the gift of the Holy Spirit, and divine direction, that we be not carried away by the many snares, temptations, and delusions to which we are greatly exposed.

15. Very cold day. Yet I rode to Mr. Charles Rice's, and preached to the society of young women on Ps. 119:59.

20. Rainy. Mr. Buel and three young men with him here. I found him willing to submit to any examinations concerning his doctrines, or opinions, or life; whereupon I made several inquiries, to which he made ready answers, and told me he had made up with Mr. Noyes at New Haven above a month after commencement, and was examined and licensed by the ministers of that association to preach. I urged him to preach; but he said he was under such obligations to preach at Concord, that he must proceed thither.

21. On 2 Cor. 6:2.—I hope there was some good success of the word today, through the blessing of God. O may it prove an accepted time and a day of salvation to us all!

22. Catechised boys A.M. at the meetinghouse. P.M. Girls at my own house.

23. P.M. Catechetical exercise with the young women. I preached on John 13:17. At Ensign Maynard's at evening, to remove his stumbling at my slippers.

27. N.B. Mr. James Fay and Mr. Francis Whipple here. P.M. A great deal of discourse about the assurance of every new convert.

29. N.B. The world full of Mr. Buel's preaching at Concord. In the judgment of some, great success; in the judgment of others, great confusion.

30. I proceeded to Cambridge.—Visited Mr. Appleton. N.B. Various accounts from Ipswich, of the state of religion there. The people are greatly enlivened and awakened there. At evening I was at Charlestown. Mr. Buel preached on Gen. 6:3. N.B. Mr. Croswell lies sick at Charlestown, after zealous preaching there for some time.

April 1. Mr. Hooper at the public lecture, on 1 John 4:13. N.B. Great disgust given by Mr. Barnard's sermon last Thursday, and now continued among some by Mr. Hooper; as appeared to me at evening at Mr. Cooper's.

9. Mr. Beriah Rice here to join the church. Neighbor Thurston here at evening. N.B. His experience of extraordinary grace, the months past. His discourse very savory and very free.

10. Mr. Williams here P.M. to join the church.

13. [He went with his daughter to Cambridge.]

14. Rainy; but yet Molly and I rode to Boston, and were at the ordination of the Rev. Mr. Andrew Eliot, at the New North Church. Dr. Sewall prayed, Mr. Eliot preached 1 Cor. 4:2, Mr.

Webb the charge, Mr. Appleton the right hand. N.B. A vast assembly, and a glorious time of God's grace.

15. [He returned home with Sarah Sparhawk, of whom more hereafter.]

20. Catechetical exercise No. 5, at the meetinghouse. Above thirty young women, I suppose, were present. N.B. Mary Bradish with me afterwards, being in some spiritual difficulties.

21. Mr. Samuel Williams here about his spiritual state, and desirous to join the church. I took pains in examining him, and hope God is doing a good work in him.

22. I had sent to Mr. Stone and to Mr. Cushing, fruitlessly, to assist me. I sent a verbal message to Mr. Burr, and, though it was a rainy day, he came and preached my lecture; a good, useful sermon on Rom. 10: part of the 14th and 15th verses, and the 17th, against exhorters among the people, &c., with a moving application.

25. Administered the Lord's Supper. Repeated on 2 Cor. 11:27, 29. P.M. on Eph. 5:14. I was in much fear and trembling, but cast myself on God. I chose to repeat in the forenoon, that I might deliver the latter part of that discourse, and likewise that I might deliver my sermon in the afternoon more entirely by itself, it not admitting to be divided, but it being the quantity of two sermons. I was much above an hour. Some number of Southborough people at meeting, and some of Hopkinton.

26. [Went to Rutland, to attend a council and fast.]

30. Mr. Grow here in spiritual distress, and Mr. Jesse Brigham's wife.

May 1. Stephen Fay here upon soul accounts.

2. On Eph. 5:14. Mrs. Bathsheba Pratt here, being greatly distressed for the hardness of her heart, notwithstanding that she had been a member in full communion above twenty years.

6. Mr. Paterson, an Irishman from Stoddardtown, here. N.B. He had been one of those that had fallen into a strange fit by the pressure of his distress at hearing the word preached. P.M. I preached at Capt. Fay's, on Eph. 5:14, sermon II.—N.B. I repeated that sermon, because of divers people being at a great loss about the doctrine held forth therein.

7. Mary Bradish with me on account of her spiritual troubles. Cousin Winchester also.

11. Mr. Bliss here, on his journey to Grafton and Sutton. I rode Mr. Benjamin How's horse to Shrewsbury, and preached to the society of lads there, on 2 Cor. 6:2.

13. I rode Mr. Burns's horse to Marlborough, and preached the lecture on Eph. 5:14.

14. Mr. [or Mrs.] Williams here again—Sarah Bellows—Daniel Stone and his wife—all of them candidates for the communion.

17. Phineas Forbush with me upon his soul distresses. N.B. News from Grafton, that Mr. Philemon Robbins preached there yesterday, and twenty or more persons fell down with distress and anguish.

18. Exercise to young women on Ps. 73:24.—Mrs. Edwards from Northampton, and Searl, a Freshman of New Haven College, here, and lodged here.

19. Sweet converse with Mrs. Edwards, a very eminent Christian. At half after eleven I left home and rode to Sutton Falls. Preached there on Eph. 5:14. After meeting, an elderly woman, one Mrs. White, whose husband is a Baptist, so overcome that she was led into Mr. Hall's. She seemed to be in great distress, but she had much joy and love.

21. My wife rode with me to Stephen Fay's, where I preached on Mat. 3:10. The assembly somewhat considerable, being there was a town meeting at the same time to choose a representative. Ensign Maynard chosen, but refused. Town then concluded not to send. I had a great cold.

23.—At eve, called at Ensign Maynard's, to visit Mrs. Wheeler of Concord (heretofore Rebecca Lee), who was under a grievous melancholy and mingled despair and distraction.

[25. Rode to Boston.]

26.—Mr. Appleton preached excellently to the Court, from Ps. 72:1, 2. P.M. When I went to Dr. Sewall's, there was but a thin appearance of ministers; upon which I heard Mr. John Caldwell, at the French meetinghouse. The drift was against false prophets, and not without bitterness, mixed with his wit and sense. I sat very uneasy, and went out as soon as it was done. Went up to Mr. Chauncy's, the convention being adjourned. Some number of ministers there, congratulating him upon his being made Doctor of Divinity by the University of Edinburgh. Our conversation was upon assurance; the ground of it, the manner of obtaining it, and the special operation of the Holy Spirit therein. A very useful conversation; Mr. Barnard and others having talked very judiciously and piously upon it. Sought Mrs. Edwards fruitlessly.

27. Mr. Loring preached to the ministers from 2 Cor. 2:16, last clause. The contribution, I understand, amounted to £230.—P.M.

I went to Dr. Chauncy's, where was a very considerable number of ministers in conversation upon the present state of things with respect to religion.

28. [Returned home.]

29. Mrs. Edwards, and young Searl with her, in her journey to Northampton.

30. On Song, 2:16. N.B. Mrs. Edwards' conversation very wonderful—her sense of divine things.

31. I rode with Mrs. Edwards to Shrewsbury, but could not proceed to Worcester, as I had purposed.

June 8. Mr. Wheeler at evening, opposing my late doctrine from Eph. 5:14—that the natural man can do nothing but what is sinful.

15. Much interrupted in the morning with Mr. Joseph Wheeler, who takes exceptions against the doctrines I deliver one Sabbath after another. I rode to Mr. Loring's of Sudbury, where the association met. There were Mr. J. Prentice, Mr. Cushing, Mr. N. Stone, and Mr. Buckminster. Mr. Buckminster offered himself to be examined. He was so, and he delivered a sermon on Luke 10:41, 42. At eve, I asked advice respecting the doctrine I had lately delivered from Eph. 5:14, and Rom. 8:8, and on that question— "Are there not some promises made to humble, fervent strivers, that they shall obtain the grace of God?"—N.B. Council at Concord, called by Ezekiel Miles and others, dissatisfied with Mr. Bliss.

16. Very useful and profitable conversations upon several heads of divinity, especially referring to the great article of conversion. Comparing several of Mr. Stoddard's writings. I also read a large paper of the experiences of a young woman, a member of the church in Westborough, which I had from her own Mss.

20. I preached at Shrewsbury, A.M. and P.M. on Eph. 5:14.

22. My sixth exposition of the catechism, to thirty-eight young women. N.B. Elizabeth Chamberlain and Mr. Joseph Green, upon soul affairs.

24. I rode over to the north of Shrewsbury, and preached to a young society there on 1 Thess. 1:10.

28. I rode over to Hopkinton, at the request of Isaac How, who lay in a low languishment. His state of mind I feared to be very dreadful, because of his insensibility of the amazing wrath of God, and being so comfortable in the apprehensions of death, notwithstanding his impenitence. Many had expected me to preach; but I

received no hint of his desiring any thing of that; besides, that there was no intimations from Rev. Mr. Barrett especially, of any thing of it.

29. Mrs. Snell was with me about her owning the covenant; as was also Mr. Jonathan Brigham and his wife.

30. [Received a request from the Rev. Mr. Barrett and Isaac How, to preach to How tomorrow.]

July 1. I rode over to Hopkinton, and Isaac How being yet alive and an assembly gathered, at the house of Mr. Josiah Rice, I preached there on 1 Tim. 1:15; followed with a moving and awakening address to the poor dying man, who seemed to take it in some suitable manner, to outward appearance; but I fear he has not really an apprehension of his astonishing danger, but is in a false peace. The assembly were very attentive, and some number affected.

6. Rode to Charlestown; made a visit to Mr. Davenport, who kept at Major Jenner's.

8. I rode to Boston. Mr. Hooper's public lecture on 1 John, 5:3. P.M. I was at Dr. Chauncy's, where was Mr. Barnard of Marblehead and his lady. Afterwards came Mr. Hooper, and Mr. Malcolm, Episcopal minister of Marblehead. The conversation turned upon Mr. Davenport, who is the subject everywhere. But few among the wise and worthy, but judge he is touched in his brain. Mr. Malcolm and I walked down to the North End, and up Snow Hill, to hear him. There had been a thunderstorm, and there were little showers in time of exercise. The sermon was from Rev. 22:17; a very fervent exhortation, and to unconverted ministers in special. Said he was then in the experience of the Divine Spirit's influences. Said he was then ready to drop down dead for the salvation of but one soul, &c. After sermon, a considerable number of ministers went to Mr. Webb's, who gave us an account of the disorders in that neighborhood last night, by people's being so late at Mr. Procter's (where Mr. Davenport lodges, and which is right over against Mr. Webb's); and he also informed us of his discourse with Mr. Davenport this morning, concerning his conduct and actions (in running out into the street among the crowd, and crying out to them in an indecent voice, gesture &c.), but to no purpose, he supposing himself to be under the immediate impressions and directions of the Divine Spirit. In a word, Mr. Webb concludes him to be crazed.

9. [Returned home.—From about this time, the "throat distemper" prevailed, and was often fatal.]

25. Mr. Jacob Amsden's wife came to meeting, who has never been at the public worship till now, ever since I was first in this town.

August 10. [He was called to Cambridge and Boston by his mother's sickness.]

19. The great disturbance last night, by means of Mr. Davenport's condemning the ministers of Boston as unconverted; and Dr. Colman, Dr. Sewall, and Dr. Chauncy, by name.

20. Mr. Davenport condemned by name nine more of the ministers. Grand Jury, I hear, have sat, and have found a bill against him as a disturber of the peace.

24. The association met at my house.

25. N.B. The account Mr. Weld gave of the remarkable work of God among them [at Attleborough].

30. Mr. Nathaniel Smith of Hopkinton here, for advice respecting his son, Nathaniel, who was so oppressed and overcome with the affairs of his soul and another world, that he would not attend to the necessary supports of life.

September 10. N.B. Mr. Davenport at Capt. Fay's, going upwards.

12. On 1 Thess. 5:19. The congregation much moved. At noon, Molly Gurfield of Shrewsbury greatly distressed, being awakened by the forenoon sermon, earnestly desired prayers P.M. for her.

13. N.B. Mr. Daniel Rogers of Ipswich, Dr. Gott, and Mr. Dodge came and dined with us. Mr. Rogers had preached three times at Marlborough.

18. Mr. Parsons of Lyme made me a kind visit, and I persuaded him to stay and keep Sabbath here.

19. I preached at Marlborough. I rode up home at eve. Found Mr. Parsons preaching with great fervency to young people, on the gathering manna in the morning. It made great impression. But the most remarkable signs were immediately after the blessing was pronounced. Mr. Stephen Fay's wife cried out, and cousin Winchester presently upon it, both of whom strove what they could to contain themselves, but burst forth with great agony of soul. Sarah Shattuck and Betsey Fay discovered also their inward distress. But Sarah Sparhawk was unbounded, and like one deprived of her reason. A great tumult ensued. Mr. Parsons advised me to compose

them, and either pray or sing a psalm. I requested him to direct to a psalm. After singing, I spoke strongly to the people, advising and beseeching them to retire to private meditation and prayer; and it had success. Sarah Sparhawk was brought away home by some young men. A number of the distressed and others came to my house, but went home about nine o'clock. Sarah Sparhawk was however often crying out, and striving much in her fits for an hour or two—then went to bed and slept well.

20. Mr. Parsons took leave. Sarah Shattuck and Betty Chamberlain here to take advice upon their spiritual concerns, and Sarah Bellows was very helpful in family business, instead of Sarah Sparhawk, who was still feeble and pensive, and could do little.

21. P.M. I preached to a number that gathered together and requested it, but no public notice had been given. I repeated, as I was desired, my last sermon on 1 Thess. 5:19. N.B. Sarah Sparhawk cried out again, and was in much distress.

30. My wife rode with me to Hopkinton. Mr. Moody of York was to preach A.M., but at 11 o'clock Mr. Barrett with a message and the Bible to me, that I must preach. Mr. Barrett prayed before sermon. I preached on Eph. 5:14. P.M. Mr. Stone prayed, and Mr. Moody preached on Prov. 1:23. At evening Mr. Barrett was requested to suffer Mr. Bliss to preach an evening lecture; but he would not allow of its being publicly in the meetinghouse. He gave way to its being at a private house.

October 4. Stephen Fay here, in various religious disquietments. His brother James here at evening; and while some young women, Sarah Shattuck, Mary Graves, and Sarah Bellows, were receiving instructions from me in singing, Mr. Fay was in much spiritual commotion; but while we were singing the 63d psalm, he was in a peculiar manner rapt in spiritual delight, and panted with the overbearing joy and admiration of the divine greatness and condescension to us, and his patience towards us; and his expressions of these things were very becoming and noticeable.

13. [Went to Boston and Cambridge.]

15. At Deacon Sparhawk's, to discourse with them concerning Sarah, and apprized them of my unwillingness to keep her. I returned home.

20. Mr. Hall preached a moving sermon on John 5:40. No crying out in the meetinghouse; but, as I was going home from the meetinghouse, Mrs. Ruth Fay, in anguish of spirit, burst out and

went into my house. I took her into my study, and gave her what instructions I could. In the mean time Sarah Sparhawk was crying and screaming upon her bed in another part of the house. Many people were in the house below. Mr. Edwards of Northampton was come, and both he and Mr. Hall assisted me in ministering to these distressed souls, and others that needed. It was an evening of great engagement.

21. Mr. Hall and Mr. Edwards went, the one to Sutton and the other to Boston.

23. N.B. I have understood there are various commotions on religious accounts among brethren on the south side of the town.

26. Mr. Secomb went with me to the Association at Marlborough. A considerable number of ministers and candidates. The conversation turned mostly of all upon the times. Mr. Marsh of Wachusett very full of his stories, to discredit those who were zealous in promoting convictions, &c.

27. N.B. Mr. Loring's angry rebuke directed to me at dinner, for opposing Mr. Marsh.

28. We have the utmost reason to celebrate the divine patience and long suffering, inasmuch as he has not only waited three years upon this church, and upon me their unworthy pastor, seeking fruit upon us; nor only three times three; but this day it is no less space than twice three times three years. O may we be humbled for our manifold defects and unprofitableness! O might I, in peculiar, who have the greatest need! And may God, of his infinite mercy, grant us grace, and to me in special, that, henceforth, we may bring some fruit to his glory! *Jejun. Priv.*[2]

31. On Hab. 6:7, 8; in which I endeavoured to improve the divine admonitions and instructions to our quickening and awakening. See the 28th day.

November 16. N.B. Mr. Stephen Fay here, and tarried and dined with me; was with me all the afternoon, and some part of the evening. He revealed several wonderful experiences which he had, both last spring and lately. He told me he had a weighty, pressing concern for two souls. I found he meant his own and mine. I asked him what he had discovered in me, that gave him reason to suspect me. He told me, my preaching and conversation; for that if I had a true sight of eternal things, he thought I should be more zealous and fervent; for, for his part, he felt as if he could cry out, &c. I

---

2. Probably an abbreviation for *Jejunitate Priver,* "I hope I'm not being dull."

confessed my dullness; yet made some appeal to my sermons, especially of late delivered. I spoke of the different tempers of men; the
diversities of gifts, but the same spirit; the different frames which
both speakers and hearers are in at different times; professed,
however, my need of divine grace and the supply of the Spirit, to
revive and quicken and furnish and assist me, and of his prayers
(and asked them), that I might obtain the presence and Spirit of
God with me; and whatever God should afford, should give in to
me, I would endeavor to give out to them. We parted in great
peace and love. May the Lord sanctify the admonition to me, and
hereby stir up in me a spirit of care and jealousy over my own soul;
and enliven me with respect to the souls committed to my care! O
might it please God to impress me deeply with the worth of
immortal souls, and my tremendous account in the day of Christ,
of those of this flock, and of all my charge!

18. Mr. Cushing here P.M. He came on the business of Sarah
Sparhawk's living here, that he might write to her grandfather
about her. But she grows so untoward, that we drew up determina-
tions to put her away, unless she will reform.

22. P.M. came Mr. Samuel Streeter, of Hopkinton, and gave me
some account of himself and his spiritual state for some years past,
but especially of his darkness and trouble till the fast at Hopkinton
last December 29, and (to God the sole glory) the help he received
by my sermon on Ps. 63:8.

26. Mr. Prentice of Grafton came to see me. I inquired whether
he had sought reconcilement with Mr. Loring of Sudbury, as he
had engaged at Rutland. He could not say he had. He brought me
his church's desire and his own, to assist them in a fast next Thursday come sennight. But I insisted upon his reconcilement with Mr.
Loring. N.B. Mr. Hall had told him and his wife, that at his late
visit to me, I received him but coldly.

December 4. [Returned home from Boston, late, and in bad
weather. Took cold, which brought on rheumatism and fever, from
which he was slowly recovering Dec. 20.]

9. A fast at Grafton.—Sarah Sparhawk very intolerable in insist-
ing to go to Grafton, though there was nobody at home but she to
take care of the business of the house, my wife waiting on me.

18. I had sent a letter to Mr. Joseph Sparhawk, but no return.
The ways heavy yet, but sent Ebenezer with Sarah to said Mr.
Sparhawk at Sutton.

12. The Second Great Awakening

WHAT IS often referred to as the Second Great Awakening was actually a series of revival movements in all parts of the United States in the early decades of the nineteenth century. In New England and the Atlantic states, the revivals were rather well-disciplined and flowed in recognized church channels under the leadership of men like Lyman Beecher (1775–1863), for many years the "field marshal" of Connecticut Congregationalism. Much of the revival work in frontier areas was not greatly dissimilar: converts were gathered in, new churches were planted, controversies erupted, and missionaries were sent about their work. But there were some striking new aspects to frontier revivalism, such as the development of vast camp meetings. At some of these, intense emotional behavior, accompanied by "physical exercises," was recorded. One of the early leaders of western revivalism was Richard McNemar (?–1839), originally a Presbyterian who moved through the "New Light" movement to find his peace in the United Society of Believers in Christ's Second Appearing, or Shakers. In 1808 McNemar prepared a history of the Kentucky revival, supplying colorful accounts of that awakening, and defending step by step the path along which his own religious pilgrimage had taken him.

SOURCE: Richard McNemar, *The Kentucky Revival: Or, a Short History of the Late Outpouring of the Spirit of God, in the Western States of America, Agreeably to Scripture-Promises, and Prophecies Concerning the Latter Day: With a Brief Account of the Entrance and Progress of What the World Calls Shakerism, among the Subjects of the Late Revival in Ohio and Kentucky* (Albany, 1808), pp. 61–66.

But there were moreover in the *schismatic* worship, a species of exercises of an involuntary kind, which seemed to have been substituted by the Great Spirit, in the room of the falling, &c. which had been among the *New-Lights*. The principal of these were the *rolling* exercise, the *jerks* and the *barks*.

1. The rolling exercise which consisted in being cast down in a violent manner, doubled with the head and feet together, and rolled over and over like a wheel, or stretched in a prostrate manner, turned swiftly over and over like a log. This was considered very debasing and mortifying, especially if the person was taken in this manner thro' the mud, and sullied therewith from head to foot.

2. Still more demeaning and mortifying were the *jerks*. Nothing in nature could better represent this strange and unaccountable operation, than for one to goad another, alternately on every side, with a piece of red hot iron. The exercise commonly began in the head which would fly backward and forward, and from side to side with a quick jolt, which the person would naturally labor to suppress, but in vain; and the more any one labored to stay himself and be sober, the more he staggered, and the more rapidly his twitches increased. He must necessarily go as he was stimulated, whether with a violent dash on the ground and bounce from place to place like a foot-ball, or hop round with head, limbs and trunk, twitching and jolting in every direction, as if they must inevitably fly asunder. And how such could escape without injury was no small wonder to spectators. By this strange operation the human frame was commonly so transformed and disfigured, as to lose every trace of its natural appearance. Sometimes the head would be twitched right and left to a half round, with such velocity, that not a feature could be discovered, but the face appear as much behind as before. And in the quick progressive jerk, it would seem as if the person was transmuted into some other species of creature. Head dresses were of little account among the female jerkers. Even handkerchiefs bound tight round the head would be flirted off almost with the first twitch, and the hair put into the utmost confusion; this was a very great inconvenience, to redress which, the generality were shorn, though directly contrary to their confession of faith. Such as were sized with the *jerks* were wrested at once, not only from under their own government, but that of every one else, so that it was dangerous to attempt confining them, or touching them in any manner, to whatever danger they were exposed; yet few were hurt, except it were such as rebelled against the operation through willful and deliberate enmity, and refused to comply with the injunctions which it came to inforce.

3. The last possible grade of mortification seemed to be couched in the *barks*, which frequently accompanied the *jerks*, nor were they the most mean and contemptible characters, who were the common victims of this disgracing operation, but persons who considered themselves in the foremost rank, possessed of the highest improvements of human nature; and yet in spite of all the efforts of nature, both men and women would be forced to personate that animal, whose name, appropriated to a human creature, is counted the most vulgar stigma.—Forced I say, for no

argument but force could induce any one of polite breeding, in a
public company, to take the position of a canine beast, move about
on all fours, growl, snap the teeth, and bark in so personating a
manner as to set the eyes and ears of the spectator at variance.—It
was commonly acknowledged by the subjects of these exercises
that they were laid upon them as a chastisement for disobedience,
or a stimulus to incite them to some duty or exercise to which they
felt opposed.—Hence it was very perceivable that the quickest
method to find releasement from the *jerks* and *barks* was to engage
in the voluntary dance; and such as refused, being inwardly moved
thereto as their duty and privilege, had to bear these afflicting
operations from month to month, and from year to year, until they
wholly lost their original design, and were converted into a badge
of honor, in the same manner as the first outward mark of human
guilt. Altho' these strange convulsions served to overawe the
heaven-daring spirits of the wicked, and stimulate the halting
Schismatic to the performance of many duties disagreeable to the
carnal mind, yet in all this, their design was not fully compre-
hended, something doubtful and awful was thought to be figured
out thereby, which would suddenly *fall with pain upon the head of
the wicked;* and nothing was more calculated to excite such fearful
apprehensions than the expressions that were sometimes mixed
with the *bow wow wow,* such as *every knee shall bow, and every
tongue confess,* &c. at least these kind of exercises served to shew
that the foundation was not yet laid for unremitting joy, and that
such as attached themselves to this people, must unite with them
as a *body* destined to *suffer* with Christ, before they could reign
with him. But however great the sufferings of the *Schismatics,*
from a sense of their own remaining depravity—the burden and
weight of distress they bore for a lost world—the hatred, contempt,
and persecuting rage of all around them—together with the spas-
modic writhings of body with which they were so generally exercised; yet they were not a little alleviated by the many extraordinary signs and gifts of the spirit, through which they were
encouraged to look for brighter days. Among these innumerable
signs and gifts may be ranked *the spirit of prophecy*—being caught
up or carried away in this spirit, and remaining for hours insensible
of any thing in nature—dreaming of dreams—seeing visions—hearing unspeakable words—the fragrant smell, and delightful singing
in the breast. This spirit of prophecy is particularly worthy of

notice, which had its foundation in a peculiar kind of faith, and grew up under the special influence of visions, dreams, &c. The first thing was to believe what God had promised, with an appropriating faith; cast anchor upon the thing promised though unseen, and hold the soul to the pursuit of it in defiance of all the tossing billows of unbelief. This faith, so contrary to the carnal heart, they concluded must be of God. It must be the spirit of Christ, or God working in the creature, both to will and to do. What is the promise but the purpose of God? And what is the purpose of my soul (says the *Schismatic*) but to have the thing promised. Has God promised?—he cannot lie: Has he purposed?—he cannot alter. Therefore what his spirit leads me to I shall possess, as certain as God is stronger than the Devil. Upon this principle all were encouraged to believe the promise, and immediately set out in cooperation with the promiser; and in proportion to the strength of their faith, to predict the certain accomplishment of that purpose of God, which they felt within them.

Notwithstanding this faith furnished a very bold foundation for predicting what should come to pass, yet it was far from comprehending the whole of that evidence, upon which the *Schismatic* looked for the purpose and promise of God to be fulfilled. It was very common for them to be caught up or carried away by the same spirit of faith, and be shewn in bright and heavenly visions, the indisputable reality of what they before contemplated in a simple belief. In those ecstasies some would seem to desert the body, and leave it for hours in a state almost or quite inanimate. Others, in their transports, would seem to use their clay tenement as a kind of instrument, to sign out and represent to the spectators, what the active spirit saw in open vision, independent of any of its mean organs. Of these extraordinary visions, nothing can be communicated here beyond an imperfect hint, and whether they ever be correctly stated on paper is a matter of doubt. Their general import respected things that were darkly hinted at in the scriptures, and hard to be understood; such things as were especially to take place in the latter days. And hence notwithstanding they had adopted the scriptures under the notion of a confession of faith, yet it was not immediately to the scriptures they applied for light, but to that transporting spirit which opened clearly to the mind, those mysterious things recorded in scripture, which the wisest men upon earth, without the spirit, could not understand. . . .

Sleeping and waking, the whole topic with these *Schismatics* was the increasing work of God, and the blessed kingdom just about to appear, and each one contemplating it through some special dream or vision, in which they felt confident they had a particular revelation of the Lord's Christ.

13. Crusading for a Christian America

ALTHOUGH REVIVALISTIC Protestants remained denominationally divided, they longed for a fully Christian America and worked for it through an intricate network of voluntary societies. Many of these benevolent institutions were officially nondenominational, for they were made up of individuals from many churches, but they represented the religious and moral concerns that evangelical Protestants held in common. Much of the energy evoked by the revivals was poured through the channels provided by the benevolent societies. There were societies for home and foreign missions, for educational causes, for the publication of Bibles and tracts, for the suppression of vice, for temperance, and for various reforming crusades. The national "anniversary" meetings of the societies each year provided a time when their interlocking leadership gathered for inspiration and mutual support. The constituencies of the societies were cultivated by field agents and by religious journals.

One of the most important of the national benevolent societies was the American Home Missionary Society, organized in 1826. Two years later its magazine, The Home Missionary and American Pastor's Journal, was launched. A regular feature was "An Address, Adapted to the Monthly Concert for Prayer," which was the agreement of many evangelicals to join in prayer on the first Monday of every month for the success of missionary efforts. The following address is typical as it urges Christians to work for a host of good causes to shape the national character and speed the millennial dawn.

SOURCE: The Home Missionary and Pastor's Journal, 2 (January 1, 1830), 137–139.

Through strength obtained of God, we have commenced another year. At this, its first monthly concert, all who enter into the spirit of the occasion, and are honestly intending to live better, to pray more, and labor more for Christ, than during the former year, are solicitous to know what are the duties and responsibilities which devolve upon them. They have labored during the months that are past, and now they come and ask respecting the future, saying, "Here are we, Lord, what wilt thou have us to do? Their inquiry is answered—"Be not weary in well-doing, for in due time ye shall reap, if ye faint not."

There is always a demand upon us for "well-doing," for benevolent action in this world of sin and suffering. But there are particular periods which require that particular departments of Christian exertion should receive special attention. In time of famine, we must feed the hungry. When pestilence stalks through the land, we should be assiduous in bearing medicine to the sick, and cheering the gloom of death with the consolations of religion. There are also peculiar states of the public mind requiring special, united, and persevering exertions in the cause of Christ. Let us, then, inquire what are the *peculiar species of well-doing* which our times and our country demand; what are the *dangers* that we shall *grow weary*, and what encouragement we have to *persevere*.

1. The particular departments of Christian action which claim special attention the ensuing year, are indicated by the aspect of the times. At the present period, men are taking strong ground on the subject of religion. The reptile passions of the sensualist and the infidel are roused into action as the light of the Church shines in upon their darkness. The enemy is alarmed—his emissaries are on the alert; nor will they again slumber till they have tried their utmost strength against the cause of truth. A general onset against the walls of Zion seems to be intended. Within the Church, corrupters are set at work to poison the stream of truth; to produce disunion, and distract the efforts of God's people in the cause of benevolence. Without, the enemies of the Church caricature her doctrines, scoff at her solemn rites, and seek to trample her institutions in the dust. Against all these forms of attack we must be prepared to take our stand. Against false teachers we must contend earnestly for the faith; with each other we must band together in inviolable league. We must rescue the Sabbath from the profane encroachments of worldliness; and assert the divine dignity of religion in opposition to those who pronounce it a mere figment of ambitious priests. And all this we must do, not in the spirit of belligerents, but in the spirit of martyrs, of apostles, of Christ—not with carnal weapons, but with fair arguments and holy lives. While we rouse up all our energies to a fearless expression of the truth, let our first and last and greatest argument be seen in the meekness of our spirit and the purity of our practice.

If ever the fair fabric of American liberty be subverted, ignorance and infidelity will be the spoilers. Religion and education are the basis of our happiness; and in a community like ours, these depend for their maintenance on the fluctuations of popular favor. For religion, the civil power can do nothing better than to let it alone, neither opposing nor establishing it. The moment religion puts on the trappings and moves in the gait prescribed by the secular power, she is debased—her native purity and loveliness are gone. In like manner, divorce learning from religion; let knowledge be cultivated without the guiding influence of the fear of God, and it tends to pride and infidelity. The conclusion is plain, therefore, that the great interests of education and morals are mainly devolved on the voluntary efforts of Christian philanthropy. If the civil power may not do this work, the Church must, or our country is lost. We must hunt the monster Ignorance from his darkest hiding places in our cities, and drive him from his remotest den in the wilderness. Our infant schools must begin the work at the threshold of the nursery. Thousands of Sabbath scholars are to be gathered and instructed. Our National Bible Society must be sustained in the heaven-descended enterprise of giving a revelation to every destitute household in the land. Look, Christian, at your Bible; for what would you barter its truths and promises? What sum would tempt you to let its doctrines and consolations be torn out, one by one, for ever from the book of God? How desolate and dead would be your soul in such a case! But virtually in just such a condition, there are now 500,000 families in these United States! living without the Bible, and therefore without Bible truth and Bible hopes. Here then is a great work to do, and one third of the time for accomplishing it has already elapsed. The new year must therefore be a year of intense effort, or this indispensable work will fail. *Fail!* let us not suffer the thought of such an event. If the Bible effort fail, it will be a reproach to the Church which a century of action will scarcely wipe away. In such an event, we might well hang our harps on the willows, and sit down and weep over the fallen glories of Zion.

But there are other departments of benevolent enterprise that must not be neglected. Who that knows the economy and efficiency of the Tract Society, can withhold his aid at a time when it is beginning to operate powerfully to the national character? The voice of our Domestic Missionary Societies, also, has reached the solitary Churches in the West, and the cheering sound has caused them to lift up their eyes in hope of seeing the salvation of God. With awakened expectations, and an importunity that might melt a heart of stone, they cry, "Come over and help us, and let our heritage be left unto us desolate no longer." From the Eastern coast to the farthest limit of our settlements in the West; from the hill country where the brooks gush pure from their native fountains, down to the distant South, where the "father of rivers" rolls his broad and turbid current into the sea—the demand is unceasing and irresistible, "Give us some one to care for our souls." The coming year, then, must witness unwonted efforts for Education and Home Missionary Societies. And no good man, we trust, will withhold his influence in urging onward that glorious and prosperous cause, which promises to deliver our land from the scourge of intemperance.

2. In these labors, there is great danger of our growing weary. The work is large. The souls for whose salvation we must labor are scattered over an immense territory; and thousands must toil in the various departments of Christian exertion, year after year, and yet the light will gain but slowly on the darkness. Another source of discouragement will be a want of mutual confidence and concert. Oh, if ever the spirit of a good man falters, and his heart dies within him, it is when he finds his motives misrepresented and his efforts counteracted by a brother's influence. Great sacrifices will be required—sacrifices of property, of personal ease and comfort, and sacrifices of feeling, more difficult than any other. Great opposition must be expected. The holiest movements of the Church will be traduced, and her motives ridiculed or held up as subjects for suspicion. The opprobrious cry of *"Church and State!"* will resound through the land. Meanwhile the very men who impute to us this unhallowed conspiracy against the national freedom are blindly taking the most direct way to render a union of Church and State inevitable. Should they succeed in trampling the Sabbath under foot, and scattering the seeds of infidelity as widely as they intend, soon would the rank licentiousness, the gathering storm of factions, treasons, and revolutions, compel the State, in self-defense, to establish by law some sort of religion, lest all sense of obligation and duty should be obliterated from the popular mind, and the mighty mass of the Republic be blown in pieces by the explosion of its own inbred fires. Therefore, let us not be frightened from our work by the din of opposition; for it is the work of freedom and humanity, as well as of religion.

3. The encouragement we have to persevere is God's own promise: "In due time ye shall reap, if ye faint not." "In *due time*"—the time that infinite wisdom and goodness prefer (and who would wish for any other?) *"ye shall reap."* This is enough. It was GOD

that spake that word, and we ask not what are the signs of the times—what are the probabilities that he will redeem his pledge—though the results of the past year are indeed most animating. The same voice that said, "Let there be light, and there was light," has assured us, that if we persevere we shall succeed. But observe the condition—*if ye faint not*. There is, then, no room for inaction or repose. It will be time enough to rest in heaven. Gird up, therefore, brethren, the loins of your minds, and let the world see, and let our Master see, that we feel ourselves committed, to live or die with the cause of Christ.

14. The Builder of Modern Revivalism

THE FOUNDATIONS of the triumph of the theology and practice of revivalism in much of American Protestantism had been laid in the first and second Awakenings, especially for the Anglo-American denominations of Puritan and Evangelical background: Congregational, Presbyterian, Methodist, and Baptist. In the 1830's a series of revivals swept across the nation in unprecedented fashion. The central figure in the work was Charles Grandison Finney (1792–1875), a Presbyterian (later Congregationalist) of little formal theological education who left his law practice to become a revivalist. Finney developed "new measures" to get a revival started and to keep it going. Actually such devices as services at unseasonable hours and protracted over a period of days, the use of exhortatory prayers and of harsh language, the scheduling of cottage and inquiry meetings, and the placing of an "anxious seat" under the piercing eye of the evangelist were not really new, but his organization of them into a system was. He also developed a theology for revival, which replaced much of the older theology in many quarters. Finney was spectacularly successful; the Rochester revival of 1830–1831 made him a national figure. During the winter of 1834–1835, he gave a series of lectures in the New York church to which he had been called. In published form the lectures ran through edition after edition and were translated into several European languages. In one of the most forceful of the lectures, "Measures to Promote Revivals," Finney described and defended his system of modern revivalism, destined to play such an important role in subsequent Protestant history. The story is told in detail by William G. McLoughlin, Modern Revivalism: Charles Grandison Finney to Billy Graham (New York, 1959). McLoughlin also prepared in 1960 a critical edition of the book from which this passage has been selected.

SOURCE: Charles G. Finney, Lectures on Revivals of Religion (New York, 1835), pp. 232–249.

Text.—"These men, being Jews, do exceedingly trouble our city, and teach customs which are not lawful for us to receive, neither to observe, being Romans."—Acts xvi. 20, 21.

"These men," here spoken of, were Paul and Silas, who went to Philippi to preach the gospel, and very much disturbed the people of that city, because they supposed the preaching would interfere with their worldly gains. As so they arraigned the preachers of the gospel before the magistrates of the city, as culprits, and charged them with teaching doctrines, and especially employing measures, that were not lawful.

In discoursing from these words I design to show,

I. That under the gospel dispensation, God has established no particular system of measures to be employed and invariably adhered to in promoting religion.

II. To show that our present forms of public worship, and every thing, so far as measures are concerned, have been arrived at by degrees, and by a succession of New Measures.

I. I am to show that under the gospel, God has established no particular measures to be used.

Under the Jewish dispensation, there were particular forms enjoined and prescribed by God himself, from which it was not lawful to depart. But these forms were all typical, and were designed to shadow forth Christ, or something connected with the new dispensation that Christ was to introduce. And therefore they were fixed, and all their details particularly prescribed by Divine authority. But it was never so under the gospel. When Christ came, the ceremonial or typical dispensation was abrogated, because the design of those forms was fulfilled, and therefore themselves of no further use. He, being the antitype, the types were of course done away at his coming. THE GOSPEL was then preached as the appointed means of promoting religion; and it was left to the discretion of the church to determine, from time to time, what measures shall be adopted, and what forms pursued, in giving the gospel its power. We are left in the dark as to the measures which were pursued by the apostles and primitive preachers, except so far as we can gather it from occasional hints in the Book of Acts. We do not know how many times they sang and how many times they prayed in public worship, nor even whether they sang or prayed at all in their ordinary meetings for preaching. When Jesus Christ was on earth, laboring among his disciples, he had nothing to do with forms or measures. He did from time to time in this respect just as it would be natural for any man to do in such cases, without any thing like a set form or mode of doing it. The Jews accused him of disregarding their forms. His object was to preach and teach mankind the true religion. And when the apostles preached afterwards, with the Holy Ghost sent down from heaven, we hear nothing about their having a particular system of measures to carry on their work, or one apostle doing a thing in a particular way because others did it in that way. Their commission was, "Go and preach the gospel, and disciple all nations." It did not prescribe any forms. It did not admit any. No person can pretend to get any set of forms or particular directions as to measures, out of this commission. Do it—the best way you can—ask wisdom from God—use the faculties he has given you—seek the direction of the Holy Ghost—go forward and do it. This was their commission. And their object was to make known the gospel in the *most effectual* way, to make the truth stand out strikingly, so as to obtain the attention and secure the obedience of the greatest number possible. No person can find any *form* of doing this laid down in the Bible. It is *preaching the gospel* that stands out prominent there as the great thing. The form is left out of the question.

It is manifest, that, in preaching the gospel, there must be some kind of measures adopted. The gospel must be gotten before the minds of the people, and measures must be taken so that they can hear it, and to induce them to attend to it. This is done by building churches, holding stated or other meetings, and so on. Without some measures, it can never be made to take effect among men.

II. I am to show that our present forms of public worship, and every thing, so far as *measures* are concerned, have been arrived at *be degrees*, and by a *succession of New Measures*.

1. I will mention some things in regard to the *ministry*.

Many years ago, ministers were accustomed to wear a *peculiar habit*. It is so now in Catholic countries. It used to be so here. Ministers had a peculiar dress as much as soldiers. They used to wear a cocked hat, and bands instead of a cravat or stock, and small clothes,[1] and a wig. No matter how much hair a man had on his head, he must cut it off and wear a wig. And then he must wear a gown. All these things were customary, and every clergyman was held bound to wear them, and it was not considered proper for him to officiate without them. All these had doubtless been introduced by a succession of innovations, for we have no good reason for believing that the apostles and primitive ministers dressed differently from other men.

But now all these things have been given up, one by one, by a succession of innovations or new measures, until now in many

1. Small clothes, or short clothes: knee breeches.

churches a minister can go into the pulpit and preach without being noticed, although dressed like any other man. And when it was done to regard to each one of them, the church complained as much as if it had been a divine institution given up. It was denounced as an *innovation*. When ministers began to lay aside their cocked hats, and wear hats like other men, it grieved the elderly people very much; it looked so "undignified," they said, for a minister to wear a round hat. When, in 1827 I wore a fur cap, a minister said, "that was too bad for a minister. . . ."

So, in like manner, when ministers laid aside their *bands*, and wore cravats or stocks, it was said they were becoming secular, and many found fault. Even now, in some places, a minister would not dare to be seen in the pulpit in a cravat or stock. The people would feel as if they had no clergyman, if he had no bands. A minister in this city asked another, but a few days since, if it would do to wear a black stock in the pulpit. He wore one in his ordinary intercourse with his people, but doubted whether it would do to wear it in the pulpit.

So in regard to short clothes; they used to be thought essential to the ministerial character. Even now, in Catholic countries, every priest wears small clothes. Even the little boys there, who are trained for the priest's office, wear their cocked hats, and black stockings, and small clothes. This would look ridiculous amongst us. But it used to be practiced in this country. . . .

Just so it was in regard to *wigs*. I remember one minister, who, though quite a young man, used to wear an enormous white wig. And the people talked as if there was a divine right about it, and it was as hard to give it up, almost, as to give up the Bible itself. *Gowns* also were considered essential to the ministerial character. And even now, in many congregations in this country, the people will not tolerate a minister in the pulpit, unless he has a flowing silk gown, with enormous sleeves as big as his body. Even in some of the Congregational churches in New England, they cannot bear to give it up. Now, how came people to suppose a minister must have a gown or a wig, in order to preach with effect? Why was it that every clergyman was held obliged to use these things? How is it that not one of these things have been given up in the churches, without producing a shock among them? They have all been given up, one by one, and many congregations have been distracted for a time by the innovation. But will any one pretend that the cause of religion has been injured by it? People felt as if they could hardly worship God without them, but plainly their attachment to them was no part of their religion, that is, no part of the Christian religion. It was mere superstition. And when these things were taken away they complained, as Micah did, "Ye have taken away my gods." But no doubt their religious character was improved, by removing these objects of superstitious reverence. So that the church, on the whole, has been greatly the gainer by the innovations. Thus you see that the present mode of a minister's dress has been gained by a series of new measures.

2. In regard to the *order of public worship*.

The same difficulties have been met in effecting every change, because the churches have felt as if God had established just the *mode which they were used to*.

(1) *Psalm books* Formerly it was customary to sing David's Psalms. By and by there was introduced a version of the Psalms in rhyme. This was very bad, to be sure. When ministers tried to introduce them, the churches were distracted, people violently opposed, and great trouble was created by the innovation. But the new measure triumphed.

Afterwards another version was brought forward in a better style of poetry, and its introduction was opposed with much contention, as a new measure. And finally Watts' version, which is still opposed in many churches. . . .

(2) *Lining the hymns* Formerly, when there were but few books, it was the custom to *line* the hymns, as it was called. The deacon used to stand up before the pulpit, and read off the psalm or hymn, a line at a time, or two lines at a time, and then sing, and the rest would all fall in. By and by, they began to introduce books, and let every one sing from his book. And what an innovation! Alas, what confusion and disorder it made! How could the good people worship God in singing, without having the deacon to line off the hymn in his holy tone, for the holiness of it seemed to consist very much in the tone, which was such that you could hardly tell whether he was reading or singing.

(3) *Choirs* Afterwards another innovation was carried. It was thought best to have a select choir of singers sit by themselves and sing, so as to give opportunity to improve the music. But this was bitterly opposed. O how many congregations were torn and rent in sunder, by the desire of ministers and some leading individuals to

bring about an improvement in the cultivation of music, by forming choirs of singers. People talked about innovations and new
measures, and thought great evils were coming to the churches,
because the singers were seated by themselves, and cultivated
music, and learned new tunes that the old people could not sing. It
did not use to be so when they were young, and they wouldn't
tolerate such new lights and novelties in the church.

(4) *Pitchpipes* When music was cultivated, and choirs seated
together, then singers wanted a pitchpipe. Formerly, when the
lines were given out by the deacon or clerk, he would strike off into
the tune, and the rest would follow as well as they could. But when
the leaders of choirs began to use pitchpipes for the purpose of
pitching all their voices on precisely the same key, what vast confusion it made! I heard a clergyman say that an elder in the town
where he used to live would get up and leave the house whenever
he heard the chorister blow his pipe. "Away with your whistle,"
said he. "What! whistle in the house of God!" He thought it a
profanation.

(5) *Instrumental music* By and by, in some congregations,
various instruments were introduced for the purpose of aiding the
singers, and improving the music. When the bass viol was first
introduced, it made a gerat commotion. . . . Who has not heard
these things talked of, as matters of the most vital importance to
the cause of religion and the purity of the church? Ministers, in
grave ecclesiastical assemblies, have spent days in discussing them.
In a synod in the Presbyterian church, only a few years ago, it was
seriously talked of by some, as a matter worthy of discipline in a
certain church, that they had an organ in the house of God. This
within a few years. And there are many churches now who would
not tolerate an organ. They would not be half so much excited to
be told that sinners are going to hell, as to be told that there is
going to be an organ in the meeting house. O, in how many places
can you get the church to do any thing else, easier than to come
along in an easy and natural way to do what is needed, and wisest,
and best, for promoting religion and saving souls! They act as if
they had a "Thus saith the Lord," for every custom and practice
that has been handed down to them, or that they have long followed themselves, however absurd or injurious.

(6) *Extempory prayers* How many people are there, who
talk just as if the Prayer Book was of divine institution! And I

suppose multitudes believe it is. And in some parts of the church a man would not be tolerated to pray without his book before him.

(7) *Preaching without notes*   A few years since, a lady in Philadelphia was invited to hear a certain minister preach and she refused, because he did not read his sermons. She seemed to think it would be profane for a man to go into the pulpit and *talk*, just as if he was talking to the people about some interesting and important subject. Just as if God had enjoined the use of notes and written sermons. They do not know that notes themselves are an innovation, and a modern one too. They were introduced in a time of political difficulties in England. The ministers were afraid they should be accused of preaching something against the government, unless they could show what they had preached, by having all written down beforehand. And with a time-serving spirit, they yielded to political considerations, and imposed a yoke of bondage upon the church.[2] And, now in many places, they cannot tolerate extempore preaching.

(8) *Kneeling in prayer*   This has made a great disturbance in many parts of the country. The time has been in the Congregational churches in New England, when a man or woman would be ashamed to be seen kneeling at a prayer meeting, for fear of being taken for a Methodist. I have prayed in families where I was the only person that would kneel. The others all stood, lest they should imitate the Methodists, I suppose, and thus countenance innovations upon the established form. Others, again, talk as if there was no other posture but kneeling, that could be acceptable in prayer.

3. *Labors of Laymen.*

(1) *Lay prayers*   Much objection was formerly made against allowing any man to pray or to take a part in managing a prayer meeting, unless he was a clergyman. It used to be said that for a layman to pray in public, was interfering with the dignity of ministers, and was not to be tolerated. A minister in Pennsylvania told me that a few years ago he appointed a prayer meeting in the church, and the elders opposed it and turned it out of the house.

2. There is some truth in Finney's point that political considerations sometimes drove men to put their thoughts on paper lest they blunder. This did not always illustrate a "time-serving spirit," however; John Knox of Scotland put some of his sermons on paper so that there could be no mistake about the stand he was taking! But the use of notes in preaching goes back to early church history.

They said they would not have such work, they had hired a minister to do the praying, and he should do it, and they were not going to have common men praying. . . .

(2) *Lay exhortation* This has been a question of vast importance, one which has agitated all New England, and many other parts of the country, whether laymen ought to be allowed to exhort in public meetings. Many ministers have labored to shut up the mouths of laymen entirely. They overlooked the practice of the primitive churches. So much opposition was made to this practice nearly a hundred years ago, that President Edwards actually had to take up the subject, and write a labored defense of the rights and duties of laymen.[3] But the opposition has not entirely ceased to this day. "What! A man that is not a minister, to talk in public! It will create confusion, it will let down the ministry; what will people think of us, ministers, if we allow common men to do the same things that we do?" Astonishing!

But now, all these things are gone by, in most places, and laymen can pray and exhort without the least objection. The evils that were feared, from the labors of laymen, have not been realized, and many ministers are glad to have them exercise their gifts in doing good.

4. *Female prayer meetings* Within the last few years, female prayer meetings have been extensively opposed in this state. What dreadful things! A minister, now dead, said that when he first attempted to establish these meetings, he had all the clergy around opposed to him. "Set women to praying? Why, the next thing, I suppose, will be to set them to preaching." And serious apprehensions were entertained for the safety of Zion, if women should be allowed to get together to pray. And even now, they are not tolerated in some churches.

So it has been in regard to all the active movements of the church. Missions, Sunday Schools, and every thing of the kind, have been opposed, and have gained their present hold in the church only by a succession of struggles and a series of innovations. A Baptist Association in Pennsylvania, some years since, disclaimed all fellowship with any minister that had been liberally educated,

---

3. It is not clear to which writing of Edwards Finney refers: perhaps to Edwards' sermon on 1 Peter 2:9, "Christians a chosen generation, a royal priesthood, a holy nation, a peculiar people."

or that supported Missions, Bible Societies, Sabbath Schools, Temperance Societies, &c. All these were denounced as new measures, not found in the Bible, and that would necessarily lead to distraction and confusion in the churches. . . .

5. I will mention *several men* who have in Divine providence been set forward as prominent *in introducing these innovations*.

(1) *The apostles* were great innovators, as you all know. After the resurrection, and after the Holy Spirit was poured out upon them, they set out to remodel the church. They broke down the Jewish system of measures and rooted it out, so as to leave scarcely a vestige.

(2) *Luther and the reformers*   You all know what difficulties they had to contend with, and the reason was, that they were trying to introduce new measures—new modes of performing the public duties of religion, and new expedients to bring the gospel with power to the hearts of men. All the strange and ridiculous things of the Roman Catholics were held to in the church with pertinacious obstinacy, as if they were of divine authority. And such an excitement was raised by the attempt to change them, as well nigh involved all Europe in blood.

(3) *Wesley and his coadjutors*   Wesley did not at first tear off from the Established Church in England, but formed little classes every where, that grew into a church within a church. He remained in the Episcopal church, but he introduced so much of new measures, as to fill all England with excitement and uproar and opposition, and he was every where denounced as an innovator and a stirrer up of sedition, and a teacher of new things which it was not lawful to receive.

Whitefield was a man of the same school, and like Wesley was an innovator. I believe he and several individuals of his associates were expelled from college for getting up such a new measure as a social prayer meeting.[4] They would pray together and expound the Scriptures, and this was such a daring novelty that it could not be borne. When Whitefield came to this country, what an astonishing opposition was raised! Often he well nigh lost his life, and barely escaped by the skin of his teeth. Now, every body looks upon him as the glory of the age in which he lived. And many of our own

4. Finney is in error here; Whitefield was graduated from Oxford in June, 1736.

denomination have so far divested themselves of prejudice as to
think Wesley not only a good but a wise and preeminently useful
man. Then almost the entire church viewed them with animosity,
fearing that the innovations they introduced would destroy the
church.

(4) *President Edwards* This great man was famous in his day
for new measures. Among other innovations, he refused to baptize
the children of impenitent parents. The practice of baptizing the
children of the ungodly had been introduced in the New England
churches in the preceding century, and had become nearly universal. President Edwards saw that the practice was wrong, and he
refused to do it, and the refusal shook all the churches of New
England.[5] A hundred ministers joined and determined to put him
down. He wrote a book on the subject, and defeated them all. It
produced one of the greatest excitements there ever was in New
England. Nothing, unless it was the revolutionary war, ever produced an equal excitement. . . .

6. *In the present generation,* many things have been introduced
which have proved useful, but have been opposed on the ground
that they were innovations. And as many as are still unsettled in
regard to them, I have thought it best to make some remarks
concerning them. There are three things in particular, which have
chiefly attracted remark, and therefore I shall speak of them. They
are *anxious meetings, protracted meetings,* and the *anxious seat.*
These are all opposed, and are called new measures.

(1) *Anxious meetings* The first I ever heard of under that
name was in New England, where they were appointed for the
purpose of holding personal conversation with anxious sinners, and
to adapt instruction to the cases of individuals, so as to lead them
immediately to Christ. The design of them is evidently philosophical, but they have been opposed because they were new. . . .

(2) *Protracted meetings* These are not new, but have always
been practiced, in some form or other, ever since there was a
church on earth. The Jewish festivals were nothing else but protracted meetings. In regard to the *manner,* they were conducted
differently from what they are now. But the *design* was the same,

5. Cf. Edwards, *An Humble Inquiry into the Rules of the Word of God
concerning the Qualifications Requisite to a Compleat Standing and Full
Communion in the Visible Christian Church* (1749), Part III.

to devote a series of days to religious services, in order to make a more powerful impression of divine things upon the minds of the people. All denominations of Christians, when religion prospers among them, hold protracted meetings. In Scotland they used to begin on Thursday, at all their communion seasons, and continue until after the Sabbath. The Episcopalians, Baptists, and Methodists, all hold protracted meetings. Yet now in our day they have been opposed, particularly among Presbyterians, and called new measures, and regarded as fraught with all manner of evil, notwithstanding they have been so manifestly and so extensively blessed. I will suggest a few things that ought to be considered in regard to them.

(a)   In appointing them, regard should be had *to the circumstances of the people*; whether the churches are able to give their attention and devote their time to carry on the meeting. In some instances this rule has been neglected. Some have thought it right to break in upon the necessary business of the community. . . . But the worldly business in which we are engaged is not our business. It is as much *God's* business, and as much our duty, as our prayers and protracted meetings are. . . . And unless God, by some special indication of his providence, indicates it to be his pleasure, that we should turn aside and have a protracted meeting at *such times*, I look upon it as tempting God to appoint them. . . .

(b)   Ordinarily a protracted meeting should be conducted through, and the labor chiefly performed, by *the same minister*, if possible. Sometimes protracted meetings have been held and dependence placed on ministers coming in from day to day. And they would have no blessing. And the reason was obvious. They did not come in a state of mind to enter into the work, and they did not know the state of people's minds, so as to know what to preach. . . .

(c)   There should not be *so many public meetings* as to interfere with the *duties of the closet and of the family*. Otherwise Christians will lose their spirituality and let go their hold of God, and the meeting will run down.

(d)   *Families* should not put themselves out so much in entertaining strangers, as to *neglect prayer and other duties*. . . . It should always be understood that it is the duty of families to have as little working and parade as possible, and to get along with their hospitality in the easiest way, so that they may all have time to pray, and go to the meeting, and to attend to the things of the kingdom.

(e) By all means guard against *unnecessarily keeping late hours*. If people keep late hours, night after night, they will inevitably wear out the body, and their health will fail, and there will be a reaction. . . .

(f) *All sectarianism* should be carefully avoided. If a sectarian spirit breaks out, either in the preaching, or praying, or conversation, it will counteract all the good of the meeting.

(g) Be watchful against *placing dependence* on a protracted meeting, *as if that of itself would produce a revival*. This is a point of great danger, and has always been so. This is the great reason why the church in successive generations has always had to give up her measures—because Christians had come to rely on them for success. So it has been in some places, in regard to *protracted meetings*. They have been so blessed, that in some places the people have thought that if they should only have a protracted meeting, they would have a blessing, and sinners would be converted of course. And so they have appointed their meeting, without any preparation in the church, and just sent abroad for some minister of note and set him to preaching, as if that would convert sinners. It is obvious that the blessing would be withheld from a meeting got up in this way.

(h) Avoid adopting the idea that a revival cannot be enjoyed *without a protracted meeting*. . . .

(3) *The anxious seat* By this I mean the appointment of some particular seat in the place of meeting, where the anxious may come and be addressed particularly, and be made subjects of prayer, and sometimes conversed with individually. Of late this measure has met with more opposition than any of the others. What is the great objection? I cannot see it. The *design* of the anxious seat is undoubtedly philosophical, and according to the laws of mind. It has two bearings:

1. When a person is seriously troubled in mind, every body knows that there is a powerful tendency to try to keep it private that he is so, and it is a great thing to get the individual willing to have the fact known to others. And as soon as you can get him willing to make known his feelings, you have accomplished a great deal. When a person is borne down with a sense of his condition, if you can get him willing to have it known, if you can get him to break away from the chains of pride, you have gained an important point towards his conversion. This is agreeable to the philosophy of the human mind. How many thousands are there who will bless

God to eternity, that when pressed by the truth they were ever brought to take this step, by which they threw off the idea that it was a dreadful thing to have any body know that they were serious about their souls.

2. Another bearing of the anxious seat is to detect deception and delusion, and thus prevent false hopes. It has been opposed on this ground, that it was calculated to create delusion and false hopes. But this objection is unreasonable. The truth is the other way. Suppose I were preaching on the subject of temperance, and that I should first show the evils of intemperance, and bring up the drunkard and his family, and show the various evils produced, till every heart is beating with emotion. Then I portray the great danger of *moderate drinking*, and show how it leads to intoxication and ruin, and that there is no safety but in TOTAL ABSTI-NENCE, till a hundred hearts are ready to say, "I will never drink another drop of ardent spirit in the world; if I do, I shall expect to find a drunkard's grave." Now I stop short, and let the pledge be circulated, and every one that is fully resolved is ready to sign it. But how many will begin to draw back and hesitate, when you begin to call on them to *sign a pledge* of total abstinence. One says to himself, "Shall I sign it, or not? I thought my mind was made up, but this signing a pledge *never* to drink again, I do not know about that." Thus you see that when a person is called upon to give a pledge, if he is found not to be decided, he makes it manifest that he was not sincere. That is, he never came to that resolution on the subject, which could be relied on to control his future life. Just so with the awakened sinner. Preach to him, and at the moment he thinks he is willing to do any thing, he thinks he is determined to serve the Lord, but bring him to the test, call on him to do one thing, to take one step, that shall identify him with the people of God, or cross his pride—his pride comes up, and he refuses; his delusion is brought out, and he finds himself a lost sinner still; whereas, if you had not done it, he might have gone away flattering himself that he was a Christian. If you say to him, "There is the anxious seat, come out and avow your determination to be on the Lord's side," and if he is not willing to do so small a thing as that, then he is not willing to do *any thing*, and there he is, brought out before his own conscience. It uncovers the delusion of the human heart, and prevents a great many spurious conversions, by showing those who might otherwise imagine themselves willing to do any thing for Christ, that in fact they are willing to do *nothing*.

The church has always felt it necessary to have something of the kind to answer this very purpose. In the days of the apostles *baptism* answered this purpose. The gospel was preached to the people, and then all those who were willing to be on the side of Christ were called on to be *baptized*. It held the precise place that the anxious seat does now, as a public manifestation of their determination to be Christians. And in modern times, those who have been violently opposed to the anxious seat have been obliged to adopt some substitute, or they could not get along in promoting a revival. . . .

Now what objection is there against taking a particular seat, or rising up, or going into the lecture-room? They all mean the same thing, when properly conducted. And they are not novelties in principle at all. The thing has always been done in substance. In Joshua's day, he called on the people to decide what they would do, and they spoke right out, in the meeting, "We will serve the Lord; the Lord our God will we serve, and his voice will we obey."

15. The Church and Slavery: A Southern View

As REVIVALISM penetrated deep into Protestant consciousness and practice, it stirred many controversies and aroused deep tensions. Yet revivalistic Protestantism succeeded in considerable measure in overcoming denominational differences through its voluntary system, and it made a deep impact on the moral and educational life of the nation. But it was not able to deal with the problem of slavery. Just as the revivalism and the benevolent empire were making progress in their many crusades, the rift in the evangelical ranks over slavery widened threateningly. In the late eighteenth century there had been a general belief that slavery was a dying institution, but that belief was changed by the invention of the cotton gin and the growth of the plantation system, combined with the fears aroused in the South by such leaders of slave revolts as Nat Turner and by the appearance of such uncompromising abolitionists as William Lloyd Garrison. Along with other Southerners, many evangelicals developed "positive good" theories of slavery, and books and sermons on the "Christian doctrine of slavery" appeared. At the same time, though often slowly and with reluctance, growing numbers of Northern evangelicals developed antislavery views. The result was the division of some of the major denominations over the slavery issue.

One of the most eloquent spokesmen for the Southern viewpoint was James Henley Thornwell (1812–1862), a professor in the Presbyterian Seminary at Columbia, South Carolina. He wrote a report on "The Church and Slavery" in 1851, reprinted in part, which was unanimously adopted by the Presbyterian Synod of South Carolina.

SOURCE: John B. Adger and John L. Girardeau (eds.), *The Collected Writings of James Henley Thornwell, D.D., LL.D.*, Vol. IV (Richmond, 1871–1873), pp. 382–388.

The relation of the Church to slavery cannot be definitely settled without an adequate apprehension of the nature and office of the Church itself. What, then, is the Church? It is not, as we fear too many are disposed to regard it, a moral institute of universal good, whose business it is to wage war upon every form of human ill, whether social, civil, political or moral, and to patronize every expedient which a romantic benevolence may suggest as likely to contribute to human comfort, or to mitigate the inconveniences of life. We freely grant, and sincerely rejoice in the truth, that the healthful operations of the Church, in its own appropriate sphere, react upon all the interests of man, and contribute to the progress and prosperity of society; but we are far from admitting either that it is the purpose of God, that, under the present dispensation of religion, all ill shall be banished from this sublunary state, and earth be converted into a paradise; or, that the proper end of the Church is the direct promotion of universal good. It has no commission to construct society afresh, to adjust its elements in different proportions, to rearrange the distribution of its classes, or to change the forms of its political constitutions. The noble schemes of philanthropy which have distinguished Christian nations, their magnificent foundations for the poor, the maimed and the blind, the efforts of the wise and good to mitigate human misery, and to temper justice with mercy in the penal visitations of the law, the various associations that have been formed to check and abate particular forms of evil, have all been quickened into life by the spirit of Christianity. But still it is not the distinctive province of the Church to build asylums for the needy or insane, to organize societies for the improvement of the penal code, or for arresting the progress of intemperance, gambling or lust. The problems, which the anomalies of our fallen state are continually forcing on philanthropy, the Church has no right directly to solve. She must leave them to the Providence of God, and to human wisdom sanctified and guided by the spiritual influences which it is her glory to foster and cherish. The Church is a very peculiar society; *voluntary* in the sense that its members become so, not by constraint, but willingly; but, not in the sense that its doctrines, discipline and order are the creatures of human will, deriving their authority and obligation from the consent of its members. On the contrary, it has a fixed and unalterable Constitution; and that Constitution is the Word of God. It is the kingdom of the Lord Jesus Christ. He is enthroned in it as a sovereign. It can hear no voice but His, obey no commands but His, pursue no ends but His. Its officers are His servants bound to execute only His will; its doctrines are His teachings, which He as a prophet has given from God; its discipline His law, which He as king has ordained. The power of the Church, accordingly, is only ministerial and declarative. The Bible, and the Bible alone, is her rule of faith and practice. She can announce what it teaches, enjoin what it commands, prohibit what it condemns, and enforce her testimonies by spiritual sanctions. Beyond the Bible she can never go, and apart from the

Bible she can never speak. To the law and to the testimony, and to them alone, she must always appeal; and when they are silent it is her duty to put her hand upon her lips.

These principles, thus abstractly stated, are not likely to provoke opposition, but the conclusion which flows from them, and for the sake of which we have here stated them, has unfortunately been too much disregarded; and that is, that the Church is not at liberty to *speculate*. She has a *creed*, but no *opinions*. When she speaks, it must be in the name of the Lord, and her only argument is *Thus it is written.*

In conformity with this principle, has the Church any authority to declare slavery to be sinful? Or, in other words, has the Bible, anywhere, either directly or indirectly, condemned the relation of master and servant as incompatible with the will of God?

We think there can be little doubt, that, if the Church had universally repressed the spirit of *speculation*, and had been content to stand by the naked testimony of God, we should have been spared many of the most effective dissertations against slavery. Deduct the opposition to it which has arisen from sympathy with imaginary sufferings, from ignorance of its nature and misapplication of the crotchets of philosophers—deduct the opposition which is due to sentiment, romance or *speculation*, and how much will be found to have originated from the humble and devout study of the Scriptures? Will any man say that he who applies to them with an honest and unprejudiced mind, and discusses their teachings upon the subject, simply as a question of language and interpretation, will rise from their pages with the sentiments or spirit of a modern abolitionist? Certain it is that no direct condemnation of slavery can anywhere be found in the Sacred Volume. A social element in all states, from the dawn of history until the present period, if it be the crying and damning sin which its enemies represent it to be, it is truly amazing that the Bible, which professes to be a lamp to our feet and a light to our path, to make the man of God perfect, thoroughly furnished unto every good work, nowhere gives the slightest caution against this tremendous evil. The master is nowhere rebuked as a monster of cruelty and tyranny, the slave nowhere exhibited as the object of peculiar compassion and sympathy. The manner in which the relation itself is spoken of and its duties prescribed—the whole tone and air of the sacred writers—convey the impression that they themselves had not the least suspicion that they were dealing with a subject full of abominations and outrages. We read their language—cool, dispassioned, didactic. We find masters exhorted in the same connection with husbands, parents, magistrates; slaves exhorted in the same connection with wives, children and subjects. The Prophet or Apostle gives no note of alarm, raises no signal of distress when he comes to the slave and his master; and the unwary reader is in serious danger of concluding, that, according to the Bible, it is not much more harm to be a master than a father, a slave than a child. But this is not all. The Scriptures not only fail to condemn slavery, they as distinctly sanction it as any other social condition of man. The Church was formally organized in the family of a slaveholder; the relation was divinely regulated among the chosen people of God; and the peculiar duties of the parties are inculcated under the Christian economy. These are facts which cannot be denied. Our argument then is this: If the Church is bound to abide by the authority of the Bible, and that alone, she discharges her whole office in regard to slavery, when she declares what the Bible teaches, and enforces its laws by her own peculiar sanctions. Where the Scriptures are silent, she must be silent too. What the Scriptures have not made essential to a Christian profession she does not undertake to make so. What the Scriptures have sanctioned she does not condemn. To this course she is shut up by the nature of her Constitution. If she had universally complied with the provisions of her charter, the angry discussions which have disgraced her courts, and produced bitterness and alienation among her own children in different countries and in different sections of the same land, would all have been prevented. The abolition excitement derives most of its fury, and all its power, from the conviction which Christian people, without warrant from God, have industriously propagated, that slavery, essentially considered, is a sin. They have armed the instincts of our moral nature against it. They have given the dignity of principle to the clamors of fanaticism; and the consequence is, that many Churches are distracted and the country reeling under a series of assaults in which treachery to man is justified as obedience to God. According to the rule of faith which gives to the Church her being, the relation of master and slave stands on the same footing with the other relations of life. In itself considered, it is not inconsistent with the will of God—it is not sinful. This is as much a doctrine of Christianity as the obligation of obedience to law.

The Church, therefore, cannot undertake to disturb the relation. The Bible further teaches that there are duties growing out of this relation—duties of the master and duties of the slave. The Church must enforce these duties upon her own members. Here her jurisdiction stops. As a *Church*, as the visible kingdom of our Lord and Savior Jesus Christ, she must venture to interfere no further, unless it be to repress the agitation of those who assume to be wiser and purer than the Word of God. Those who corrupt the Scriptures, who profanely add to the duties of the Decalogue, are no more entitled to exemption from ecclesiastical discipline than any other disturbers of the peace or fomenters of faction and discord. It is not a question whether masters can be received into the communion of the saints, but it is a question whether those who exclude them should not themselves be rejected. We are far from insinuating that abolitionists, *as such*, are unfit to be members of the Church. Slavery may evidently be contemplated in various aspects—as a social arrangement, involving a distinction of classes, like Oriental caste, or European gradation of ranks; as a civil relation, involving rights and obligations corresponding to its own nature; as a political condition, bearing upon the prosperity, happiness and growth of communities. In any or in all of these aspects, it may be opposed upon considerations of policy and prudence—as the despotism of Asia, the aristocracy of Europe, or the free institutions of America are opposed—without the imputation of sin upon the nature of the relation itself. The members of the Church, as citizens and as men, have the same right to judge of the expediency or inexpediency of introducing and perpetuating in their own soil this institution, as any other element of their social economy. But they transcend their sphere, and bring reproach upon the Scriptures as a rule of faith, when they go beyond these political considerations, and condemn slavery as essentially repugnant to the will of God. They then corrupt the Scriptures, and are exposed to the malediction of those who trifle with the divine testimony. The Southern churches have never asked their brethren in Europe, or in the nonslaveholding sections of their own land, to introduce slavery among them; they have never asked them to approve it as the wisest and best constitution of society. All they have demanded is, that their brethren would leave it where God has left it, and deal with it, where it is found, as God has dealt with it. We insist upon it, that they should not disturb the tranquillity of the state by attempting to readjust our social fabric according to their own crotchets, when we ourselves, the only parties who have a right to meddle, are satisfied with our condition. We do not recognize them as political apostles, to whom God has transferred from us the right inherent in every other people to manage their affairs in their own way, so long as they keep within the limits of the divine law. If we fail in our social and political organizations, if, by consequence, we lag behind in the progress of nations, we do not forfeit our right to self-government and become the minors and wards of wiser and stronger states. It is as preposterous in our Northern and European brethren to undertake to force their system upon us, or to break up our own in obedience to their notions, as it would be in us to wage a war upon theirs, on the ground that ours is better. Slavery, as a *political* question, is one in regard to which communities and states may honestly differ. But as a *moral* question, the Bible has settled it; and all we contend for is, that as *that* is a matter of liberty, we should not break fellowship for difference upon other grounds. If any man, however, is not content to stand by the Word of God, if any church will not tolerate the liberty wherewith Christ has made us free, that man and that church cannot be vindicated from the charge of fomenting schism. They become justly exposed to censure. He who would debar a slaveholder from the table of the Lord, upon the simple and naked ground that he is a slaveholder, deserves himself to be excluded for usurping the prerogatives of Christ, and introducing terms of communion which cast reproach upon the conduct of Jesus and the Apostles. He violates the very charter of the Church—is a traitor to its fundamental law. . . .

16. The Church and Slavery: A Northern View

ALBERT BARNES (1798–1870), pastor of the First Presbyterian Church of Philadelphia, a prominent member of the "new school" division of his denomination, wrote extensively on the slavery issue. A good summary of the views of this spokesman for the northern antislavery position is his chapter in which he undertook to state "The Position of the Church at Large on the Subject of Slavery."

SOURCE: Albert Barnes, The Church and Slavery (Philadelphia, 1857), pp. 41–48.

Such being the case, it is important to inquire what is the actual position of the church in relation to slavery. The infidel has a right to ask this question; the Christian ought to be able to answer it.

The influence of the church is not, and has not been, what it might be; it is not what it should be. But, then, it should not be held responsible for what it cannot do; nor should its general influence be measured by the views of a small portion of its members. No body of men should be judged by the errors of a portion of its own body, or be charged as a whole with that which properly belongs only to a part. In respect to a portion of the church, we may admit that we have no words of apology to offer; while in the movements of other portions of it, and in the general effect of Christianity on the system for a period of one thousand eight hundred years, we may find much to justify the hope that its influence will be ultimately direct and decided in hastening the period when all mankind shall be free.

It would be wholly foreign to the design which I have in view, and would be a work which could not be accomplished in a volume of a few pages, to examine the general influence of the Christian church on the subject of slavery; and it would be equally apart from my design to examine in detail the position of other denominations of Christians than the one with which I am connected. My main object is to inquire into the actual position of my own denomination in regard to slavery, and the particular duty of that branch of the church of Christ. Yet, as connected with the general subject, and as tending to correct some prevalent misapprehensions in regard to the influence of the church on this great evil, and to meet some of the aspersions which are quite freely lavished upon the church by its enemies, it may be proper to make a few remarks on the general influence of the church on the subject.

The following facts, then, I suppose, do not admit of dispute:—

1. The *spirit* of the New Testament is against slavery, and the principles of the New Testament, if fairly applied, would abolish it. In the New Testament, no man is commanded to purchase and own a slave; no man is commended as adding any thing to the evidences of his Christian character, or as performing the appropriate duty of a Christian, for owning one. Nowhere in the New Testament is the institution referred to as a good one, or as a desirable one. It is commonly—indeed, it is almost universally—conceded that the proper application of the principles of the New Testament would abolish slavery everywhere, or that, in the state of things which will exist when the gospel shall be fairly applied to all the relations of life, slavery will not be found among those relations. This is admitted even by most of those who apologize for slavery, and who, at other times, speak of it as on the same basis as the relation of husband and wife, or of master and apprentice. Moreover, it has not been often alleged by the enemies of Christianity that the New Testament sustains and sanctions slavery; that its spirit would be opposed to emancipation; or that the fair application of the gospel in the world would extend and perpetuate the system. There have been, and there are, keen-sighted and sagacious enemies of the Christian religion; there have been those who have had every disposition to show, if possible, that its influence in the world is evil; but it has not often occurred, so far as I know, that they have made it an objection to Christianity that its spirit was favorable to slavery, or that its fair application in the world would tend to perpetuate and extend it. Neither Celsus, Porphyry, nor Julian urged this as an objection to the New Testament; nor have the keen and sagacious enemies of Christianity in more modern times alleged that they have discovered that slavery was either originated by Christianity or that it lends its sanction to the system. If the question were submitted to any number of intelligent and impartial men whether the spirit of the New Testament is adverse to or favorable to slavery, and whether the fair application of the principles of the New Testament would perpetuate slavery or abolish it, it is presumed that on these points there would be no material difference of opinion. This conclusion would

seem to be confirmed by the facts just adverted to,—that infidels
have never made it an objection to the New Testament that it
countenances or would perpetuate slavery, and that it is admitted,
by even those who attempt to apologize for the system, that the
fair application of Christianity would remove it from the world.[1]

2. The *general* course of the Christian church has been against
slavery. This was undeniably true in the early history of the church.
I know not that it has ever been alleged that any of the prominent
defenders of the Christian faith among the "fathers" were advocates of slavery, or that any decree of synods or councils can be
adduced in favor of the system. The influence of Christianity, also,
on slavery in the Roman empire is well known. Christianity *found*
slavery everywhere existing; it introduced it nowhere. By a gradual
but certain process it meliorated the system as it existed, and was
among the most efficient causes of its being ultimately abolished in
the Roman empire.[2] While there may have been a gradual tendency toward freedom in the opinions of the world, yet there can
be no doubt that this was fostered, if not originated, by the preva-
lence of Christianity; and that when the time occurred, as it did,

1. The only exception of these remarks which I recollect to have ever met
with is the case of Professor Francis William Newman, in his work on the
"Phases of Faith," in assigning his reasons for renouncing his early opinions
and rejecting the Bible as a revelation. One of those reasons for his change
of views (and the passage deserves to be quoted as illustrating and confirm-
ing the remark which I have made, that an appeal to the Bible as sustaining
slavery tends to promote infidelity) is that the New Testament sanctions
slavery, and is, in fact, the stronghold of those who defend the accursed
system.
    The passage in the "Phases of Faith" (pp. 166–167) in which this occurs
is the following:—"Undue credit has been claimed for Christianity as the foe
and extirpator of slavery. Englishmen of the nineteenth century boldly de-
nounce slavery as an immoral and abominable system. There may be a little
fanaticism in the fervour which this sometimes assumes; but not one of the
Christian apostles ever opens his lips at all against slavery. Paul sent back
the fugitive Onesimus to his master Philemon, with kind recommendations
and apologies for the slave, but without a hint to the master that he ought
to make him legally free. *At this day, inconsequence, the New Testament is
the argumentative stronghold of those in the United States who are trying
to keep up the accursed system.*" For an answer to this, the reader may
refer to the "Defence of the Eclipse of Faith," pp. 159, *et seq.*
2. For proof of this I may be permitted to refer to my work on the "Scriptural Views of Slavery," pp. 368–372.

when slavery ceased to exist in what had been the Roman empire, one of the main causes which led to this was the silent influence of the Christian religion.

3. Efforts for emancipation have occurred usually in close connection with the Christian church, and under the influence of Christian men. The efforts which were made in England, and which resulted in emancipation throughout the British empire, were commenced and conducted under the influence of Christian men—not of mere statesmen; not of infidels. Clarkson and Wilberforce and Buxton were Christian men; William Penn was a Christian; and all that has been done in the cause by the society of Friends has been originated by the fact that they regard the system as opposed to the gospel. Without any fear of contradiction, it may be affirmed that the efforts which have been made in the world to break the fetters of slavery; to suppress the slave trade; and to give to all persons held in bondage the blessings of freedom, have been owing mainly to the influence of Christians, and that if it had not been for their influence those efforts would not have been made. The rejecters of the Bible have not been the movers in this cause; nor out of the church has there ever been enough power, under the mere promptings of humanity, to induce men to abandon the slave traffic or to set the oppressed free. Whatever aid such men may have rendered to the cause, the moving power has always come originally from the bosom of the church:—from the silent influence of Christianity on the hearts of many men, or from the untiring energy, the tact, the eloquence, the self-denial, of some distinguished leader or leaders in the cause of emancipation, who have been made what they were by the power of the gospel of Christ.

4. It is true, also, that the great body of Christians in this land, and in all other lands, are opposed to slavery. It is not true that the authority of the best Christian writers can be adduced in favor of the system; nor is it true that the mass of Christians and of Christian ministers in the world are the advocates of slavery. A very large majority of Christians in this land own no slaves, and are, on principle, opposed to the owning of slaves. The whole number of slave holders in the United States does not amount to four hundred thousand; and of these a small portion only are professors of religion. Not a few of those also who are slave holders profess to be opposed to the system, and express a desire to be delivered from it. They see its evils and wrongs; they would not favor its introduction

if it were not already in existence; they endeavor to meliorate the condition of the slave; and they would sincerely rejoice if, consistently, as they suppose, with the best interests of the slaves themselves, they could all be made free. While they perceive difficulties in the way of emancipation, which to them appear insuperable at present, and which they see no prospect of being able soon to overcome, they feel the system to be a burden—a burden to themselves, a burden to the slave. Not a few are so oppressed with this state of things that they leave the slave states, and emigrate to states where freedom prevails; and not a few more would, if we may credit their own testimony, rejoice if all that dwell in the land were free. The men who are connected with the church who openly advocate the system of slavery, and who would wish to make it perpetual, are comparatively few in number; and it is not a little remarkable that the apologists for slavery are not always those who are connected with the system, but men who sustain no relation to it whatever, and who voluntarily become advocates for a system which they who are connected with it regard as an unmitigated curse. Such men *deserve* no thanks from the world; and they *receive* no thanks from those who are suffering under the evils of the system, and who sigh for the day when they may be wholly delivered from it.

There is much indeed to lament in the feelings entertained in the church on the subject. There is much indifference to the evils of the system. There is much that pains the heart of philanthropy when we reflect how many there are, in the aggregate, in the church who apologize for the evil; much to lament in the fact that there are any professed Christians who are holders of slaves. But, still, the church does not deserve unmitigated denunciation. The church, as such, is *not* the "bulwark of slavery"; the church, as such, is not the advocate for slavery; the church, as such, is not the apologist for slavery. The whole society of Friends is detached from it, and their sentiments are well known to the world. One half of the Methodist church in this country, and the whole of the Methodist denomination abroad, is opposed to slavery. All the branches, it is believed, of the Scotch church are opposed to the system. The German churches are equally opposed to it; the great body of Congregationalists are opposed to it, and their influence is that of decided hostility to it. The churches abroad—the Established church and the Dissenting churches in England; the two great bodies of the Presbyterian churches, and all the smaller bodies of Presbyterians in Scotland; the Presbyterians in Ireland, and all the churches on the continent, so far as any expression of opinion has been made, are opposed to the system. Not a few of these foreign Christians, with entire propriety, utter a loud voice of remonstrance and appeal to their transatlantic brethren, and urge upon them, in language which cannot be misunderstood, the duty of detaching themselves entirely from the system, and assuming, in regard to it, the position occupied by the churches of other lands.

17. Controversy over Evolution

FOLLOWING THE Civil War, the Protestant world was soon torn again by controversy, this time over the way modern scientific and historical knowledge should be handled within the church. The tensions did not lead to major schisms as the slavery controversy had, though some of the prominent liberals left or were driven out of their denominational homes. But the tensions over modern scientific scholarship did lead to the development of self-conscious liberal and conservative parties in the denominations, and introduced a polarization that has characterized Protestant life ever since. As the controversies over the theory of evolution and the historical criticism of the Bible raged, some dissatisfied groups did withdraw into conservative fellowships.

Some conspicuous Protestant churchmen rather quickly espoused the theory of evolution, such as the most conspicuous preacher of his day, Henry Ward Beecher of Brooklyn, and President James McCosh of Princeton. One of the most prolific spokesmen for a religious interpretation of the theory of evolution, Minot J. Savage (1841–1918), had begun his career as a Congregationalist but switched to the more liberal Unitarian fold in 1873. The Religion of Evolution, first published in 1876, was reprinted many times. The selection is quite typical of those who felt that theistic religion could be in conformity with the most advanced scientific thinking of the times.

SOURCE: Minot J. Savage, The Religion of Evolution (Boston, 1891), pp. 40–48.

It would transcend our limits to attempt even an outline of the proofs of this theory. These are to be found in the works of the masters of science, specially prepared for that purpose. I must, therefore, content myself with remarking some of the surface probabilities, and then placing the theory alongside the Mosaic, that you may compare them.

1. It is a fact that ought to make men stop and think, before rejecting it, that almost every trained scientific man living, who is competent to give a judgment on the question, is a believer in evolution. If all the skillful doctors were agreed about a certain disease, it would hardly be modest for us to say they were wrong. When all the generals are at one about a military question, the probabilities are decidedly their way. When all the architects agree about a building, and when all the painters unite in defense of a

question in art, outsiders should at least hesitate. Nearly all the present opposition to evolution comes from theology; but theology does not happen to know anything about it. As though I should attempt to settle a disputed point in music by the sense of smell, or a case of color (red or white) by hearing! The men who opposed evolution may be generally divided into two classes—those actuated by theological prejudice, and those who know nothing about it.

2. The theory of evolution is constructed out of the observed and accumulated facts of the universe: it is not guess-work. The men who have elaborated this answer to the old question, How did things come to be as they are? are men who have gone to the facts themselves, and asked the question. They went to the earth and studied it, and so developed the science of geology: they looked at the stars to see how they moved, and so made astronomy: they studied animals to see how they grew, and so made zoology: they studied man, and so made physiology and anthropology. If anybody, then, in the world, has any right to an opinion on the subject, it is those who have looked at the facts to find out about them. And it is simply absurd to see people offer an opinion, who have no better stuff than ignorance or prejudice to make it out of.

3. It stands the very highest test of a good theory; that is, it takes into itself, accounts for, and adjusts, almost every known fact; while there is not one single fact known that makes it unreasonable for a man to be an evolutionist.

Now, what is the theory? Simply this: that the whole universe, suns, planets, moons, our earth, and every form of life upon it, vegetable and animal, up to man, together with all our civilization, has developed from a primitive fire-mist or nebulae that once filled all the space now occupied by the worlds; and that this development has been according to laws and methods and forces still active, and working about us today. It calls in no unknown agency. It does not offer to explain a natural fact by a miracle which only deepens the mystery it attempts to solve. It says, "I accept and ask for only the forces that are going on right before my eyes, and with these I will explain the visible universe." Certainly a magnificent pretension, and, if accomplished, a magnificent achievement, of the mind of man.

Look at the theory a little more in detail. Evolution teaches that the space now occupied by suns and planets was once filled with a fire-mist, or flaming gas. This mist, or gas, by the process of cooling and condensation, and in accordance with the laws of motion naturally set up in it, in the course of ages was solidified into the stars and worlds, taking on gradually their present motions, shapes, and conditions. This is the famous "nebular hypothesis." In favor of this theory is the fact that the earth is now in precisely the condition we should expect it to be, on this supposition. The moon, being smaller than the earth, has now become cold and dead. Jupiter and Saturn, being larger, are still hot—halfway between the sun's flaming condition and the earth's habitable one. And then all through the sky are clouds of nebulae, still in the condition of flaming gas, whirling, and assuming just such shapes as the evolution theory alone can explain. The theory further teaches that, when the cooling earth had come into such a condition that there were land and water and an atmosphere, then life appeared. But how? By any special act of creation? No. It introduces no new or unknown force, and calls for no miracle. Science discovers no impassable gulf between what we ignorantly call dead matter, and that which is alive. It does not believe any matter is dead: so it finds in it "the promise and potency of every form of life." It has discovered a little viscous globule, or cell, made up chiefly of nitrogen and albumen. It is a chemical compound, the coming into existence of which is no more wonderful than the formation of a crystal, and calls no more urgently for a miracle than a crystal does. This little mass, or cell, is not only the lowest and most original form of life, but it is the basis of every form. There is no single form of life on the globe, from the moss on a stone up to the brain of Sir Isaac Newton, that is not a more or less complex compound or combination of this primary, tiny cell; and there is no stage in the process of development, where ascertained laws and forces are not competent to produce the results. There is no barrier between the vegetable and animal kingdom. No naturalist living can tell where the one leaves off, and the other begins, so insensibly do they merge into each other, like day passing through twilight into night. Neither is there any barrier between species, either of plants or animals. This point is now settled. Evolution also (what no other theory does) explains the distribution of plants and animals over the surface of the earth. It explains the present condition of the races of mankind—the progress of some, the stagnation of others, and the cases of gradual decay and dying out. It explains social, political, and religious movements and changes, rises and falls. It is gradually proving its capacity to grapple with and solve the great enigmas and questions of the ages. And when generally understood and accepted, it will modify and direct all the forces and movements of the modern world.

From the primeval fire-mist, then, until today, the world has grown, without any necessity for, or help from, special creations, miracles, or any other forces than those known and recognized as at work right around us. It has taken millions of years to do this; but what are they in eternity? There have been no cataclysms, nor breaks, nor leaps. The sun has shone, the rain has fallen, the winds have blown, the rivers have run, the oceans have worn the shores, the continents have risen and sunk, just as they are doing now; and all these things have come to pass.

But some one will say, "This is blank and outright atheism. You have left God entirely out of the question. Where has he been, and what has he been doing, all these millions of years? From the fire-mist until today, all has gone along on purely natural principles, and by natural laws, you say?" Yes, that is just what evolution says. But, before we call it atheism, let me ask you a question. Here is a century-old oak tree. The acorn from which it sprang was the natural product of some other oak. It fell to the earth, and the young oak sprouted. From that day to this—a hundred years—the oak has simply grown by natural law. You want no miracle to explain it. Is your theory of the oak, then, atheistic? Is it any less strange that the oak should grow than that thousands of other oaks, and other forms of life, should do the same? When a child is born, it grows, you say, by natural law. Is it any more wonderful that it should be born by natural law? and that all life should be born, and should develop, by natural law? You are just as atheistic to say that a tree or a child grows by natural law, as evolution is, when it says the world did the same. Suppose science should put its God back in the past some millions of ages, while Moses puts his back only six thousand years, would the difference in time make one theory more atheistic than the other? But I should call pushing him back six thousand years, or a hundred million years, or five minutes, even, more atheistic than I should like to believe. So I would do neither the one nor the other. What if we see the life and power and movement of God in the fire-mist, in all the growing worlds, in the first appearance of life on the planet, in the forms that climb up through all grades to man? What if we see him in the dust of the street, in the grasses and flowers, in the clouds and the light, in the ocean and the storms, in the trees and the birds, in the animals, lifting up through countless forms to humanity? What if we see him in the family, in society, in the state, in all religions, up to the highest outflowerings of Christianity? What if we see him in art, literature, and science? What if we make the whole world his temple, and all life a worship? All this we may not only do in evolution, but evolution helps us do it. I shall be greatly mistaken, if the radicalism of evolution does not prove to be the grandest of all conservatism in society and politics not only, but in religion as well. It will turn out to be the most theistic of all theisms. It will give us the grandest conception of God that the world has ever known. It is inconsistent with "orthodoxy," but not with religion. It is charged by the thoughtless with being material-istic; but in reality it is any thing else. It so changes our conception of matter as utterly to destroy the old "materialism." It not only does not touch any one of the essential elements of true religion, but, on the other hand, it gives a firm and broad foundation on which to establish it beyond the possibility of overthrow. To illus-trate this will be the work of future treatment of the special topics.

It only remains for me now to suggest a comparison as to grandeur and divinity between the two theories of creation. So many thoughtless sneers have been flung at the theory that dared talk of man's relationship to the ape, that a comparison like this may help change the sneer to admiration.

We marvel at Watt, the first constructor of a steam engine; but it has taken many a brain beside his to bring it to its present perfection. What if he had been able to build it on such a plan, and put into it such a generative force, that it should go on, through long intervals of time, developing from itself improve-ments on itself, until it had become adapted to all the needs of man? It should fit itself for rails; it should grow into adaptation for country roads and city streets; it should swim the water, and fly the air; it should shape itself to all elements and uses that could make it available for the service of man. Suppose that all this should develop from the first simple engine that Watt constructed; and should do it by virtue of power that Watt himself implanted in it? The simple thought of such a mechanism makes us feel how superhuman it would be, and how worthy of divinity. Is it not infinitely more than the separate construction of each separate improvement? And yet this supposition is simplicity and ease itself, compared with the grand magnificence of creation after the Darwinian idea. Who can pick an acorn from the ground, and, looking up to the tree from which it has fallen, try to conceive all the grand and century-grown beauty and power of the oak as contained in the tiny cone in his hand, and not feel overwhelmed by the might and the mystery of the works of God? How unutterably grander is the thought that the world-wide banyan tree of life, with all its million-times-multiplied variety of form and function, and beauty and power, standing with its roots in the dust, and with its top "commercing with the skies," and bearing on its upper boughs the eternal light of God's spiritual glory, is all the godlike growth of one little seed in which the divine finger planted such fructifying force!

18. Conflict over Biblical Criticism

THE EMERGING liberal parties in the evangelical denominations were further consolidated during the late nineteenth-century controversies over biblical interpretation. The liberal leaders explained that to approach the Bible in a scholarly way as one approached other books was to allow its real message to be more fully understood, for by seeing it in the context of its time its original meanings could be better grasped. The conservative reaction was that such procedures subjected the Word of God to tests devised by human reason. The struggle, highlighted by the suspension of Professor Charles H. Briggs of Union Theological Seminary from the Presbyterian ministry in 1893, was further intensified during the fundamentalist-modernist controversy of the 1920's. Useful interpretations of this deeply rooted tension in Protestantism can be found in such books as William R. Hutchinson (ed.), American Protestant Thought: The Liberal Era (New York, 1968), Ernest R. Sandeen, The Roots of Fundamentalism: British and American Millenarianism, 1800–1930 (Chicago, 1970), Martin E. Marty, Righteous Empire, and H. Shelton Smith, Robert T. Handy, and Lefferts A. Loetscher, American Christianity, Vol. II, chaps. 17 and 18.

One of the most influential leaders of evangelical liberal theology was William Newton Clarke (1840–1912), a Baptist pastor who became a seminary teacher of theology and wrote the first liberal systematic theology in the United States, An Outline of Christian Theology (New York, 1898). In his spiritual autobiography, Clarke traced the steps by which he moved from the traditional acceptance of the Bible as inerrant, a view which he held in the 1860's, to a historical and critical approach to it in the next decade. Some of the consequences of this shift in the understanding of biblical authority are traced, in particular the role of women in the church.

SOURCE: William Newton Clarke, Sixty Years with the Bible: A Record of Experience (New York, 1909), pp. 42–48, 102–108, 149–155.

I looked upon the Bible as so inspired by God that its writers were not capable of error. I did not feel myself at liberty to dissent from its teachings, to doubt the accuracy of its statements, or to question the validity of its reasonings. This was not the result of a theory of the manner of inspiration: it was my working principle in use of the Bible, inherited from earlier times. Anywhere else, I should not have taken seriously the great age of the patriarchs; but since it was written in the Bible I thought that nothing but skepticism would doubt it. If I doubted that, I might doubt anything that was written there. So I believed that Methuselah lived his nine hundred and sixty-nine years. The hand of Paul, I saw, lay heavily upon the activities of Christian women, but I distrusted the arguments by which some were endeavoring to lift it off—or rather, I distrusted the entire business of tampering with such matters. Paul was an inspired man, and his prohibitions were not to be set aside. As a witness to truth, Paul, or any other inspired writer, was the same as God. Hence the presumption was that his commands were universal and permanent in their scope, and to argue these prohibitions down to a local and temporary application in Corinth seemed to me to belittle the Bible and degrade it from its high estate. God's written requirements were presumably universal. And of this reasoning I do not think so badly, even now. If I still held the same premises, I am inclined to think that I should be compelled to hold the same conclusions.

As to the character of inspiration, however, I remember the rising of one rather startling question. No one heard it but myself, but I heard it and it went far into my mind. In the sixties the famous book called "Essays and Reviews, by Clergymen of the Church of England," created a stir that now seems incredible. At present it would seem gentle as a summer's breeze, but then it was a veritable storm-center in English theology. I did not read the book, but I picked it up one day in the library, and read the statement, in effect, that any theory of inspiration, or divine influence in writing, that can be true of the Bible must be true of all parts of the Bible: it must account for the qualities of Judges as well as of John, of Esther as well as of Isaiah, of the Song of Solomon as well as of the Epistle to the Romans, of the Apocalypse as well as of the Gospel of Luke. That startled me, and I laid down the book with the feeling that I had read enough for once. "Of course that is true," I said to myself, for there was nothing else to say. The statement proved itself. A good theory of inspiration must be good all round, fitting all the inspired writings. But before I had closed the book the conviction had flashed upon me that I knew no theory of inspiration that could stand this reasonable test. The theories that I had studied might account for some books, but were transparently impossible for others. They were framed to account for the highest quality of the Bible in its noblest parts, and assume that that high quality ran through the whole—which it does not. I felt pretty certain also that it would be impossible to construct a theory of inspiration that would meet this reasonable demand, if inspiration was to bear anything more than a very general and indefinite meaning. I was not able to imagine a divine influence in writing that would equally account for the composition of Galatians, Proverbs, Job, and the Gospels, to say nothing of other books. I went away from the library "under conviction" that these things were so. No immediate results followed upon this silent episode, but it had its lasting influence upon my life. Strong confidence in definite theories of inspiration was not to be expected of me after that.

Although I did not in my student days depart from my inherited manner of dealing with the Scriptures, I can now see plainly that suggestions of the historical method, unnamed and unrecognized, were creeping in. My studies in theology and history were preparing me for larger methods though I did not know it yet, and so was my work upon the Bible itself. Textual criticism is a revolutionary thing: I have often wondered that advocates of verbal inspiration were so tolerant of it. If we cannot be perfectly sure of the very words that first were written, we cannot claim that any text in our possession is verbally inspired; and as for the idea that there was a verbally inspired and faultless text whose faultlessness was lost as soon as it was copied, the wonder is that any one ever took it seriously at all. Exegesis is revolutionary, too, and quite incompatible with permanent confidence in verbal inspiration. The practice of tracing out each writer's thought, with earnest endeavor to do justice to all his peculiarities of every kind, is enough to bring other ideas of inspiration into view. . . .

During the seventies I was usually in attendance upon a weekly conference of ministers living in and about a city, at which all sorts of religious and theological topics were discussed. More than once in the decade the advent question was taken up, being a question that men were interested in discussing as they are not now, and on both sides of it I heard as able advocates as our denomination contained. The premillennial and postmillennial views of the advent were presented, elaborated, and defended, sometimes with conspicuous power. It was not in vain, though the results were not such as the disputants were seeking. In consequence of the discussion several things became clear to me, some at once and some on further reflection.

The first thing that I observed was that neither of the two theories could be better defended from the Bible than the other. Either could be defended perfectly well, by making proper selection of proof texts. The Bible contained the confident prediction of an early advent, and at the same time it contained an outlook upon the future that neither included an early advent nor had place for one. I observed that both doctrines were obtainable from the Bible, but was impressed by the fact that neither one was the doctrine of the Bible as a whole. In the sense of being found in the Scriptures, both were scriptural; but in the better sense of rightly representing the Scriptures, neither was scriptural. The contesting theories had been too successful in debate: each by its very success had destroyed not only the other but itself.

At first I did not see how much this meant, but gradually it came to me, and a very important change in my convictions was a necessary result. It was borne in upon me that the Bible contains material for two opposite and irreconcilable doctrines about the early return of Christ to this world. Both doctrines cannot be true: one of them at least must rest upon misjudgment. Since this is the fact, it certainly cannot be that I am required to believe all that the Bible says because the Bible says it. If either one of the theories is true, no matter which, I certainly am not bound by the testimony that the Bible bears in favor of the other. Whatever its nature may be, the book in which these facts are found cannot have been given me by God as a book that bears his own authority in support of all its statements. The book from which these two theories can be drawn is of necessity a different book from that. Thus the Bible itself, upon examination, shows me that it is not a book infallible throughout, in which error does not exist, and that I am not required to say that it is. This negative statement followed plainly from the discussion.

Of course the corresponding positive statement was just as evidently true. The discussion showed that upon one point at least the early Christians, including apostles and writers of the New Testament, were mistaken—not only could be mistaken, but were. They believed that their Lord was soon to return to this world in visible glory. He did not so return: hence they cherished an expectation that was wrong. This I was required to affirm on the authority of facts, even though the disappointed expectations stands recorded on the pages of the Bible. I was required to affirm it in fact; on the authority of the Bible itself. Of this I could have no doubt. It is true that I heard some of the best men I knew laboring hard to show that the expectation did not exist, but their labor was in vain. I saw that it did exist, and that it proved to be a false expectation. Arguments to the contrary were quibbles, well-meant though they were. At present, of course, the intense vitality of the advent hope is one of the commonplaces of New Testament knowledge. No one who professes scholarship at all ever thinks of doubting it. At that time, however, understanding of the matter was less advanced, and it is less surprising than it would be now that the fact could be argued against. Nevertheless, upon me the truth was dawning: how could it fail to dawn? I perceived that writers in the Bible had recorded unquestioning expectation of the almost immediate occurrence of an event that has never occurred at all. Certainly they were in error on that point. Their inspiration, of whatever kind it was, was not a safeguard against this error, but allowed them, or rather perhaps impelled them, to work their mistaken view of the immediate future into our holy book.

From all this it followed that I was not obliged to agree with these writers in all that they had written, or to look upon them as infallible guides. It did not follow that therefore I ought to throw the Bible away, and I am thankful that that foolish suggestion so often supposed to attend upon such discoveries did not occur to me. But it did follow that I was not required to accept all state-ments in the Bible as true and all views that it contained as correct. Apparently I was a free reader, not a reader upon whom assent was obligatory. Apparently I might judge its statements in view of facts. And it was not some outside heretic or unbeliever that was persuading me to this conclusion: I was led to it by examination of the book itself. Its own contents bore witness to its errancy—to use a word with which I afterward became familiar. In coming to this judgment I was simply going whither the Bible led me. As I look back I wonder on what ground I ought to have proceeded if I was to judge otherwise. What would any friend advise? How, starting from the facts that I first encountered, should I have reached the conclusion that all statements in the Bible were binding upon me?

I have said that I moved slowly and unevenly in the change that I am now recording. I have dated this conviction against the inerrancy of the Bible here in the seventies, and here it belongs, for at this time it was planted in my mind and I began to be aware of its presence and its importance. But its growth was gradual, and its victory over my thinking was slow in coming—surer perhaps for being slow. Years passed before it came to its own. This is no wonder, in view of my early training. Nevertheless, when the new conception had made so valid an entrance it deserved well of the future, and was sure to do its work. . . .

I have spoken of the hand of Paul as lying heavily upon the activities of Christian women. For me the traditional deference for the Pauline prohibition long continued; but in the three parishes that I have spoken of there was a curious succession of attitudes on the subject of women in the church, which became an element in my biblical education.

In the first parish the general understanding was that Paul forbade the women to take part in the meetings of the church; and yet there was a peculiar line of unconscious compromise. The women seemed to have a habit of confidence in the pastor as interpreter and representative of Paul. If he thought that Paul's prohibition was not binding upon them, they would feel free to speak; but if he disapproved on Pauline grounds, the most of them would not speak at all, and those who did would have some constraint in doing so, or at least some consciousness. In this way my opinion obtained an exaggerated importance. I was not understood to be very rigid in judgment against the woman's right, and I was not, for in fact I wanted all the gifts in the little church to be in use, and did not conceal the desire—and a large half of the gifts were feminine. But at the same time Paul made me timid and half-hearted about it: it became known that I understood him to be against us, and there was constraint upon the women. There were exceptions, but this was the rule. Their activity did not increase in my day. I think it rather diminished.

The training of my second parish had been rigidly Pauline for generations, and the atmosphere was full of the great apostle's influence. Rarely was a woman's voice heard in the church, his judgment of silence being accepted as the judgment of God. There was some private dissent, but the public sentiment, so to call it, was of one effect. The women of the parish were nobly going out into activities of larger and more important significance, against which no inspired voice had been lifted up; in fact, a large missionary organization of women had its origin there in my time; but in the church, with rare exceptions, even the women of the largest gifts were silent. In this parish, however, the young people's meeting came in as an institution in my time, and in this the girls began freely and simply to do what their mothers had not dared, or even desired, in the face of an inspired apostle. Various excuses were made for this, though not by the young people themselves. Some used to suggest in those days that perhaps this was not a meeting of the church, and did not come under Paul's prohibition. Similar excuses were offered for the larger use of women in public work which was coming in. As to my understanding of Paul's words and intention, I had not changed; but gradually there was dawning upon me the improbability of God's intending to govern our movements in America through Paul's directions to the church in Corinth two thousand years ago. The method did not seem like the reasonable God. At the same time the quibbling arguments by which I heard good men evading the prohibition wearied me, and were almost enough to convert me. Thus the old influence was slipping away, and I did not blame myself.

In my third parish, with its brisker movement of life, all was changed. The women were taking part in the meetings of the church, as many of them as wished to do so, with perfect freedom. They knew all about the arguments for reading Paul's prohibition as local and temporary, at least the Corinthian one, and so had no fear that they were sinning against the Scriptures. But the real reason of their freedom was that in this matter they were not governed by Paul any more. Some of them had fine gifts for speaking and something to say, and would have found some way to speak their minds if Paul himself had been there with all the weapons that he was supposed to carry. They were acting out their real life from the heart, and the ancient hand was off from them. A few years of such freedom lifted it from me. I came to the conviction that the Christian life of women, as of men, must have free course in the activities that are normal to the age in which they live, and that Paul would be the first to have it so. In fact, I think he would have cancelled the prohibition, if he had foreseen what would come of it through long centuries. Better a little disorder in Corinth, he would have said, than such a handicap on the sex of Phœbe and Priscilla. In later years I have had no trouble with these Corinthian counsels; and since I ceased to believe myself required to accept all arguments in the Bible as valid because they are there, I have not been troubled by the inconclusive reasons for enforcing silence upon women that are found in the Pastoral Epistles. Thus by a long and slow evolution I have come to recognize the normal freedom of the Christian life. It seems a pity that I had to unlearn so much upon the way.

III

Indigenous Patterns of Religion

19. Religion among American Indians—
Two Accounts

THE EUROPEAN *settlers of North America with rare exceptions had little respect for Indian religion, which they dismissed as heathen superstition. Converts to Christianity were expected to renounce their past and to adopt both the civilization and the religion of the white man. Yet Indian religious attitudes and practices survived in various ways through the tragic centuries that saw the defeat and displacement of the Indians. The legends and rituals of the Indians varied considerably among the many tribes. The explanations of Indian religion that follow were given by Indian chiefs in the nineteenth century to white men. Pawnee religion was explained by Secret Pipe Chief to George Bird Grinnell (1849–1938), editor, author, and explorer who had served with General Custer's expedition to the Black Hills in 1874. Potawotamie beliefs were described by Potogojecs to a Catholic missionary, Peter J. De Smet, S.J., and included by him in one of his letters, which were collected in book form.*

SOURCE: George Bird Grinnell, *Pawnee Hero Stories and Folk Tales, with Notes on the Origin, Customs and Character of the Pawnee People* (New York, 1889), pp. 350–359.

Peter J. De Smet, *Oregon Missions and Travels over the Rocky Mountains in 1845–46* (New York, 1847), pp. 343–354.

A

It is generally believed that, among the Indians of North America, the priests and the shamans, "medicine men," or doctors, are the same. This is not the case with the Pawnees. Among them the priestly office was entirely distinct from that of the doctor, and had nothing in common with it. The priest was in a sense the medium of communication with Ti-ra'-wa; he prayed to the deity more efficaciously than could a common person, acted, in fact, as an intercessor; he knew the secrets of the sacred bundles, and when he asked anything good for the tribe, or for an individual, it was likely to be granted. His education and the power given him from above brought him into specially close relations with Ti-ra'-wa, who seemed to watch over him and to listen to him when he interceded for the tribe. He was an intermediary between Ti-ra'-wa and the people, and held a relation to the Pawnees and their deity not unlike that occupied by Moses to Jehovah and the Israelites.

The office of the "medicine man," shaman or doctor, had to do only with sickness or injury. He was the healer. Disease was caused by bad spirits, and it was the doctor's part to drive off these evil influences.

In the lodge or house of every Pawnee of influence, hanging on the west side, and so opposite the door, is the sacred bundle neatly wrapped in buckskin, and black with smoke and age. What these bundles contain we do not know. Sometimes, from the ends, protrude bits of scalps, and the tips of pipe stems and slender sticks, but the whole contents of the bundle are known only to the priests and to its owner—perhaps, not always even to him. The sacred bundles are kept on the west side of the lodge, because, being thus furthest from the door, fewer people will pass by them than if they were hung in any other part of the lodge. Various superstitions attach to these bundles. In the lodges where certain of them are kept it is forbidden to put a knife in the fire; in others, a knife may not be thrown; in others, it is not permitted to enter the lodge with the face painted; or again, a man cannot go in if he has feathers tied in his head.

On certain sacred occasions the bundles are opened, and their contents form part of the ceremonial of worship.

No one knows whence the bundles came. Many of them are very old; too old even to have a history. Their origin is lost in the haze of the long ago. They say, "The sacred bundles were given us long ago. No one knows when they came to us." Secret Pipe Chief, one of the very oldest men in the tribe, and its high priest, said to me:

"All the sacred bundles are from the far-off country in the southwest, from which we came long ago. They were handed down to the people before they started on their journey. Then they had never seen anything like iron, but they had discovered how to make the flint knives and arrow points. There was nothing that came to us through the whites. It all came to us through the power of Ti-ra'-wa. Through his power we were taught how to make bows and stone knives and arrow heads.

"It was through the Ruler of the universe that the sacred bundles were given to us. We look to them, because, through them and the buffalo and the corn, we worship Ti-ra'-wa. We all, even the chiefs, respect the sacred bundles. When a man goes on the warpath, and has led many scouts and brought the scalps, he has done it through the sacred bundles. There were many different ceremonies that they used to go through. The high priest performs these ceremonies.

"The high priestship was founded in this way: The black eagle spoke to a person, and said to him, 'I am one of those nearest to Ti-ra'-wa, and you must look to me to be helped; to the birds and the animals—look to me, the black eagle, to the white-headed eagle, to the otter and the buffalo.'

"The black eagle sent the buzzard as a messenger to this person, and he gave him the corn. The secrets of the high priestship and the other secrets were handed down at the same time. The buzzard, because he is bald, stands for the old men who have little hair. The white-headed eagle also represents the old men, those whose hair is white. These are the messengers through whom Ti-ra'-wa sends his words to the people. The Wichitas also had these secrets, and so have the Rees."

The Pawnees believe that they were created by Ti-ra'-wa, but that there had been people on the earth before them. They say, "The first men who lived on the earth were very large Indians. They were giants; very big and very strong. The animals that lived then were the same that we know now, and of the same size. These giants used to hunt the buffalo on foot. They were so swift and strong that a man could run down a buffalo, and kill it with a great stone, or a club, or even with his flint knife. Then, when he had killed it, if it was a big buffalo bull, he would tie it up, throw it over his back, and carry it into camp, just as a man today would carry in an antelope. When one killed a yearling, he would push its head up under his belt, and let its body swing by his side, just as we would carry a rabbit.

"These people did not believe in Ti-ra'-wa. When it would thunder and rain, they would shake their fists at the sky and call out bad words. In these days all people, wherever they live—all Indians, all white men, all Mexicans and all black men—when they smoke up, speak to A-ti'-us Ti-ra'-wa, and ask that he will give them the right kind of a mind, and that he will bless them, so that they may have plenty to eat, and may be successful in war, and may be made chiefs and head men. When we smoke toward the earth we say, 'Father of the dead, you see us.' This means that this is Ti-ra'-wa's ground. It belongs to him, and we ask him that he will let us walk on it, and will let us be buried in it. We believe that after we are dead we will live again with Ti-ra'-wa up in the sky. We fear nothing after death worse than we know now. All will live again with Ti-ra'-wa and be happy. A thief, one who steals from others in the camp, one who is bad, dies, and that is the end of him. He goes into the ground, and does not live again. One reason why we believe that there is a life after death is that sometimes, when asleep, we dream and see these things. We see ourselves living with Ti-ra'-wa. Then, too, we often dream of our people whom we have known, and who have died. We dream of being dead ourselves, and of meeting these people and talking with them, and going to war with them.

"Now, these giants did not believe in any of these things. They did not pray to Ti-ra'-wa, and they thought that they were very strong, and that nothing could overcome them. They grew worse and worse. At last Ti-ra'-wa got angry, and he made the water rise up level with the land, and all the ground became soft, and these great people sank down into the mud and were drowned. The great bones found on the prairie are the bones of these people, and we have been in deep cañons, and have seen big bones under ground, which convinces us that these people did sink into the soft ground.

"After the destruction of the race of giants, Ti-ra'-wa created a new race of men, small, like those of today. He made first a man and a woman. They lived on the earth and were good. To them was given the corn. From this man and this woman the Pawnees sprung, and they have always cultivated the corn from the earliest times."

There can be no doubt as to the belief of the Pawnees in a future life. The spirits of the dead live after their bodies have become dust. The stories of the Ghost Bride and the Ghost Wife . . . are examples of this belief. Secret Pipe Chief told me of himself:

"I was dead once. Just as I died, I found my way leading to an Indian village. I entered it, and went straight to the lodge of my friends and my relations. I saw them, and when I saw them I knew them again. I even knew my old relations, whom I had never looked on when I was alive. I went into a lodge, but I was not offered a seat, and I thought that I was not welcome. I came out of the lodge, and went out of the village toward the west. Then I came back to life again. In the morning I had died, and I came to life in the afternoon. That must be the reason that I still live, and am getting old. I was not welcome yet. They did not receive me. From this I am convinced that there is a life after we are dead."

Sometimes ghosts appear to them, but more often they merely speak to them; only a voice is heard. They believe that the little whirlwinds often seen in summer are ghosts. The reason for this is that once a person shot at a whirlwind with his arrow. The arrow passed through it, and it all disappeared and came to nothing. Then the man was convinced that it was a ghost, and that he had killed it.

The different bands of the Pawnees had not all the same beliefs. Thus the Skidi band offered up the human sacrifice—a captive taken in war—to the morning star. This is thought to have been a propitiatory offering to avert the evil influences exerted by that planet. At the present day the Indians speak of the sacrifice as having been made to Ti-ra'-wa. None of the other tribes had this form of worship, and in this fact we have another indication that the separation of the Skidi from the Pawnees had been a long one. The Ka-wa-ra-kish band of the Pita-hau-erat are said to have been "the only ones of the Pawnees who did not worship Ti-ra'-wa. They worshiped toward the west."

Mention has been made of the Nahu'rac, or animals, which possess miraculous attributes given them by Ti-ra'-wa. The Pawnees know of five places where these animals meet to hold council —five of these Nahu'rac lodges. One of these is at Pa-hŭk', on the south side of the Platte River, opposite the town of Fremont, in Nebraska. The word Pa-hŭk' means "hill island." Another animal home is under an island in the Platte River, near the town of Central City. It is called by the Pawnees La-la-wa-koh-ti-to, meaning "dark island." The third of these sacred places is on the Loup Fork, opposite the mouth of the Cedar River, and under a high, white cut bank. It is called Ah-ka-wit-akol, "white bank." Another is on the Solomon River, Kitz-a-witz-ŭk, "water on a bank"; it is called Pa'howa sometimes. This is a mound, shaped like a dirt lodge. At the top of the mound, in the middle, is a round hole, in which, down below, can be seen water. At certain times, the people gather there, and throw into this hole their offerings to Ti-ra'-wa, blankets and robes, blue beads, tobacco, eagle feathers and moccasins. Sometimes, when they are gathered there, the water rises to the top of the hole, and flows out, running down the side of the mound into the river. Then the mothers take their little children and sprinkle the water over them, and pray to *Ti-ra'-wa* to bless them. The water running out of the hole often carries with it the offerings, and the ground is covered with the old rotten things that have been thrown in. The fifth place is a hard, smooth, flinty rock, sticking up out of the ground. They call it *Pa-hur'*, "hill that points the way." In the side of the hill there is a great hole, where the *Nahu'rac* hold councils. This hill is in Kansas, and can be seen from the Burlington & Missouri River Railroad. It is known to the whites as Guide Rock.

B

Legend of the Potawotomie Indians

St. Louis University
January 10, 1847.

Very Rev. and Dear Father Provincial,—Agreeably to my promise, I send you the account given by the Potawotomies, residing at Council Bluffs, respecting their own origin, and the causes which gave rise to their "great medicine," and juggling, considered by them as of the highest antiquity. Such superstitions, indeed, are found to exist among all the tribes of the American continent, differing only in the form and the accompanying ceremonies. The Nanaboojoo of the Potawotomies, the Wieska of the Objibbeways the Wizakeshak of the Crees, the Sauteux and the Black-Feet, the Etalapasse of the Tchinouks on the coast of the Pacific, can, among these different tribes, be traced up to the same personage.

I send it *verbatim*, as it was communicated to me by Potogojecs, one of the most intelligent chiefs of the Potawotomie nation. Though fabulous, it is not entirely devoid of interest; it should excite us to offer up our prayers the more fervently to the Great Father of Light, for these poor benighted children of the forest, and beg of Him to send good and worthy laborers into this vast vineyard. Having inquired of this chief what he thought of the Great Spirit, of the Creator, and of the origin of his religion, or great medicine, he replied as follows: "I will give you a faithful account of what my tribe believes in these matters. We have not, like you, books to transmit our traditions to our children; it is the duty of the old men of the nation to instruct the young people in whatever relates to their belief, and their happiness.

"Many among us believe that there are two Great Spirits who govern the universe, but who are constantly at war with each other. One is called the Kchemnito, that is, the Great Spirit, the other Mchemnito, or the Wicked Spirit. The first is goodness itself, and his beneficent influence is felt everywhere; but the second is wickedness personified, and does nothing but evil. Some believe that they are equally powerful, and, through fear of the Wicked Spirit, offer to him their homage and adoration. Others, again, are doubtful which of them should be considered the more powerful, and accordingly endeavor to propitiate both, by offering to each an appropriate worship. The greater part, however, believe as I do, that Kchemnito is the first principle, the first great cause, and consequently ought to be all-powerful, and to whom alone is due all worship and adoration; and that Mchemnito ought to be despised and rejected!

"Kchemnito at first created a world, which he filled with a race of beings having nothing but the appearance of men—perverse, ungrateful, wicked dogs—that never raised their eyes to heaven to implore the assistance of the Great Spirit. Such ingratitude aroused him to anger, and he plunged the world in a great lake, where they were all drowned. His anger thus appeased, he withdrew it from the waters, and created anew a beautiful young man, who, however, appeared very sad, and being dissatisfied with his solitary condition, grew weary of life. Kchemnito took pity on him, and gave him, during sleep, a sister, as a companion to cheer his loneliness. When he awoke and saw his sister he rejoiced exceedingly—his melancholy instantly disappeared. They spent their time in agreeable conversation and amusement, living for many years together in a state of innocence and perfect harmony, without the slightest incident to mar the happiness of their peaceful solitude.

"The young man had a dream, for the first time, which he communicated to his sister. 'Five young men,' said he, 'will come this night, and rap at the door of the lodge—the Great Spirit forbids you to laugh, to look at them, or give an answer to any of the first four, but laugh, look, and speak, when the fifth presents himself.' She acted according to his advice. When she heard the voice of the fifth, she opened the door to him, laughing at the same time very heartily; he entered immediately, and became her husband. The first of the five strangers, called Sama (tobacco), having received no answer, died of grief; the three others, Wapekone (pumpkin), Eshketamok (watermelon), and Kojees (the bean), shared the fate of their companion. Taaman (maize), the bridegroom, buried his four companions, and from their graves there sprung up, shortly after, pumpkins, watermelons, beans, and tobacco plants in sufficient abundance to supply their wants during the whole year, and enable them to smoke to the manitous, and in the council. From this union are descended the American Indian nations.

"A great manitou came on earth, and chose a wife from among the children of men. He had four sons at a birth; the first born was called Nanaboojoo, the friend of the human race, the mediator between man and the Great Spirit; the second was named Chipiapoos, the man of the dead, who presides over the country of the souls; the third, Wabosso, as soon as he saw the light, fled towards the north, where he was changed into a white rabbit, and under that name is considered there as a great manitou; the fourth was Chakekenapok, the man of flint, or fire-stone. In coming into the world he caused the death of his mother.

"Nanaboojoo, having arrived at the age of manhood, resolved to avenge the death of his mother (for among us revenge is considered honorable); he pursued Chakekenapok all over the globe. Whenever he could come within reach of his brother, he fractured some member of his body, and after several rencounters, finally destroyed him by tearing out his entrails. All fragments broken from the body of this man of stone then grew up into large rocks; his entrails were changed into vines of every species, and took deep root in all the forests; the flint-stones scattered around the earth indicate where the different combats took place. Before fire was introduced among us, Nanaboojoo taught our ancestors how to form hatchets, lances, and the points of arrows, in order to assist us in killing our enemies in war, and animals for our food. Nanaboojoo and his brother, Chipiapoos, lived together retired from the rest of mankind, and were distinguished from all other beings by their superior qualities of body and mind. The manitous that dwell in the air, as well as those who inhabit the earth and the waters, envied the power of these brothers, and conspired to destroy them. Nanaboojoo discovered and eluded their snares, and warned Chipiapoos not to separate himself from him a single moment. Notwithstanding this admonition, Chipiapoos ventured alone one day upon Lake Michigan; the manitous broke the ice, and he sank to the bottom, where they hid the body. Nanaboojoo became inconsolable when he missed his brother from his lodge; he sought him everywhere in vain, he waged war against all the manitous, and precipitated an infinite number of them into the deepest abyss. He then wept, disfigured his person, and covered his head, as a sign of his grief, during six years, pronouncing from time to time, in sad and mournful tones, the name of the unhappy Chipiapoos.

"While this truce continued, the manitous consulted upon the means best calculated to appease the anger of Nanaboojoo, without, however, coming to any conclusion; when four of the oldest and wisest, who had had no hand in the death of Chipiapoos, offered to accomplish the difficult task. They built a lodge close to that of Nanaboojoo, prepared an excellent repast, and filled a calumet with the most exquisite tobacco. They journeyed in silence towards their redoubted enemy, each carrying under his arm a bag, formed of the entire skin of some animal, an otter, a lynx, or a beaver, well provided with the most precious medicines (to which, in their superstitious practices, they attach a supernatural power). With many kind expressions, they begged that he would condescend to accompany them. He arose immediately, uncovered his head, washed himself, and followed them. When arrived at their lodge, they offered him a cup containing a dose of their medicine, preparatory to his initiation. Nanaboojoo swallowed the contents at a single draught, and found himself completely restored. They then commenced their dances and their songs; they also applied their medicine bags, which, after gently blowing them at him, they would then cast on the ground; at each fall of the medicine bag, Nanaboojoo perceived that his melancholy, sadness, hatred, and anger disappeared, and affections of an opposite nature took possession of his soul. They all joined in the dance and song—they ate and smoked together. Nanaboojoo thanked them for having initiated him in the mysteries of their grand medicine.

"The manitous brought back the lost Chipiapoos, but it was forbidden him to enter the lodge; he received, through a chink, a burning coal, and was ordered to go and preside over the region of souls, and there, for the happiness of his uncles and aunts, that is, for all men and women, who should repair thither, kindle with this coal a fire which should never be extinguished.

"Nanaboojoo then re-descended upon earth, and, by order, of the Great Spirit, initiated all his family in the mysteries of the grand medicine. He procured for each of them a bag well furnished with medicines, giving them strict orders to perpetuate these ceremonies among their descendants, adding at the same time, that these practices, religiously observed, would cure their maladies, procure them abundance in the chase, and give them complete victory over their enemies. (All their religion consists in these superstitious practices, dances and songs; they have the most implicit faith in these strange reveries.)

"Nanaboojoo is our principal intercessor with the Great Spirit; he it was that obtained for us the creation of animals for our food and raiment. He has caused to grow those roots and herbs which are endowed with the virtue of curing our maladies, and of enabling us, in time of famine, to kill the wild animals. He has left the care of them to Mesakkummikokwi, the great-grandmother of the human race, and in order that we should never invoke her in vain, it has been strictly enjoined on the old woman never to quit the dwelling. Hence, when an Indian makes the collection of roots and herbs which are to serve him as medicines, he deposits, at the same time, on the earth, a small offering to Mesakkummikokwi. During his different excursions over the surface of the earth, Nanaboojoo killed all such animals as were hurtful to us, as the mastodon, the mammoth, etc. He has placed four beneficial spirits at the four cardinal points of the earth, for the purpose of contributing to the happiness of the human race. That of the north procures for us ice and snow, in order to aid us in discovering and following the wild animals. That of the south gives us that which occasions the growth of our pumpkins, melons, maize and tobacco. The spirit placed at the west gives us rain, and that of the east gives us light, and commands the sun to make his daily walks around the globe. The thunder we hear is the voice of spirits, having the form of large birds, which Nanaboojoo has placed in the clouds. When they cry very loud we burn some tobacco in our cabins, to make them a smoke offering and appease them.

"Nanaboojoo yet lives, resting himself after his labors, upon an immense flake of ice, in the Great Lake (the North Sea). We fear that the whites will one day discover his retreat, and drive him off, then the end of the world is at hand, for as soon as he puts foot on the earth, the whole universe will take fire, and every living creature will perish in the flames!"

In their festivities and religious assemblies, all their songs turn upon some one or other of these fables. When the chief had finished this history, I asked him whether he had any faith in what he had just related. "Assuredly I have, for I have had the happiness to see and entertain three old men of my nation, who penetrated far into the north, and were admitted into the presence of Nana-boojoo, with whom they conversed a long time. He confirmed all that I have recounted to you!"

Our savages believe that the souls of the dead, in their journey to the great prairie of their ancestors, pass a rapid current, over which the only bridge is a single tree, kept constantly in violent agitation, managed, however, in such a way that the souls of perfect men pass it in safety, whilst those of the wicked slip off the tree into the water and are lost forever.

Such is the narration given to me by the Potawotomi chief, comprising all the articles of the creed held by this tribe, we can hardly fail to recognize in it, much obscured by the accumulation of ages, the tradition of the universal deluge, of the creation of the universe, of Adam and Eve; even some traces of the incarnation are found in the birth of Nanaboojoo, he was descended of parents, one of whom only, his mother, was of the human race; he is, moreover, the intercessor between God and man.

20. Joseph Smith:
A New Revelation and a New Church

THE REVIVALISM that swept back and forth across upstate New York in the early decades of the nineteenth century intensified rivalries between the denominations. Joseph Smith (1805–1844) moved into the area from New England at the age of ten. His religious feelings were aroused by the emotional piety that swirled around him, but he was troubled by the claims and counterclaims of the various groups. Seeking divine guidance alone in the forest, he claimed to have been led to discover the mysterious golden plates of the Book of Mormon. In 1830 he published a translation of the plates and founded a new church, which soon became known as the Church of Jesus Christ of Latter-Day Saints. Although critics quickly pointed out that the Book of Mormon showed strong internal marks of nineteenth-century authorship in its references to places and ideas, believers in the new movement found that it provided a satisfying world view and offered comforting explanations of spiritual difficulties. The young prophet also continued to have revelations, introducing a plurality of gods and of wives. Meeting hostility as its distinctive doctrines became known, the young church moved to Kirtland, Ohio, and then on to Independence, Missouri, where the new city of Zion was to be built. Driven out again to Nauvoo, Illinois, the prophet was murdered in jail in 1844. Under the leadership of Brigham Young, the long trek westward to Salt Lake City, Utah, began.

In addition to the Book of Mormon, the authoritative documents of this indigenous American church include The Doctrine and Covenants and The Pearl of Great Price. The selection is from the latter work, and was itself originally extracted from the History of Joseph Smith, the Prophet, by Himself.

SOURCE: *The Pearl of Great Price: Being a Choice Selection from the Revelations, Translations and Narrations of Joseph Smith, First Prophet, Seer, and Revelator to the Church of Jesus Christ of Latter-Day Saints* (Salt Lake City, 1891), pp. 56–70.

Extracts from the History of Joseph Smith

CONTAINING AN ACCOUNT OF THE FIRST VISIONS AND REVELATIONS WHICH HE RECEIVED, ALSO OF HIS DISCOVERING AND OBTAINING THE PLATES OF GOLD WHICH CONTAIN THE RECORD OF MORMON —ITS TRANSLATION—HIS BAPTISM AND ORDINATION BY THE ANGEL.

Owing to the many reports which have been put in circulation by evil designing persons in relation to the rise and progress of the Church of Jesus Christ of Latter-Day Saints, all of which have been designed by the authors thereof to militate against its character as a church, and its progress in the world, I have been induced to write this history, so as to disabuse the public mind, and put all inquirers after truth in possession of the facts as they have transpired in relation both to myself and the church so far as I have such facts in possession.

In this history I will present the various events in relation to this church, in truth and righteousness, as they have transpired, or as they at present exist, being now the eighth year since the organization of the said church.

I was born in the year of our Lord one thousand eight hundred and five, on the twenty-third day of December, in the town of Sharon, Windsor County, state of Vermont. My father, Joseph Smith, senior, left the state of Vermont, and moved to Palmyra, Ontario (now Wayne) County, in the state of New York, when I was in my tenth year. In about four years after my father's arrival at Palmyra, he moved with his family into Manchester, in the same county of Ontario. His family consisted of eleven souls, namely: my father, Joseph Smith, my mother, Lucy Smith (whose name previous to her marriage was Mack, daughter of Solomon Mack), my brothers Alvin (who is now dead), Hyrum, myself, Samuel Harrison, William, Don Carlos, and my sisters Sophronia, Catherine, and Lucy.

Some time in the second year after our removal to Manchester, there was in the place where we lived an unusual excitement on the subject of religion. It commenced with the Methodists, but soon became general among all the sects in that region of country; indeed the whole district of country seemed affected by it, and great multitudes united themselves to the different religious parties, which created no small stir and division amongst the people, some crying, Lo here, and some, Lo there; some were contending for the Methodist faith, some for the Presbyterian, and some for the Baptists.' For notwithstanding the great love which the converts for these different faiths expressed at the time of their conversion, and the great zeal manifested by their respected clergy, who were active in getting up and promoting this extraordinary scene of religious feeling, in order to have everybody converted, as they were pleased to call it, let them join what sect they pleased; yet when the converts began to file off, some to one party, and some to another, it was seen that the seemingly good feelings of both the priests and the converts were more pretended than real, for a scene of great confusion and bad feeling ensued—priest contending against priest, and convert against convert, so that all the good feelings one for another, if they ever had any, were entirely lost in a strife of words, and a contest about opinions.

I was at this time in my fifteenth year. My father's family was proselyted to the Presbyterian faith, and four of them joined that church, namely, my mother, Lucy, my brothers Hyrum, Samuel Harrison, and my sister Sophronia.

During this time of great excitement, my mind was called up to serious reflection and great uneasiness; but though my feelings were deep and often pungent, still I kept myself aloof from all those parties, though I attended their several meetings as often as occasion would permit; but in process of time my mind became somewhat partial to the Methodist sect, and I felt some desire to be united with them, but so great was the confusion and strife among the different denominations, that it was impossible for a person, young as I was, and so unacquainted with men and things, to come to any certain conclusion who was right, and who was wrong. My mind at different times was greatly excited, the cry and tumult was so great and incessant. The Presbyterians were most decided against the Baptists and Methodists, and used all their powers of either reason or sophistry to prove their errors, or, at least, to make the people think they were in error. On the other hand the Baptists and Methodists, in their turn, were equally zealous to establish their own tenets and disprove all others.

In the midst of this war of words and tumult of opinions, I often said to myself, What is to be done? Who of all these parties are right? Or, are they all wrong together? If any one of them be right, which is it, and how shall I know it?

While I was laboring under the extreme difficulties, caused by the contests of these parties of religionists, I was one day reading the Epistle of James, first chapter, and fifth verse, which reads, If any of you lack wisdom, let him ask of God, that giveth unto all men liberally and upbraideth not, and it shall be given him. Never did any passage of Scripture come with more power to the heart of man than this did at this time to mine. It seemed to enter with great force into every feeling of my heart. I reflected on it again and again, knowing that if any person needed wisdom from God, I did; for how to act I did not know, and unless I could get more wisdom than I then had, would never know; for the teachers of religion of the different sects understood the same passage so differently as to destroy all confidence in settling the question by an appeal to the Bible. At length I came to the conclusion that I must either remain in darkness and confusion, or else I must do as James directs, that is, ask of God. I at length came to the determination to ask of God, concluding that if he gave wisdom to them that lacked wisdom, and would give liberally and not upbraid, I might venture. So, in accordance with this, my determination to ask of God, I retired to the woods to make the attempt. It was on the morning of a beautiful clear day, early in the spring of eighteen hundred and twenty. It was the first time in my life that I had made such an attempt, for amidst all my anxieties I had never as yet made the attempt to pray vocally.

After I had retired into the place where I had previously designed to go, having looked around me and finding myself alone, I kneeled down and began to offer up the desires of my heart to God. I had scarcely done so, when immediately I was seized upon by some power which entirely overcame me, and had such astonishing influence over me as to bind my tongue so that I could not speak. Thick darkness gathered around me, and it seemed to me for a time as if I were doomed to sudden destruction. But exerting all my powers to call upon God to deliver me out of the power of this enemy which had seized upon me, and at the very moment when I was ready to sink into despair and abandon myself to destruction, not to an imaginary ruin, but to the power of some actual being from the unseen world, who had such a marvelous power as I had never before felt in any being. Just at this moment of great alarm, I saw a pillar of light exactly over my head, above the brightness of the sun, which descended gradually until it fell upon me. It no sooner appeared than I found myself delivered from the enemy which held me bound. When the light rested upon me, I saw two personages, whose brightness and glory defy all description, standing above me in the air. One of them spake unto me, calling me by name, and said (pointing to the other), THIS IS MY BELOVED SON, HEAR HIM.

My object in going to inquire of the Lord, was to know which of all the sects was right, that I might know which to join. No sooner, therefore, did I get possession of myself, so as to be able to speak, than I asked the personages who stood above me in the light, which of all the sects was right (for at this time it had never entered into my heart that all were wrong), and which I should join. I was answered that I must join none of them, for they were all wrong, and the personage who addressed me said that all their creeds were an abomination in his sight; that those professors were all corrupt. They draw near to me with their lips, but their hearts are far from me; they teach for doctrine the commandments of man, having a form of godliness, but they deny the power thereof.

He again forbade me to join with any of them; and many other things did he say unto me which I cannot write at this time. When I came to myself again, I found myself lying on my back, looking up into heaven.

Some few days after I had this vision, I happened to be in company with one of the Methodist preachers, who was very active in the before mentioned religious excitement, and conversing with him on the subject of religion, I took occasion to give him an account of the vision which I had had. I was greatly surprised at his behavior; he treated my communication not only lightly, but with great contempt, saying it was all of the devil, that there were no such things as visions or revelations in these days; that all such things had ceased with the apostles, and that there never would be any more of them.

I soon found, however, that my telling the story had excited a great deal of prejudice against me among professors of religion, and was the cause of great persecution, which continued to increase; and though I was an obscure boy, only between fourteen and fifteen years of age, and my circumstances in life such as to make a boy of no consequence in the world, yet men of high standing would take notice sufficient to excite the public mind against me, and create a hot persecution, and this was common among all the sects; all united to persecute me.

It has often caused me serious reflection, both then and since, how very strange it was that an obscure boy, of a little over fourteen years of age, and one, too, who was doomed to the necessity of obtaining a scanty maintenance by his daily labor, should be thought a character of sufficient importance to attract the attention of the great ones of the most popular sects of the day, so as to create in them a spirit of the hottest persecution and reviling. But strange or not, so it was, and was often a cause of great sorrow to myself. However it was, nevertheless, a fact, that I had had a vision. I have thought since, that I felt much like Paul when he made his defense before King Agrippa, and related the account of the vision he had when he saw a light and heard a voice, but still there were but few who believed him; some said he was dishonest, others said he was mad, and he was ridiculed and reviled; but all this did not destroy the reality of his vision. He had seen a vision, he knew he had, and all the persecution under heaven could not make it otherwise; and though they should persecute him unto death, yet he knew and would know unto his latest breath, that he had both seen a light, and heard a voice speaking to him, and all the world could not make him think or believe otherwise.

So it was with me; I had actually seen a light, and in the midst of that light I saw two personages, and they did in reality speak unto me, or one of them did; and though I was hated and persecuted for saying that I had seen a vision, yet it was true; and while they were persecuting me, reviling me and speaking all manner of evil against me, falsely, for so saying, I was led to say in my heart, Why persecute for telling the truth? I have actually seen a vision, and who am I that I can withstand God? Or why does the world think to make me deny what I have actually seen? For I had seen a vision. I knew it, and I knew that God knew it, and I could not deny it, neither dare I do it; at least I knew that by so doing I would offend God and come under condemnation.

I had now got my mind satisfied so far as the sectarian world was concerned, that it was not my duty to join with any of them, but continue as I was until further directed; I had found the testimony of James to be true, that a man who lacked wisdom might ask of God, and obtain and not be upbraided. I continued to pursue my common avocations in life until the twenty-first of September, one thousand eight hundred and twenty-three, all the time suffering severe persecution at the hands of all classes of men, both religious and irreligious, because I continued to affirm that I had seen a vision.

During the space of time which intervened between the time I had the vision, and the year eighteen hundred and twenty-three (having been forbidden to join any of the religious sects of the day, and being of very tender years, and persecuted by those who ought to have been my friends, and to have treated me kindly, and if they supposed me to be deluded to have endeavored, in a proper and affectionate manner, to have reclaimed me), I was left to all kinds of temptations, and mingling with all kinds of society, I frequently fell into many foolish errors, and displayed the weakness of youth, and the corruption of human nature, which I am sorry to say led me into divers temptations, to the gratification of many appetites offensive in the sight of God. In consequence of these things I often felt condemned for my weakness and imperfections; when on the evening of the above mentioned twenty-first of September, after I had retired to my bed for the night, I betook myself to prayer and supplication to Almighty God, for forgiveness of all my sins and follies, and also for a manifestation to me, that I might know of my state and standing before him; for I had full confidence in obtaining a divine manifestation, as I had previously had one.

While I was thus in the act of calling upon God, I discovered a light appearing in the room, which continued to increase until the room was lighter than at noonday, when immediately a personage appeared at my bedside, standing in the air, for his feet did not touch the floor. He had on a loose robe of most exquisite whiteness. It was a whiteness beyond anything earthly I had ever seen; nor do I believe that any earthly thing could be made to appear so exceedingly white and brilliant; his hands were naked, and his arms also, a little above the wrist; so also were his feet naked, as were his legs, a little above the ankles. His head and neck were also bare. I could discover that he had no other clothing on but this robe, as it was open, so that I could see into his bosom.

Not only was his robe exceedingly white, but his whole person was glorious beyond description, and his countenance truly like lightning. The room was exceedingly light, but not so very bright as immediately around his person. When I first looked upon him I was afraid, but the fear soon left me. He called me by name and said unto me that he was a messenger sent from the presence of God to me, and that his name was Moroni. That God had a work for me to do, and that my name should be had for good and evil among all nations, kindreds, and tongues; or that it should be both good and evil spoken of among all people. He said there was a book deposited, written upon gold plates, giving an account of the former inhabitants of this continent, and the source from whence they sprang. He also said that the fullness of the everlasting Gospel was contained in it, as delivered by the Savior to the ancient inhabitants. Also, that there were two stones in silver bows (and these stones, fastened to a breastplate, constituted what is called the Urim and Thummim) deposited with the plates, and the possession and use of these stones was what constituted seers in ancient or former times, and that God had prepared them for the purpose of translating the book.

After telling me these things, he commenced quoting the prophecies of the Old Testament. He first quoted part of the third chapter of Malachi, and he quoted also the fourth or last chapter of the same prophecy, though with a little variation from the way it reads in our Bibles. Instead of quoting the first verse as it reads in our books, he quoted it thus: "For behold, the day cometh that shall burn as an oven, and all the proud, yea, and all that do wickedly, shall burn as stubble, for they that come shall burn them, saith the Lord of Hosts, that it shall leave them neither root nor branch." And again, he quoted the fifth verse thus: "Behold, I will reveal unto you the Priesthood, by the hand of Elijah the Prophet, before the coming of the great and dreadful day of the Lord." He also quoted the next verse differently: "And he shall plant in the hearts of the children, the promises made to the fathers, and the hearts of the children shall turn to their fathers; if it were not so, the whole earth would be utterly wasted at his coming."

In addition to these, he quoted the eleventh chapter of Isaiah, saying that it was about to be fulfilled. He quoted also the third chapter of Acts, twenty-second and twenty-third verses, precisely as they stand in our New Testament. He said that prophet was Christ, but the day had not yet come when they who would not hear his voice should be cut off from among the people, but soon would come.

He also quoted the second chapter of Joel, from the twenty-eighth to the last verse. He also said that this was not yet fulfilled, but was soon to be. And he further stated, the fullness of the Gentiles was soon to come in. He quoted many other passages of Scripture, and offered many explanations which cannot be mentioned here. Again, he told me that when I got those plates of which he had spoken (for the time that they should be obtained was not yet fulfilled) I should not show them to any person, neither the breastplate with the Urim and Thummim, only to those to whom I should be commanded to show them; if I did, I should be destroyed. While he was conversing with me about the plates, the vision was opened to my mind that I could see the place where the plates were deposited, and that so clearly and distinctly, that I knew the place again when I visited it.

After this communication, I saw the light in the room begin to gather immediately around the person of him who had been speaking to me, and it continued to do so, until the room was again left dark, except just around him, when instantly I saw, as it were, a conduit open right up into heaven, and he ascended up till he entirely disappeared, and the room was left as it had been before this heavenly light had made its appearance.

I lay musing on the singularity of the scene, and marveling greatly at what had been told me by this extraordinary messenger, when, in the midst of my meditation, I suddenly discovered that my room was again beginning to get lighted, and in an instant, as it were, the same heavenly messenger was again by my bedside. He commenced, and again related the very same things which he had done at his first visit, without the least variation, which having done, he informed me of great judgments which were coming upon the earth, with great desolations by famine, sword, and pestilence, and that these grievous judgments would come on the earth in this generation. Having related these things, he again ascended as he had done before.

By this time, so deep were the impressions made on my mind, that sleep had fled from my eyes, and I lay overwhelmed in astonishment at what I had both seen and heard; but what was my surprise when again I beheld the same messenger at my bedside, and heard him rehearse or repeat over again to me the same things as before, and added a caution to me, telling me that Satan would try to tempt me (in consequence of the indigent circumstances of my father's family) to get the plates for the purpose of getting rich. This he forbade me, saying that I must have no other object in view in getting the plates but to glorify God, and must not be influenced by any other motive but that of building his kingdom, otherwise I could not get them. After this third visit, he again ascended up into heaven as before, and I was again left to ponder on the strangeness of what I had just experienced, when almost immediately after the heavenly messenger had ascended from me the third time, the cock crew, and I found that day was approaching, so that our interviews must have occupied the whole of that night. I shortly after arose from my bed, and, as usual, went to the necessary labors of the day, but, in attempting to labor as at other times, I found my strength so exhausted as rendered me entirely unable. My father, who was laboring along with me, discovered something to be wrong with me, and told me to go home. I started with the intention of going to the house, but, in attempting to cross the fence out of the field where we were, my strength entirely failed me, and I fell helpless on the ground, and for a time was quite unconscious of anything. The first thing that I can recollect, was a voice speaking unto me, calling me by name; I looked up and beheld the same messenger standing over my head, surrounded by light, as before. He then again related unto me all that he had related to me the previous night, and commanded me to go to my father, and tell him of the vision and commandment which I had received.

I obeyed, I returned back to my father in the field and rehearsed the whole matter to him. He replied to me that it was of God, and to go and do as commanded by the messenger. I left the field and went to the place where the messenger had told me the plates were deposited, and owing to the distinctness of the vision which I had had concerning it, I knew the place the instant that I arrived there. Convenient to the village of Manchester, Ontario County, New York, stands a hill of considerable size, and the most elevated of any in the neighborhood. On the west side of this hill, not far from the top, under a stone of considerable size, lay the plates, deposited in a stone box; this stone was thick and rounding in the middle on the upper side, and thinner towards the edges, so that the middle part of it was visible above the ground, but the edge all round was covered with earth. Having removed the earth and obtained a lever, which I got fixed under the edge of the stone, and with a little exertion raised it up; I looked in, and there indeed did I behold the plates, the Urim and Thummim, and the breastplate as stated by the messenger. The box in which they lay was formed by laying stones together in some kind of cement. In the bottom of the box were laid two stones crossways of the box, and on these stones lay the plates and the other things with them. I made an attempt to take them out, but was forbidden by the messenger, and was again informed that the time for bringing them forth had not yet arrived, neither would arrive until four years from that time; but he told me that I should come to that place precisely in one year from that time, and that he would there meet with me, and that I should continue to do so, until the time should come for obtaining the plates.

Accordingly as I had been commanded, I went at the end of each year; and at each time I found the same messenger there, and received instruction and intelligence from him at each of our interviews, respecting what the Lord was going to do, and how and in what manner his kingdom was to be conducted in the last days.

As my father's worldly circumstances were very limited, we were under the necessity of laboring with our hands, hiring by day's work and otherwise as we could get opportunity; sometimes we were at home and sometimes abroad, and by continued labor were enabled to get a comfortable maintenance.

In the year 1824, my father's family met with a great affliction, by the death of my eldest brother, Alvin. In the month of October, 1825, I hired with an old gentleman, by the name of Josiah Stoal, who lived in Chenango County, state of New York. He had heard something of a silver mine having been opened by the Spaniards, in Harmony, Susquehanna County, state of Pennsylvania, and had, previous to my hiring with him, been digging, in order, if possible, to discover the mine. After I went to live with him he took me among the rest of his hands to dig for the silver mine, at which I continued to work for nearly a month without success in our undertaking, and finally I prevailed with the old gentleman to cease digging after it. Hence arose the very prevalent story of my having been a money digger.

During the time that I was thus employed, I was put to board with a Mr. Isaac Hale, of that place; it was there that I first saw my wife (his daughter) Emma Hale. On the 18th of January, 1827, we were married, while yet I was employed in the service of Mr. Stoal.

Owing to my still continuing to assert that I had seen a vision, persecution still followed me, and my wife's father's family were very much opposed to our being married. I was therefore under the necessity of taking her elsewhere, so we went and were married at the house of Squire Tarbill, in South Bainbridge, Chenango County, New York. Immediately after my marriage, I left Mr. Stoal's and went to my father's and farmed with him that season.

At length the time arrived for obtaining the plates, the Urim and Thummim, and the Breastplate. On the 22nd day of September,

1827, having gone, as usual, at the end of another year, to the place where they were deposited, the same heavenly messenger delivered them up to me with this charge, that I should be responsible for them; that if I should let them go carelessly or through any neglect of mine, I should be cut off; but that if I would use all my endeavors to preserve them, until he, the messenger, should call for them, they should be protected.

I soon found out the reason why I had received such strict charges to keep them safe, and why it was that the messenger had said, that when I had done what was required at my hand, he would call for them; for no sooner was it known that I had them, than the most strenuous exertions were used to get them from me; every stratagem that could be invented was resorted to for that purpose; the persecution became more bitter and severe than before, and multitudes were on the alert continually to get them from me if possible; but, by the wisdom of God, they remained safe in my hands, until I had accomplished by them what was required at my hand; when, according to arrangements, the messenger called for them, I delivered them up to him, and he has them in his charge until this day, being the 2d day of May, 1838.

The excitement, however, still continued, and rumor, with her thousand tongues, was all the time employed in circulating tales about my father's family, and about myself. If I were to relate a thousandth part of them, it would fill up volumes. The persecution, however, became so intolerable that I was under the necessity of leaving Manchester, and going with my wife to Susquehanna County, in the state of Pennsylvania; while preparing to start (being very poor, and the persecution so heavy upon us, that there was no probability that we would ever be otherwise), in the midst of our afflictions we found a friend in a gentleman, by the name of Martin Harris, who came to us and gave me fifty dollars to assist us in our afflictions. Mr. Harris was a resident of Palmyra Township, Wayne County, in the state of New York, and a farmer of respectability. By this timely aid was I enabled to reach the place of my destination in Pennsylvania, and immediately after my arrival there, I commenced copying the characters of the plates. I copied a considerable number of them, and by means of the Urim and Thummim I translated some of them, which I did between the time I arrived at the house of my wife's father in the month of December, and the February following.

Some time in this month of February, the aforementioned Mr.

Martin Harris came to our place, got the characters which I had drawn off the plates, and started with them to the city of New York. For what took place relative to him and the characters, I refer to his own account of the circumstances as he related them to me after his return, which was as follows—

I went to the city of New York, and presented the characters which had been translated, with the translation thereof, to Professor Anthon, a gentleman celebrated for his literary attainments. Professor Anthon stated that the translation was correct, more so than any he had before seen translated from the Egyptian. I then showed him those which were not yet translated, and he said that they were Egyptian, Chaldaic, Assyric, and Arabic, and he said that they were the true characters. He gave me a certificate, certifying to the people of Palmyra that they were true characters, and that the translation of such of them as had been translated was also correct. I took the certificate and put it into my pocket, and was just leaving the house, when Mr. Anthon called me back, and asked me how the young man found out that there were gold plates in the place where he found them. I answered that an angel of God had revealed it unto him.

He then said unto me, Let me see that certificate. I accordingly took it out of my pocket and gave it to him, when he took it and tore it to pieces, saying that there was no such thing now as ministering of angels, and that if I would bring the plates to him, he would translate them. I informed him that part of the plates were sealed, and that I was forbidden to bring them; he replied, "I cannot read a sealed book." I left him and went to Dr. Mitchell, who sanctioned what Professor Anthon had said respecting both the characters and the translation.

On the 15th day of April, 1829, Oliver Cowdery came to my house, until when I had never seen him. He stated to me that having been teaching school in the neighborhood where my father resided, and my father being one of those who sent to the school, he went to board for a season at his house, and while there, the family related to him the circumstances of my having the plates, and accordingly he had come to make inquiries of me.

Two days after the arrival of Mr. Cowdery (being the 17th of April), I commenced to translate the Book of Mormon, and he commenced to write for me.

We still continued the work of translation, when, in the ensuing month (May 1829), we on a certain day went into the woods to pray and inquire of the Lord respecting baptism for the remission of sins, as we found mentioned in the translation of the plates. While we were thus employed, praying and calling upon the Lord, a messenger from heaven descended in a cloud of light, and having laid his hands upon us, he ordained us, saying unto us, "*Upon you, my fellow-servants, in the name of Messiah, I confer the Priesthood of Aaron, which holds the keys of the ministering of angels, and of the Gospel of repentance, and of baptism by immersion for the remission of sins; and this shall never be taken again from the earth, until the sons of Levi do offer again an offering unto the Lord in righteousness.*" He said this Aaronic Priesthood had not the power of laying on of hands for the gift of the Holy Ghost, but that this should be conferred on us hereafter; and he commanded us to go and be baptized, and gave us directions that I should baptize Oliver Cowdery, and afterwards that he should baptize me.

Accordingly we went and were baptized—I baptized him first, and afterwards he baptized me—after which I laid my hands upon his head and ordained him to the Aaronic Priesthood, and afterwards he laid his hands on me and ordained me to the same Priesthood—for so we were commanded.

The messenger who visited us on this occasion, and conferred this Priesthood upon us, said his name was John, the same that is called John the Baptist in the New Testament, and that he acted under the direction of Peter, James, and John, who held the keys of the Priesthood of Melchisedeck, which Priesthood, he said, should in due time be conferred on us, and that I should be called the first elder and he the second. It was on the 15th day of May, 1829, that we were baptized; and ordained under the hand of the messenger.

Immediately upon our coming up out of the water, after we had been baptized, we experienced great and glorious blessings from our heavenly Father. No sooner had I baptized Oliver Cowdery than the Holy Ghost fell upon him, and he stood up and prophesied many things which would shortly come to pass. And again, so soon as I had been baptized by him, I also had the spirit of prophecy, when, standing up, I prophesied concerning the rise of the church, and many other things connected with the church and this generation of the children of men. We were filled with the Holy Ghost, and rejoiced in the God of our salvation.

Our minds being now enlightened, we began to have the Scriptures laid open to our understandings, and the true meaning of their more mysterious passages revealed unto us in a manner which we never could attain to previously, nor ever before had thought of. In the meantime we were forced to keep secret the circumstances of our having been baptized and having received the Priesthood, owing to a spirit of persecution which had already manifested itself in the neighborhood. We had been threatened with being mobbed, from time to time, and this too by professors of religion. And their intentions of mobbing us were only counteracted by the influence of my wife's father's family (under divine providence), who had become very friendly to me, and who were opposed to mobs, and were willing that I should be allowed to continue the work of translation without interruption; and therefore offered and promised us protection from all unlawful proceedings as far as in them lay.

21. Alexander Campbell
and the Disciples of Christ

ONE OF the earliest critics of Joseph Smith was Alexander Campbell (1788–1866), who published in 1832 Delusions: An Analysis of the Book of Mormon. But Campbell, too, was seeking the true Christian church amid the competing claims of the sects. He had arrived in the United States from Scotland in 1809, and enthusiastically joined with his father, who had broken from the conservative Seceder Presbyterian Church, to form a free Christian association. This soon grew into an independent church. Recognizing an affinity with the Baptists, the growing numbers of Campbellites associated with them for more than a decade, but then broke the connection to merge with the bulk of the "Christian" movement under Barton W. Stone in a new denomination, the Disciples of Christ, in 1832. The new brotherhood had about 25,000 members, but by the opening of the twentieth century it had grown to more than a million. Close kin of the mainline evangelical denominations, the Disciples, seeking to provide a church structured after the primitive New Testament pattern in which all true Christians could unite, gained strength especially in the South and Southwest.

In 1835, when his new movement was young, Campbell wrote a precise description of it for an encyclopedia. The article was reprinted with an introduction by Roscoe M. Pierson in 1951 by the College of the Bible, Lexington, Kentucky.

SOURCE: John Newton Brown (ed.), Fessenden and Co.'s Encyclopedia of Religious Knowledge (Boston, 1835), pp. 462–464.

DISCIPLES OF CHRIST (sometimes called CAMPBELLITES, or REFORMERS). As is usual in similar cases, the brethren who unite under the name of Disciples of Christ, or Christians, are nicknamed after those who have been prominent in gathering them together: they choose, however, to be recognised by the above simple and unassuming name.

The rise of this society, if we only look back to the drawing of the lines of demarcation between it and other professors, is of recent origin. About the commencement of the present century, the Bible alone, without any human addition in the form of creeds or confessions of faith, began to be pled and preached by many distinguished ministers of different denominations, both in Europe and America.

With various success, and with many of the opinions of the various sects imperceptibly carried with them from the denominations to which they once belonged, did the advocates of the Bible cause plead for the union of Christians of every name on the broad basis of the apostles' teaching. But it was not until the year 1823, that a restoration of the original gospel and order of things began to be pled in a periodical, edited by Alexander Campbell, of Bethany, Virginia, entitled, "the Christian Baptist."

He and his father, Thomas Campbell, renounced the Presbyterian system, and were immersed in the year 1812. They, and the congregation which they had formed, united with the Redstone Baptist association; protesting against all human creeds as bonds of union, and professing subjection to the Bible alone. This union took place in the year 1813. But in pressing upon the attention of that society and the public the all-sufficiency of the sacred Scriptures for every thing necessary to the perfection of Christian character, whether in the private or social relations of life, in the church or in the world, they began to be opposed by a strong creed-party in that association. After some ten years' debating and contending for the Bible alone and the apostles' doctrine, Alexander Campbell and the church to which he belonged, united with the Mahoning association, in the Western Reserve of Ohio, that association being more favorable to his views of reform.

In his debates on the subject and action of baptism with Mr. Walker, a seceding minister, in the year 1820, and with Mr. M'Calla, a Presbyterian minister, of Kentucky, in the year 1823, his views of reformation began to be developed, and were very generally received by the Baptist society, as far as these works were read.

But in his "Christian Baptist," which began July 4, 1823, his views of the need of reformation were more fully exposed; and as these gained ground by the pleading of various ministers of the Baptist denomination, a party in opposition began to exert itself, and to oppose the spread of what they were pleased to call heterodoxy. But not till after great numbers began to act upon these principles, was there any attempt towards separation. After the Mahoning association appointed Mr. Walter Scott as evangelist, in the year 1827, and when great numbers began to be immersed into Christ under his labors, and new churches began to be erected by him and other laborers in the field, did the Baptist associations begin to declare nonfellowship with the brethren of the reformation. Thus by constraint, not of choice, they were obliged to form societies out of those communities that split upon the ground of adherence to the apostles' doctrine. Within the last seven years, they have increased with the most unprecedented rapidity; and during the present year (1833), not much less than ten thousand have joined the standard of reformation. They probably at this time, in the United States alone, amount to at least one hundred thousand. The distinguishing characteristics of their views and practices are the following:

They regard all the sects and parties of the Christian world as having, in greater or less degrees, departed from the simplicity of faith and manners of the first Christians, and as forming what the apostle Paul calls "the apostasy." This defection they attribute to the great varieties of speculation and metaphysical dogmatism of the countless creeds, formularies, liturgies, and books of discipline adopted and inculcated as bonds of union and platforms of communion in all the parties which have sprung from the Lutheran reformation. The effects of these synodical covenants, conventional articles of belief, and rules of ecclesiastical polity, has been the introduction of a new nomenclature, a human vocabulary of religious words, phrases and technicalities, which has displaced the style of the living oracles, and affixed to the sacred diction ideas wholly unknown to the apostles of Christ.

To remedy and obviate these aberrations, they propose to ascertain from the holy Scriptures, according to the commonly received and well-established rules of interpretation, the ideas attached to the leading terms and sentences found in the holy Scriptures, and then to use the words of the Holy Spirit in the apostolic acceptation of them.

By thus expressing the ideas communicated by the Holy Spirit in the terms and phrases learned from the apostles, and by avoiding the artificial and technical language of scholastic theory, they propose to restore a pure speech to the household of faith; and by accustoming the family of God to use the language and dialect of the heavenly Father, they expect to promote the santification of one another through the truth, and to terminate those discords and debates which have always originated from the words which man's wisdom teaches, and from a reverential regard and esteem for the style of the great masters of polemic divinity; believing that speaking the same things in the same style, is the only certain way to thinking the same things.

They make a very marked difference between faith and opinion; between the testimony of God and the reasonings of men; the words of the Spirit and human inferences. Faith in the testimony of God and obedience to the commandments of Jesus are their bond of union; and not an agreement in any abstract views or opinions upon what is written or spoken by divine authority. Hence all the speculations, questions, debates of words, and abstract reasonings found in human creeds, have no place in their religious fellowship. Regarding Calvinism and Arminianism, Trinitarianism and Unitarianism, and all the opposing theories of religious sectaries, as *extremes* begotten by each other, they cautiously avoid them, as equidistant from the simplicity and practical tendency of the promises and precepts, of the doctrine and facts, of the exhortations and precedents of the Christian institution.

They look for unity of spirit and the bonds of peace in the practical acknowledgment of one faith, one Lord, one immersion, one hope, one body, one Spirit, one God and Father of all; not in unity of opinions, nor in unity of forms, ceremonies, or modes of worship.

The holy Scriptures of both Testaments they regard as containing revelations from God, and as all necessary to make the man of God perfect, and accomplished for every good word and work; the New Testament, or the living oracles of Jesus Christ, they understand as containing the Christian religion; the testimonies of Matthew, Mark, Luke, and John, they view as illustrating and proving the great proposition on which our religion rests, viz. *that Jesus of Nazareth is the Messiah, the only-begotten and well-beloved Son of God, and the only Savior of the world;* the Acts of the Apostles as a divinely authorized narrative of the beginning and progress of the reign or kingdom of Jesus Christ, recording the full development of *the gospel* by the Holy Spirit sent down from heaven, and the procedure of the apostles in setting up the church of Christ on earth; the Epistles as carrying out and applying the doctrine of the apostles to the practice of individuals and congregations, and as developing the tendencies of the gospel in the behavior of its professors; and all as forming a complete standard of Christian faith and morals, adapted to the interval between the ascension of Christ and his return with the kingdom which he has received from God; the Apocalypse, or Revelation of Jesus Christ to John in Patmos, as a figurative and prospective view of all the fortunes of Christianity, from its date to the return of the Savior.

Every one who sincerely believes the testimony which God gave of Jesus of Nazareth, saying, *"This is my Son, the beloved, in whom I delight,"* or, in other words, believes what the evangelists and apostles have testified concerning him, from his conception to his coronation in heaven as Lord of all, and who is willing to obey him in every thing, they regard as a proper subject of immersion, and no one else. They consider immersion into the name of the Father, Son and Holy Spirit, after a public, sincere, and intelligent confession of the faith in Jesus, as necessary to admission to the privileges of the kingdom of the Messiah, and as a solemn pledge on the part of heaven, of the actual remission of all past sins and of adoptions into the family of God.

The Holy Spirit is promised only to those who believe and obey the Savior. No one is taught to expect the reception of that heavenly Monitor and Comforter as a resident in his heart till he obeys the gospel.

Thus while they proclaim faith and repentance, or faith and a change of heart, as preparatory to immersion, remission, and the Holy Spirit, they say to all penitents, or all those who believe and repent of their sins, as Peter said to the first audience addressed after the Holy Spirit was bestowed after the glorification of Jesus, "Be immersed, every one of you, in the name of the Lord Jesus, for the remission of sins, and you shall receive the gift of the Holy Spirit." They teach sinners that God commands all men everywhere to reform or to turn to God, that the Holy Spirit strives with them so to do by the apostles and prophets, that God beseeches them to be reconciled through Jesus Christ, and that is the duty of all men to believe the gospel and to turn to God.

The immersed believers are congregated into societies according to their propinquity to each other, and taught to meet every first day of the week in honor and commemoration of the resurrection of Jesus, and to break the loaf which commemorates the death of the Son of God, to read and hear the living oracles, to teach and admonish one another, to unite in all prayer and praise, to contribute to the necessities of saints, and to perfect holiness in the fear of the Lord.

Every congregation chooses its own overseers and deacons, who

preside over and administer the affairs of the congregations; and
every church, either from itself or in cooperation with others, sends
out, as opportunity offers, one or more evangelists, or proclaimers
of the word, to preach the word and to immerse those who believe,
to gather congregations, and to extend the knowledge of salvation
where it is necessary, as far as their means extend. But every church
regards these evangelists as its servants, and therefore they have no
control over any congregation, each congregation being subject to
its own choice of presidents or elders whom they have appointed.
Perseverance in all the work of faith, labor of love, and patience of
hope is inculcated by all the disciples as essential to admission into
the heavenly kingdom.

Such are the prominent outlines of the faith and practices of
those who wish to be known as the Disciples of Christ: but no
society among them would agree to make the preceding items
either a confession of faith or a standard of practice; but, for the
information of those who wish an acquaintance with them, are
willing to give at any time a reason for their faith, hope and
practice.

The views of reformation in faith and practice of "the Disciples
of Christ" may be seen at great length, by those desiring a more
particular acquaintance, in the *Christian Baptist and Millennial
Harbinger*, edited by Alexander Campbell, of Bethany, Brooke
county, Virginia; also in the *Evangelist*, published by Walter Scott,
Carthage, Ohio; and the *Christian Messenger*, published by Barton
W. Stone and J. T. Johnson, Georgetown, Kentucky. The *Christian Baptist and Millennial Harbinger*, being the first publication
of these sentiments, contains a history of this reformation, as well
as a full development of all things from the beginning.

22. William Miller and the Adventists

WILLIAM MILLER (1782-1849) was a Deist in his youth, but encounters with death by disease and battle during the War of 1812 turned his thoughts toward religion. He joined the Low Hampton Baptist church in New York. Seeking to meet the criticism of the skeptics that the Bible was inconsistent, he found the solution in the millenarian prophecies of the Books of Daniel and Revelation. When the whole Bible was viewed as pointing to the return of Christ, he found that the problems were resolved and harmony found. Miller attracted great attention when he prophesied that the second coming of Christ would occur in 1843 (later revised to 1844). As the 1840's dawned, he was constantly in demand as a revivalist. When the final day passed, some of the Adventists returned to their previous church homes, some lapsed, but others regrouped and in time formed a number of Adventist churches, such as the Advent Christian Church and the Seventh-Day Adventist Church. At the height of his popularity, Miller penned this synopsis of his views.

SOURCE: Joshua V. Himes, Views of the Prophecies and Prophetic Chronology, Selected from the Manuscripts of William Miller; with a Memoir of His Life (Boston, 1841), pp. 32-35.

MY DEAR BROTHER,—You have requested a synopsis of my views of the Christian faith. The following sketch will give you some idea of the religious opinions I have formed by a careful study of the Word of God.

I believe all men, coming to years of discretion, do and will disobey God, and this is, in some measure, owing to corrupted nature by the sin of our parent. I believe God will not condemn us for any pollution in our father, but the soul that sinneth shall die. All pollution of which we may be partakers from the sins of our ancestors, in which we would have no agency, can and will be washed away in the blood and sacrifice of Jesus Christ, without our agency. But all sins committed by us as rational, intelligent agents can only be cleansed by the blood of Jesus Christ, through our repentance and faith. I believe in the salvation of all men who receive the grace of God by repentance and faith in the mediation of Jesus Christ. I believe in the condemnation of all men who reject the gospel and mediation of Christ, and thereby lose the efficacy of the blood and righteousness of our Redeemer, as proffered to us in the gospel. I believe in practical godliness as commanded us in the Scriptures (which are our only rule of faith and practice), and that they only will be entitled to heaven and future blessedness, who obey and keep the commandments of God as given us in the Bible, which is the Word of God. I believe in God, the Father of our Lord Jesus Christ, who is a Spirit, omnipresent, omniscient, having all power, creator, preserver, and self-existent. As being holy, just and beneficent, I believe in Jesus Christ, the Son of God, having a body in fashion and form like man, divine in his nature, human in his person, godlike in his character and power. He is a Savior for sinners, a priest to God, a mediator between God and man, and King in Zion. He will be all to his people, God with us forever. The spirit of the Most High is in him, the power of the Most High is given him, the people of the Most High are purchased by him, the glory of the Most High shall be with him, and the kingdom of the Most High is his on earth.

I believe the Bible is the revealed will of God to man, and all therein is necessary to be understood by Christians in the several ages and circumstances to which they may refer—for instance, what may be understood today might not have been necessary to have been understood 1,000 years ago. For its object is to reveal things new and old, that the man of God may be thoroughly furnished for, and perfected in, every good word and work, for the age in which he lives. I believe it is revealed in the best possible manner for all people in every age and under every circumstance to understand, and that it is to be understood as literal as it can be and make good sense—and that in every case where the language is figurative, we must let the Bible explain its own figures. We are in no case allowed to speculate on the Scriptures, and suppose things which are not clearly expressed, nor reject things which are plainly taught. I believe all of the prophecies are revealed to try our faith, and to give us hope, without which we could have no reasonable hope. I believe that the Scriptures do reveal unto us, in plain language, that Jesus Christ will appear again on this earth, that he will come in the glory of God, in the clouds of heaven, with all his saints and angels; that he will raise the dead bodies of all his saints who have slept, change the bodies of all that are alive on earth that are his, and both these living and raised saints will be caught up to meet the Lord in the air. There the saints will be judged and presented to the Father, without spot or wrinkle. Then the gospel kingdom will be given up to God the Father. Then will the Father give the bride to the Son Jesus Christ; and when the marriage takes place, the church will become the "New Jerusalem," the "beloved city." And while this is being done in the air, the earth will be cleansed by fire, the elements will melt with fervent heat, the works of men will be destroyed, the bodies of the wicked will be burned to ashes, the devil and all evil spirits, with the souls and spirits of those who have rejected the gospel, will be banished from the earth, shut up in the pit or place prepared for the devil and his angels, and will not be permitted to visit the earth again until 1,000 years. This is the first resurrection, and first judgment. Then Christ and his people will come down from the heavens, or middle air, and live with his saints on the new earth in a new heaven, or dispensation, forever, even forever and ever. This will be the restitution of the right owners to the earth.

Then will the promise of God, to his Son, be accomplished: "I will give him the heathen for his inheritance, and the utmost parts of the earth for his possession." Then "the whole earth shall be full of his glory." And then, will the holy people take possession of their joint heirship with Christ, and his promise be verified, "the meek shall inherit the earth," and the kingdom of God will have come, and "his will done in earth as in heaven." After 1,000 years shall have passed away, the saints will all be gathered and encamped in the beloved city. The sea, death and hell will give up their dead, which will rise up on the breadths of the earth, out of the city, a great company like the sand of the seashore. The devil will be let loose, to go out and deceive this wicked host. He will tell them of a battle against the saints, the beloved city; he will gather them in the battle around the camp of the saints. But there is no battle; the devil has deceived them. The saints will judge them, the justice of God will drive them from the earth into the lake of fire and brimstone, where they will be tormented day and night, forever and ever. "This is the second death." After the second resurrection, second judgment, the righteous will then possess the earth forever.

I understand that the judgment day will be a thousand years long. The righteous are raised and judged in the commencement of that day, the wicked in the end of that day. I believe that the saints will be raised and judged about the year 1843; according to Moses' prophecy, Lev. xxvi., Exek. xxxix., Daniel ii., vii., viii–xii. Hos. v.

1–3., Rev. the whole book; and many other prophets have spoken of these things. Time will soon tell if I am right, and soon he that is righteous will be righteous still, and he that is filthy will be filthy still. I do most solemnly entreat mankind to make their peace with God, be ready for these things. "The end of all things is at hand." I do ask my brethren in the gospel ministry to consider well what they say before they oppose these things. Say not in your hearts, "my Lord delayeth his coming." Let all do as they would wish they had if it does come, and none will say they have not done right if it does not come. I believe it will come; but if it should not come, then I will wait and look until it does come. Yet I must pray, "Come, Lord Jesus, come quickly."

This is a synopsis of my views. I give it as a matter of faith. I know of no scripture to contradict any view given in the above sketch. Men's theories may oppose. The ancients believed in a temporal and personal reign of Christ on earth. The moderns believe in a temporal, spiritual reign as a millennium. Both views are wrong—both are too gross and carnal. I believe in a glorious, immortal and personal reign of Jesus Christ with all his people on the purified earth forever. I believe the millennium is between the two resurrections and two judgments: the righteous and the wicked, the just and the unjust. I hope the dear friends of Christ will lay by all prejudice, and look at and examine these three views by the only rule and standard, the BIBLE.

23. Mary Baker Eddy and Christian Science

In 1866, Mary Baker Eddy (1821–1910), after a fall on the ice, claimed to be remarkably healed, and to have found the way to cure others. She believed that she had been led through her experience to a discovery of the deeper meaning of the Bible. Others have pointed out that many of her ideas were quite similar to those of Phineas P. Quimby, a mental healer by whom she had been helped. She also drew much in a general way from the thought of New England transcendentalism. But whatever the source of her ideas, she cast them in her own distinctive form. In 1875 Mrs. Eddy organized a society which soon became the Church of Christ (Scientist) with headquarters in Boston; in half a century the new church reportedly had about 200,000 members. That same year she published the first edition of Science and Health with Key to the Scriptures, the basic book of the new church. In addition, Mrs. Eddy wrote a number of small books, including a little one in 1891 which endeavored to state the central teachings of Christian Science succinctly. The early portions of a 1908 reprint of this book follow.

SOURCE: Mary Baker G. Eddy, *Rudimental Divine Science* (Boston, 1908), pp. 7–17.

How Would You Define Christian Science?

As the law of God, the law of Good, interpreting and demonstrating the Principle and rule of universal harmony.

What Is the Principle of Christian Science?

It is God, the Supreme Being, Infinite and Immortal Mind, the Soul of man and the universe. It is our Father which is in heaven. It is Substance, Spirit, Life, Truth, and Love—these are the Deific Principle.

Do You Mean by This That God Is a Person?

The word *person* affords a large margin for misapprehension, as well as definition. In French the equivalent word is *personne*. In Spanish, Italian, and Latin, it is *persona*. The Latin verb *personare* is compounded of the prefix *per* (through) and *sonare* (to sound).

In law, Blackstone applies the word *personal* to *bodily presence*, in distinction from one's appearance (in court, for example) by deputy or proxy.

Other definitions of *person*, as given by Webster, are "a living soul; a self-conscious being; a moral agent; especially, a living human being, a corporeal man, woman, or child; an individual of the human race."

He adds, that among Trinitarian Christians the word stands for one of the three subjects, or agents, constituting the Godhead.

In Christian Science we learn that God is definitely individual, and not a *person*, as that word is used by the best authorities, if our lexicographers are right in defining *person* as especially a finite *human being*; but God is personal, if by *person* is meant Infinite Soul.

We do not conceive rightly of God, if we think of Him as less than infinite. The human person is finite; and therefore I prefer to retain the proper sense of Deity, by using the phrase *an individual* God, rather than a *personal* God; for there is and can be but one Infinite Individual Spirit, whom mortals have named God.

Science defines the individuality of God, as supreme Good. This term enlarged our sense of Deity, takes away the trammels assigned to God by finite thought, and introduces us to higher definitions.

Is Healing the Sick the Whole of Science?

Healing physical sickness is the smallest part of Christian Science. It is only the bugle-call to thought and action, in the higher range of infinite goodness. The emphatic purpose of Christian Science is the healing of sin; and this task, sometimes, may be harder than the cure of disease; because, while mortals love to sin, they do not love to be sick. Hence their comparative acquiescence in your endeavors to heal them of bodily ills, and their obstinate resistance to all efforts to save them from sin through Christ, spiritual Truth and Love, which redeem them, and become their Savior through the flesh, from the flesh, the material world and evil.

This Life, Truth, and Love—this Trinity of Good—was individualized, to the perception of mortal sense, in the man Jesus. His history is emphatic in our hearts, and it lives more because of his spiritual than his physical healing. His example is, to Christian Scientists, what the models of the masters in music and painting are to artists.

Genuine Christian Scientists will no more deviate morally from that divine digest of Science called the Sermon on the Mount, than they will manipulate invalids, prescribe drugs, or deny God. Jesus' healing was spiritual in its nature, method, and design. He wrought the cure of disease through the Divine Mind, which gives all true volition, impulse, and action; and destroys the mental error made manifest physically, and establishes the opposite manifestation of Truth upon the body in harmony and health.

By the Individuality of God, Do You Mean That God Has a Finite Form?

No. I mean the Infinite and Divine Principle of all Being, the ever-present I Am, filling all space, including in Itself all Mind, the One Father and Mother God. Life, Truth, and Love are this Trinity in Unity, and their universe is spiritual, peopled with perfect beings, harmonious and eternal, of which our material universe and men are the counterfeits.

Is God the Principle of All Science, or Only of Divine or Christian Science?

Science is Mind manifested. It is not material; neither is it of human origin.

All true Science represents a moral and spiritual force, which holds the earth in its orbit. This force is Spirit, that "can bind the sweet influences of the Pleiades, and loose the bands of Orion."

There is no Material Science, if by that term you mean material intelligence. God is Mind, and there is no other Mind. Good is Mind, but evil is not Mind. God is not in evil, but in God only. Spirit is not in matter, but in Spirit only. Law is not in matter, but in Mind only.

Is There No Matter?

All is Mind. According to the Scriptures and Christian Science, all is God, and there is naught beside Him. "God is Spirit"; and we can only learn and love Him through his Spirit, which brings out the fruits of Spirit, and extinguishes forever the works of darkness, by His marvelous Light.

The five material senses testify to the existence of matter. The spiritual senses afford no such evidence, but deny the testimony of the material senses. Which testimony is correct? The Bible says: "Let God be true, and every man a liar." If, as the Scriptures declare, God is All-in-all, then all must be Mind, since God is Mind. Therefore in divine Science there is no material mortal man, for man is spiritual and eternal, he being made in the image of Spirit, or God.

There is no material sense. Matter is inert, inanimate, and sensationless—considered apart from Mind. Lives there a man who has ever found Soul in the body or in matter, who has ever seen spiritual substance with the eye, who has found sight in matter, hearing in the material ear, or intelligence in nonintelligence? If there is any such thing as matter, it must be either Mind which is called matter, or matter without Mind.

Matter without Mind is a moral impossibility. Mind in matter is pantheism. Soul is the only real consciousness which cognizes Being. The body does not see, hear, smell, or taste. Human belief says that it does; but destroy this belief of seeing with the eye, and we could not see materially; and so it is with each of the physical senses.

Accepting the verdict of these material senses we should believe man and the universe to be the football of chance, and sinking into oblivion. Destroy the five senses as organized matter, and you must either become non-existent, or exist in Mind only; and this latter conclusion is the simple solution of the Problem of Being, and leads to the equal inference that there is no matter.

The Sweet Sounds and Glories of Earth and Sky,
Assuming Manifold Forms and Colors—
Are They Not Tangible and Material?

As Mind they are real, but not as matter. All beauty and goodness are in and of Mind, emanating from God; but when we change the nature of beauty and goodness from Mind to matter, the beauty is marred, through a false conception, and, to the material sense, evil takes the place of good.

Has not the Truth in Christian Science met a response from Prof. S. P. Langley, the young American astronomer? He says that "color is in us," not "in the rose"; and he adds that this is not "any metaphysical subtlety," but a fact "almost universally accepted, within the last few years, by physicists."

Is Not the Basis of Mind-Healing a Destruction of the Evidence of the Material Senses, and Restoration of the True Evidence of Spiritual Sense?

It is, so far as you perceive and understand this predicate and postulate of Mind-healing; but the Science of Mind-healing is best understood in practical demonstration. The proof of what you apprehend, in the simplest definite and absolute form of healing, can alone answer this question of how much you understand of Christian Science Mind-healing. Not that all healing is Science, by any means; but that the simplest case, healed in Science, is as demonstrably Scientific, in a small degree, as the most difficult case so treated.

The infinite and subtler conceptions and consistencies of Christian Science are set forth in my work, "Science and Health."

Is Man Material or Spiritual?

In Science, man is the manifest reflection of God, perfect and immortal Mind. He is the likeness of God; and His likeness would be lost if inverted or perverted.

According to the evidence of the so-called physical senses, man is material, fallen, sick, depraved, mortal. Science and spiritual sense contradict this, and they afford the only true evidence of the Being of God and man, the material evidence being wholly false.

Jesus said of personal evil, that "the Truth abode not in him," because there is no material sense. Matter, as matter, has neither sensation nor personal intelligence. As a pretension to be Mind, matter is a lie, and "the father of lies"; Mind is not in matter and Spirit cannot originate its opposite, named matter.

According to Divine Science, Spirit no more changes its species, by evolving matter from Spirit, than natural science, so-called, or material laws, bring about alteration of species, by transforming minerals into vegetables, or plants into animals—thus confusing and confounding the three great kingdoms. No rock brings forth an apple; no pine tree produces a mammal, or provides breast milk for babes.

To sense, the lion of today is the lion of six thousand years ago; but in Science, Spirit sends forth its own harmless likeness.

24. New Thought for a New Age

CHRISTIAN SCIENCE was but one manifestation of a broad stream of religious thinking rooted in idealistic metaphysics and popular scientism which gained considerable following by the opening of the twentieth century. The "New Thought" movement stressed self-improvement, health, serenity, and prosperity. It exerted a liberalizing influence on the older denominations and contributed to the rise of a number of new religious bodies, such as the Unity School of Christianity, founded by Charles and Myrtle Fillmore in 1889. One of the most prolific popularizers of New Thought was Ralph Waldo Trine (1866–1958), author of "The Life Books." His In Tune with the Infinite (1897) sold well for more than fifty years. On the title page appear words that summarize the content: "Within yourself lies the cause of whatever enters into your life. To come into the full realization of your own awakened interior powers, is to be able to condition your life in exact accord with what you would have it."

SOURCE: Ralph Waldo Trine, In Tune with the Infinite, or Fullness of Peace, Power, and Plenty (New York, 1897), pp. 11–15.

The great central fact of the universe is that Spirit of Infinite Life and Power that is back of all, that animates all, that manifests itself in and through all; that self-existent principle of life from which all has come, and not only from which all has come, but from which all is continually coming. If there is an individual life, there must of necessity be an infinite source of life from which it comes. If there is a quality or a force of love, there must of necessity be an infinite source of love whence it comes. If there is wisdom, there must be the all-wise source back of it from which it springs. The same is true in regard to peace, the same in regard to power, the same in regard to what we call material things.

There is, then, this Spirit of Infinite Life and Power back of all which is the source of all. This Infinite Power is creating, working, ruling through the agency of great immutable laws and forces that run through all the universe, that surround us on every side. Every act of our everyday lives is governed by these same great laws and forces. Every flower that blooms by the wayside, springs up, grows, blooms, fades, according to certain great immutable laws. Every snowflake that plays between earth and heaven, forms, falls, melts, according to certain great unchangeable laws.

In a sense there is nothing in all the great universe but law. If this is true there must of necessity be a force behind it all that is the maker of these laws and a force greater than the laws that are made. This Spirit of Infinite Life and Power that is back of all is what I call God. I care not what term you may use, be it Kindly Light, Providence, the Over Soul, Omnipotence, or whatever term may be most convenient. I care not what the term may be as long as we are agreed in regard to the great central fact itself.

God, then, is this Infinite Spirit which fills all the universe with Himself alone, so that all is from Him and in Him, and there is nothing that is outside. Indeed and in truth, then, in Him we live and move and have our being. He is the life of our life, our very life itself. We have received, we are continually receiving our life from Him. We are partakers of the life of God; and though we differ from Him in that we are individualized spirits, while He is the Infinite Spirit including us as well as all else besides, yet *in essence the life of God and the life of man are identically the same, and so are one.* They differ not in essence, in quality; they differ in degree.

There have been and are highly illumined souls who believe that we receive our life from God after the manner of a divine inflow. And again, there have been and are those who believe that our life is one with the life of God, and so that God and man are one. Which is right? Both are right; both right when rightly understood.

In regard to the first: if God is the Infinite Spirit of Life back of all, whence all comes, then clearly our life as individualized spirits is continually coming from this Infinite Source by means of this divine inflow. In the second place, if our lives as individualized spirits are directly from, are parts of this Infinite Spirit of life, then the degree of the Infinite Spirit that is manifested in the life of each must be identical in quality with that Source, the same as a drop of water taken from the ocean is, in nature, in characteristics, identical with that ocean, its source. And how could it be otherwise? The liability to misunderstanding in this latter case, however, is this: in that although the life of God and the life of man in essence are identically the same, the life of God so far transcends the life of individual man that it includes all else beside. In other words, so far as the quality of life is concerned, in essence they are the same; so far as the degree of life is concerned, they are vastly different.

In this light is it not then evident that both conceptions are true? and more, that they are one and the same? Both conceptions may be typified by one and the same illustration.

There is a reservoir in a valley which receives its supply from an inexhaustible reservoir on the mountain side. It is then true that the reservoir in the valley receives its supply by virtue of the inflow of the water from the larger reservoir on the mountain side. It is also true that the water in this smaller reservoir is in nature, in quality, in characteristics identically the same as that in the larger reservoir which is its source. The difference, however, is this: the reservoir on the mountain side, in the *amount* of its water, so far transcends the reservoir in the valley that it can supply an innumerable number of like reservoirs and still be unexhausted.

And so in the life of man. If, as I think we have already agreed, however we may differ in regard to anything else, there is this Infinite Spirit of Life back of all, the life of all, and so, from which all comes, then the life of individual man, your life and mine, must come by a divine inflow from this Infinite Source. And if this is true, then the life that comes by this inflow to man is necessarily the same in essence as is this Infinite Spirit of Life. There is a difference. It is not a difference in essence. It is a difference in degree.

If this is true, does it not then follow that in the degree that man opens himself to this divine inflow does he approach to God? If so, it then necessarily follows that in the degree that he makes this approach does he take on the God-powers. And if the God-powers are without limit, does it not then follow that the only limitations man has are the limitations he sets to himself, by virtue of not knowing himself?

25. Black Protestantism
as Indigenous Religious Expression

BECAUSE THE majority of American Negro Christians were to be found
in their own Baptist and Methodist bodies by the dawn of the twentieth
century, they have often been considered as offshoots of mainline Christianity. Clearly, the Negro churches did have many of the features of
the conservative, revivalistic evangelicalism that characterized the popular Protestant denominations. Yet the black denominations probably
were not wholly untouched by African religious consciousness, and
they were certainly marked by the distinct hungers and needs of the
Negroes both before and after emancipation. E. Franklin Frazier has
written of the distinctive characteristics of the "invisible institution" of
the Negro church among the enslaved blacks in The Negro Church in
America (New York, 1964). As the black churches burgeoned in the
Reconstruction period as the main form of public life wholly under
black control, the religious style that emerged had some distinctive indigenous qualities of its own. This is perceptively described in the following essay from the pen of one of the great early scholars of black
history, life, and religion in America—W. E. Burghardt Du Bois (1868–
1963), who was educated at Fisk, Berlin, and Harvard (Ph.D., 1895).
Du Bois wrote this piece while he was engaged in teaching sociology at
Atlanta University and working on what proved to be his most successful volume, The Souls of Black Folk (1903).

SOURCE: W. E. Burghardt Du Bois, "The Religion of the American
    Negro," *The New World: A Quarterly Review of Religion,
    Ethics, and Theology*, IX (1900), 614–625.

It was out in the country, far from home, far from my foster
home, on a dark Sunday night. The road wandered from our ram-
bling log house up the stony bed of a creek, past wheat and corn,
until we could hear dimly across the fields a rhythmic cadence of
song—soft, thrilling, powerful, that swelled and died sorrowfully in
our ears. I was a country school teacher then, fresh from the East,
and had never seen a southern Negro revival. To be sure, we in
Berkshire were not perhaps as stiff and formal as they in Suffolk of
olden time; yet we were very quiet and subdued, and I know not
what would have happened those clear Sabbath mornings had
some one punctuated the sermon with a wild scream, or interrupted the long prayer with a loud Amen! And so most striking to

me, as I approached the village and the little plain church perched aloft, was the air of intense excitement that possessed that mass of black folk. A sort of suppressed terror hung in the air and seemed to seize us—a pythian madness, a demoniac possession, that lent terrible reality to song and word. The black and massive form of the preacher swayed and quivered as the words crowded to his lips and flew at us in singular eloquence. The people moaned and fluttered, and then the gaunt-cheeked brown woman beside me suddenly leaped straight into the air and shrieked like a lost soul, while round about came wail and groan and outcry, and a scene of human passion such as I had never conceived before.

Those who have not thus witnessed the frenzy of a Negro revival in the untouched backwoods of the South can but dimly realize the religious feeling of the slave; as described, such scenes appear grotesque and funny, but as seen they are awful. Three things characterized this religion of the slave—the preacher, the music and the frenzy. The Preacher is the most unique personality developed by the Negro on American soil. A leader, a politician, an orator, a "boss," an intriguer, an idealist—all these he is, and ever, too, the center of a group of men, now twenty, now a thousand in number. The combination of a certain adroitness with deep-seated earnestness, of tact with consummate ability, gave him his preeminence, and helps him maintain it. The type, of course, varies according to time and place, from the West Indies in the sixteenth century to New England in the nineteenth, and from the Mississippi bottoms to cities like New Orleans or New York.

The music of Negro religion is that plaintive rhythmic melody with its touching minor cadences, which, despite caricature and defilement, still remains the most original and beautiful expression of human life and longing yet born on American soil. Sprung from the African forests, where its counterpart can still be heard, it was adapted, changed and intensified by the tragic soul-life of the slave, until, under the stress of law and whip, it became the one true expression of a people's sorrow, despair and hope.

Finally the frenzy or "shouting," when the Spirit of the Lord passed by, and, seizing the devotee, made him mad with supernatural joy, was the last essential of Negro religion and the one more devoutly believed in than all the rest. It varied in expression from the silent rapt countenance or the low murmur and moan to the mad abandon of physical fervor—the stamping, shrieking and shouting, the rushing to and fro and wild waving of arms, the weeping and laughing, the vision and the trance. All this is nothing new in the world, but old as religion, as Delphi and Endor. And so firm a hold did it have on the Negro that many generations firmly believed that without this visible manifestation of the god, there could be no true communion with the Invisible.

These were the characteristics of Negro religious life as developed up to the time of Emancipation. Since under the peculiar circumstances of the black man's environment, they were the one expression of his higher life, they are of deep interest to the student of his development, both socially and psychologically. Numerous are the attractive lines of inquiry that here group themselves. What did slavery mean to the African savage? What was his attitude toward the World and Life? What seemed to him good and evil— God and Devil? Whither went his longings and strivings, and wherefore were his heart-burnings and disappointments? Answers to such questions can come only from a study of Negro religion as a development, through its gradual changes from the heathenism of the Gold Coast to the institutional Negro church of Chicago.

Moreover, the religious growth of millions of men, even though they be slaves, cannot be without potent influence upon their contemporaries. The Methodists and Baptists of America owe much of their condition to the silent but potent influence of their millions of Negro converts. Especially is this noticeable in the South, where theology and religious philosophy are on this account a full half century behind the North, and where the religion of the poor whites is a plain copy of Negro thought and methods. The mass of "gospel" hymns which has swept through American churches and well-nigh ruined our sense of song, consists largely of debased imitations of Negro melodies made by ears that caught the jingle but not the music, the body but not the soul, of the Jubilee songs. It is thus clear that the study of Negro religion is not only a vital part of the history of the Negro in America, but no uninteresting part of American history.

The Negro church of today is the social center of Negro life in the United States, and the most characteristic expression of African character. Take a typical church in a small Virginian town: it is the "First Baptist"—a roomy brick edifice seating five hundred or more persons, tastefully finished in Georgia pine, with a carpet, a small organ and stained-glass windows. Underneath is a large assembly room with benches. This building is the central club-house of a community of a thousand or more Negroes. Various organizations meet here—the church proper, the Sunday school, two or three insurance societies, women's societies, secret societies and mass meetings of various kinds. Entertainments, suppers and lectures are held beside the five or six regular weekly religious services. Considerable sums of money are collected and expended here, employment is found for the idle, strangers are introduced, news is disseminated and charity distributed. At the same time this social, intellectual and economic center is a religious center of great power. Depravity, Sin, Redemption, Heaven, Hell and Damnation are preached twice a Sunday with much fervor, and revivals take place every year after the crops are laid by; and few indeed of the community have the hardihood to withstand conversion. Back of this more formal religion, the Church stands as a real conserver of morals, a strengthener of family life, and the final authority on what is Good and Right.

Thus one can see in the Negro church today, reproduced in microcosm, all that great world from which the Negro is cut off by color prejudice and social condition. In the great city churches the same tendency is noticeable and in many respects emphasized. A great church like the Bethel of Philadelphia has 1,104 members, an edifice seating 1,500 persons and valued at $100,000, an annual budget of $5,000 and a government consisting of a pastor with several assisting local preachers, an executive and legislative board, financial boards and tax collectors; general church meetings for making laws; subdivided groups led by class leaders, a company of militia, and twenty-four auxiliary societies. The activity of such a church is immense and far-reaching, and the bishops who preside over these organizations throughout the land are among the most powerful Negro rulers in the world.

Such churches are really governments of men, and consequently a little investigation reveals the curious fact that, in the South, at least, practically every American Negro is a church member. Some, to be sure, are not regularly enrolled, and a few do not habitually attend services; but, practically, a proscribed people must have a social center, and that center for this people is the Negro church. The census of 1890 showed nearly 24,000 Negro churches in the country, with a total enrolled membership of over two and a half million, or ten actual church members to every twenty-eight persons, and in some Southern states one in every two persons. Besides these there is the large number who, while not enrolled as members, attend and take part in many of the activities of the church. There is an organized Negro church for every sixty black families in the nation, and in some states for every forty families, owning, on an average, $1,000 worth of property each, or nearly $26,000,000 in all.

Such, then, is the large development of the Negro church since Emancipation. The question now is, What have been the successive steps of this social history and what are the present tendencies? First, we must realize that no such institution as the Negro church could rear itself without definite historical foundations. These foundations we can find if we remember that the social history of the Negro did not start in America. He was brought from a definite social environment—the polygamous clan life under the headship of the chief and the potent influence of the priest. His religion was nature worship, with profound belief in invisible surrounding influences, good and bad, and his worship was through incantation and sacrifice. The first rude change in this life was the slave ship and the West Indian sugar fields. The plantation organization replaced the clan and tribe, and the white master replaced the chief with far greater and more despotic powers. Forced and long-continued toil became the rule of life, the old ties of blood relationship and kinship disappeared, and instead of the family appeared a new polygamy and polyandry, which, in some cases, almost reached promiscuity. It was a terrific social revolution, and yet some traces were retained of the former group life, and the chief remaining institution was the Priest or Medicine man. He early appeared on the plantation and found his function as the healer of the sick, the interpreter of the Unknown, the comforter of the sorrowing, the supernatural avenger of wrong, and the one who rudely but picturesquely expressed the longing, disappointment and resentment of a stolen and oppressed people. Thus, as bard, physician, judge and priest, within the narrow limits allowed by the slave system, rose the Negro preacher, and under him the first Afro-American institution, the Negro church. This church was not at first by any means Christian nor definitely organized; rather it was an adaptation and mingling of heathen rites among the members of each plantation, and roughly designated as Voodooism. Association with the masters, missionary effort and motives of expediency gave these rites an early veneer of Christianity, and after the lapse of many generations the Negro church became Christian.

Two characteristic things must be noticed in regard to this church. First, it became almost entirely Baptist and Methodist in faith; secondly, as a social institution it anedated by many decades the monogamic Negro home. From the very circumstances of its beginning, the church was confined to the plantation, and consisted primarily of a series of disconnected units; although, later on, some freedom of movement was allowed, still this geographical limitation was always important and was one cause of the spread of the decentralized and democratic Baptist faith among the slaves. At the same time, the visible rite of baptism appealed strongly to their mystic temperament. Today the Baptist church is still largest in membership among Negroes, and has a million and a half communicants. Next in popularity came the churches organized in connection with the white neighboring churches, chiefly Baptist and Methodist, with a few Episcopalian and others. The Methodists still form the second greatest denomination, with nearly a million members. The faith of these two leading denominations was more suited to the slave church from the prominence they gave to religious feeling and fervor. The Negro membership in other denominations has always been small and relatively unimportant, although the Episcopalians and Presbyterians are gaining among the more intelligent classes today, and the Catholic church is making headway in certain sections. After emancipation, and still earlier in the North, the Negro churches largely severed such affiliations as they had had with the white churches, either by choice or by compulsion. The Baptist churches became independent, but the Methodists were compelled early to unite for purposes of episcopal government. This gave rise to the great African Methodist church, the greatest Negro organization in the world, to the Zion church and the Colored Methodist, and to the black conferences and churches in this and other denominations.

The second fact noted, namely, that the Negro church antedates the Negro home, leads to an explanation of much that is paradoxical in this communistic institution and in the morals of its members. But especially it leads us to regard this institution as peculiarly the expression of the inner ethical life of a people in a sense seldom true elsewhere. Let us turn then from the outer physical development of the church to the more important inner ethical life of the people who compose it. The Negro has already been pointed out many times as a religious animal—a being of that deep emotional nature which turns instinctively toward the supernatural. Endowed with a rich tropical imagination and a keen, delicate appreciation of Nature, the transplanted African lived in a world animate with gods and devils, elves and witches; full of strange influences—of Good to be implored, of Evil to be propitiated. Slavery, then, was to him the dark triumph of Evil over him. All the hateful powers of the underworld were striving against him, and a spirit of revolt and revenge filled his heart. He called up all the resources of heathenism to aid—exorcism and witchcraft, the mysterious Obi worship with its barbarous rites, spells and blood sacrifice even, now and then, of human victims. Weird midnight orgies and mystic conjurations were invoked, the witch woman and the voodoo priest became the center of Negro group life, and that vein of vague superstition which characterizes the unlettered Negro even today was deepened and strengthened.

In spite, however, of such success as that of the fierce Maroons, the Danish blacks and others, the spirit of revolt gradually died away under the untiring energy and superior strength of the slave masters. By the middle of the eighteenth century the black slave had sunk, with hushed murmurs, to his place at the bottom of a new economic system, and was unconsciously ripe for a new philosophy of life. Nothing suited his condition then better than the doctrines of passive submission embodied in the newly learned Christianity. Slave masters early realized this, and cheerfully aided religious propaganda within certain bounds. The long system of repression and degradation of the Negro tended to emphasize the elements in his character which made him a valuable chattel: courtesy became humility, moral strength degenerated into submission, and the exquisite native appreciation of the beautiful became an infinite capacity for dumb suffering. The Negro, losing the joy of this world, eagerly seized upon the offered conceptions of the next; the avenging Spirit of the Lord enjoining patience in this world, under sorrow and tribulation until the Great Day when He should lead His dark children home—this became his comforting dream. His Preacher repeated the prophecy, and his bards sang:

> Children, we all shall be free
> When the Lord shall appear!

This deep religious fatalism, painted so beautifully in Uncle Tom, came soon to breed, as all fatalistic faiths will, the sensualist side by side with the martyr. Under the lax moral life of the plantation, where marriage was a farce, laziness a virtue, and property a theft, a religion of resignation and submission degenerated easily, in less strenuous minds, into a philosophy of indulgence and crime. Many of the worst characteristics of the Negro masses of today had their seed in this period of the slave's ethical growth. Here it was that the home was ruined under the very shadow of the church, white and black; here habits of shiftlessness took root, and sullen hopelessness replaced hopeful strife.

With the beginning of the abolition movement and the gradual growth of a class of free Negroes came a change. We often neglect the influence of the freedman before the war, because of the paucity of his numbers and the small weight he had in the history of the nation. But we must not forget that his chief influence was internal—was exerted on the black world, and that there he was the ethical and social leader. Huddled as he was in a few centers like Philadelphia, New York and New Orleans, his chief characteristic was intense earnestness and deep feeling on the slavery question. Freedom became to him a real thing and not a dream. His religion became darker and more intense, and into his ethics crept a note of revenge, into his songs a day of reckoning close at hand. The "Coming of the Lord" swept this side of death, and came to be a thing to be hoped for in this day. Through fugitive slaves and irrepressible discussion this desire for freedom seized the black millions still in bondage, and became their one ideal of life. The black bards caught new notes, and sometimes even dared to sing:

> Before I'll be a slave
> I'll be buried in my grave,
> An go home to my Jesus
> And be saved.

For fifty years Negro religion thus transformed itself and identified itself with the dream of abolition until that which was a radical fad in the white North and an anarchistic plot in the white South had become a religion to the black world. Thus, when Emancipation finally came, it seemed to the freedman a literal Coming of the Lord. His fervid imagination was stirred, as never before, by the tramp of armies, the blood and dust of battle and the wail and whirl of social upheaval. He stood dumb and motion-less before the whirlwind—what had he to do with it? Was it not the Lord's doing and marvelous in his eyes? Joyed and bewildered with what came, he stood awaiting new wonders till the inevitable age of reaction swept over the nation and brought the crisis of today.

It is difficult to explain clearly the present critical stage of Negro religion. First, we must remember that living as the blacks do in close contact with a great modern nation and sharing, although imperfectly, the soul-life of that nation, they must necessarily be affected more or less directly by all the religious and ethical forces that are today moving the United States. These questions and movements are, however, overshadowed and dwarfed by the all-important question (to them) of their civil, political and economic status. They must perpetually discuss the "Negro problem"—live, move, and have their being in it, and interpret all else in its light or darkness. With this come, too, peculiar problems of their inner life—of the status of women, the maintenance of home, the train-ing of children, the accumulation of wealth and the prevention of crime. All this must mean a time of intense ethical ferment, of religious heart-searching and intellectual unrest. From the double life every American Negro must live, as a Negro and as an Ameri-can, as swept on by the current of the nineteenth while yet struggling in the eddies of the fifteenth century—from this must arise a painful self-consciousness, an almost morbid sense of per-sonality and a moral hesitancy which is fatal to self-confidence. The worlds within and without the Veil of Color are changing, and changing rapidly, but not at the same rate, not in the same way; and this must produce a peculiar wrenching of the soul, a peculiar sense of doubt and bewilderment. Such a double life, with double thoughts, double duties and double social classes, must give rise to double words and double ideals, and tempt the mind to pretense or to revolt, to hypocrisy or to radicalism.

In some such doubtful words and phrases can one perhaps most clearly picture the peculiar ethical paradox that faces the Negro of today and is tingeing and changing his religious life. Feeling that his rights and his dearest ideals are being trampled upon, that the public conscience is even more deaf to his righteous appeal, and that all the reactionary forces of prejudice, greed and revenge are daily gaining new strength and fresh allies, the Negro faces no enviable dilemma. Conscious of his impotence, and pessimistic, he often becomes bitter and vindictive, and his religion, instead of a worship, is a complaint and a curse, a wail rather than a hope, a sneer rather than a faith. On the other hand, another type of mind, shrewder and keener and more tortuous too, sees in the very strength of the anti-Negro movement its patent weaknesses, and with Jesuitic casuistry is deterred by no ethical considerations in the endeavor to turn this weakness to the black man's strength. Thus we have two great and hardly reconcilable streams of thought and ethical strivings; the danger of the one lies in anarchy, that of the other in hypocrisy. The one type of Negro stands almost ready to curse God and die, and the other is too often found a traitor to right and a coward before force; the one is wedded to ideals remote, whimsical, perhaps impossible of realization; the other forgets that life is more than meat and the body more than raiment. But, after all, is not all this simply the writhing of the age translated into black? The triumph of the Lie which today, with its false culture, faces the hideousness of the anarchist assassin?

Today the two groups of Negroes, the one in the North, the other in the South, represent these divergent ethical tendencies, the first tending toward radicalism, the other toward hypocritical compromise. It is no idle regret with which the white South mourns the loss of the old-time Negro—the frank, honest, simple old servant who stood for the earlier religious age of submission and humility. With all his laziness and lack of many elements of true manhood he was at least open-hearted, faithful and sincere. Today he is gone, but who is to blame for his going? Is it not those very persons who mourn for him? Is it not the tendency born of Reconstruction and reaction to found a society on lawlessness and deception, to tamper with the moral fiber of a naturally honest and straightforward people until the whites threaten to become ungovernable tyrants and the blacks criminals and hypocrites? Deception is the natural defense of the weak against the strong, and the South used it for many years against its conquerors; today it must be prepared to see its black proletariat turn that same two-edged weapon against itself. And how natural this is! The death of Nat Turner and John Brown proved long since to the Negro the present hopelessness of physical defense. Political defense is becoming less and less available, and economic defense is still only partially effective. But there is a patent defense at hand—the defense of deception and flattery, of cajoling and lying. It is the same defense which the Jews of the Middle Age used and which left its stamp on their character for centuries. Today the young Negro of the South who would succeed cannot be frank and outspoken, honest and self-assertive; but rather he is daily tempted to be silent and wary, politic and sly; he must flatter and be pleasant, endure petty insults with a smile, shut his eyes to wrong; in too many cases he sees positive personal advantage in deception and lying. His real thoughts, his real aspirations must be guarded in whispers; he must not criticise, he must not complain. Patience, humility and adroitness must, in these growing black youth, re-place impulse, manliness and courage. With this sacrifice there is an economic opening, and perhaps peace and some prosperity. Without this there is riot, migration or crime. Nor is this situation peculiar to the Southern United States—is it not rather the only method by which undeveloped races have gained the right to share modern culture? The price of culture is a lie.

On the other hand, in the North the tendency is to emphasize the radicalism of the Negro. Driven from his birthright in the South by a situation at which every fiber of his more outspoken and assertive nature revolts, he finds himself in a land where he can scarcely earn a decent living amid the harsh competition and the color discrimination. At the same time, through schools and peri-odicals, discussions and lectures, he is intellectually quickened and awakened. The soul, long pent up and dwarfed, suddenly expanded in new-found freedom. What wonder that every tendency is to excess—radical complaint, radical remedies, bitter denunciation or angry silence. Some sink, some rise. The criminal and the sensualist leave the church for the gambling hall and the bawdy-house, and fill the slums of Chicago and Baltimore; the better classes segregate themselves from the group life of both white and black, and form an aristocracy, cultured but pessimistic, whose bitter criticism stings while it points out no way of escape. They despise the sub-mission and subserviency of the Southern Negroes, but offer no other means by which a poor and oppressed minority can exist side by side with its masters. Feeling deeply and keenly the tendencies and opportunities of the age in which they live, their souls are bitter at the fate which drops the Veil between, and the very fact that this bitterness is natural and justifiable only serves to intensify it and make it more maddening.

Between the two extreme types of ethical attitude which I have thus sought to make clear, wavers the mass of the millions of Negroes North and South; and their religious life and activity partake of this social conflict within their ranks. Their churches are differentiating; now into groups of cold, fashionable devotees, in no way distinguishable from similar white groups save in color of skin; now into large social and business institutions catering to the desire for information and amusement of their members, warily avoiding unpleasant questions both within and without the black world and preaching in effect if not in word: *Dum vivimus, vivamus.*[1]

But, back of this, still brood silently the deep religious feeling of the real Negro heart, the stirring, unguided might of powerful human souls who have lost the guiding star of the past and are seeking in the great night a new religious ideal. Some day the Awakening will come, when the pent-up vigor of ten million souls shall sweep irresistibly toward the Goal, out of the Valley of the Shadow of Death, where all that makes life worth living—Liberty, Justice and Right—is marked "For White People Only."

1. While we live, let us live.

IV

The Search for Unity

26. An Evangelical Interpretation of the Religious Situation—1893

IN THE nineteenth and especially in the twentieth centuries there have been many efforts to find larger unities among the many religious bodies. There have been reunions of divided denominational families, and unions across denominational lines. Cooperative agencies of many kinds have been launched. Often in the hope of preparing the way for closer contacts among those who have affinities, the pluralistic picture has at times been interpreted to show that one of the major traditions— usually Protestantism—is in fact the dominant faith and that it will continue to increase. Such an effort was the following essay on "The Present Religious Condition of America," prepared by Henry King Carroll for the World's Parliament of Religion in Chicago in 1893. Carroll (1848–1931), an editor of the Independent for many years, was in charge of the 1890 census of the churches. He later became an associate secretary of the Federal Council of Churches.

SOURCE: John Henry Barrows (ed.), The World's Parliament of Religions, Vol. II (Chicago, 1893), pp. 1162–1165.

There are so many religious bodies in America that it is desirable, if we would get a comprehensive idea of them, to arrange them, first, in grand divisions; secondly, in classes; and thirdly, in families. I would specify three grand divisions: 1. The Christian. 2. The Jewish. 3. Miscellaneous. Under the last head come the Chinese Buddhists, the Theosophists, the Ethical Culturists, some communistic societies and pagan Indians. The Jewish division embraces simply the Orthodox and Reformed Jews. The Christian division contains, of course, the great majority of denominations and believers, Catholics, Protestants, Latter-Day Saints—all bodies not Jewish, pagan or anti-Christian.

We commonly divide the Christian bodies into classes, as, Catholic and Protestant, Evangelical and non-Evangelical. In the Catholic class there are seven representatives in this country; the Roman Catholic, the United Greek Catholic, the Russian Orthodox, the Greek Orthodox, the Armenian, the Old Catholic and the Reformed Catholic. All the Catholic bodies, except the Roman, are small and unimportant as represented in the United States, ranging in numbers of communicants from 100 to less than 14,000.

No denomination of Protestantism has thus far proved to be too small for division. Denominations appear in the census returns with as few as twenty-five members. I was reluctantly compelled to exclude one with twenty-one members.

We count in all 143 denominations in the United States, besides 150 or more congregations which are independent, or unassociated with any church. Of the 143 separate denominational bodies six are Adventist, thirteen Baptist, three (River) Brethren, four (Plymouth) Brethren, seven Catholic, two Christian Connection, nine Communistic, four Dunkard, four Quaker, two Jewish, two Mormon, sixteen Lutheran, twelve Mennonite, seventeen Methodist, twelve Presbyterian, two Episcopalian, three Reformed, and two United Brethren, with twenty-three single denominations, such as the Congregationalists, Moravians, Disciples of Christ, Christadelphians, Christian Scientists and Salvation Army. Many of the 143 separate bodies are very small and unimportant. We can pick out ninety-seven, of which no one has as many as 25,000 communicants; seventy-five have less than 10,000 communicants each; fifty-four less than 2,500, and thirty-two less than 1,000, ranging between 20 and 937. Of bodies having 25,000 and upwards there are only forty-six, or about one third of the whole number. The other two-thirds is made up of denominations having from 20 to 25,000. It is the little bodies, therefore, that give religion in the United States such a divided aspect. If most of them were blotted out we should lose little that is very valuable, but much that is queer in belief and practice. What is it has caused these numerous divisions? Among the Methodists ten of the seventeen divisions were due to the race or the slavery question, and six to controversies over practical questions. The other was imported. Of the twelve Presbyterian bodies all are consistently Calvinistic but two, the Cumberland and the Cumberland colored, which hold to a modified Calvinism. All use the Presbyterian system of government with little variation. What, then, is it that divides them? Slavery divided the Northern and Southern, the race question the two Cumberland bodies. One branch is Welsh and the rest are kept apart largely by Scotch obstinacy. They have close points of agreement, but they differ on questions that seem to others utterly insignificant. We may, I think, sum up the causes of division under four heads: (1) Controversies over doctrine; (2) controversies over administration or discipline; (3) controversies over moral questions; (4) ambitious and disputatious persons.

The last census, that of 1890, embraced all religious bodies among its greatly extended inquiries, and we have, therefore, for the first time, complete returns for all forms of religion represented in the United States. These returns show how many ministers, organizations or congregations, church edifices and communicants each denomination has, together with the seating capacity of its edifices and their value; also how they are distributed among the counties, states and territories.

The Roman Catholic is now the largest of the churches in number of communicants, having, in round numbers, 6,231,000. A hundred years ago it had only about 25,000; fifty years ago it had about 1,200,000. According to this it has increased, in the last half century, five-fold. This enormous growth is due chiefly to immigration. The Methodist Episcopal Church comes second, with more than 2,240,000; the Regular Baptists (colored) third with 1,362,000; the Regular Baptists (South) fourth, with 1,308,000; and the Methodist Episcopal (South) fifth, with 1,210,000.

Taking value of church property as our next item, that is, the value of houses of worship, their furnishings and the lots on which they stand, we find that the Catholic Church is first again, its property being valued at $118,000,000. The Methodist Episcopal Church is second, reporting $97,000,000; the Protestant Episcopal third, $81,000,000; the Northern Presbyterian fourth, $74,000,000; and the Southern Baptists fifth, $49,000,000. Two of these denominations, the Episcopal and the Presbyterian, are not among the five I have just mentioned as having the largest number of communicants. They stand third and fourth, respectively, in the table of church property, showing that they are much more wealthy in proportion to communicants than the other denominations.

In number of organizations, or congregations, the Methodist Episcopal Church comes first, with 25,861, and the Roman Catholic last, with 10,231. The Southern Baptists are second, with 16,450; the Southern Methodists third, with 15,000; and the Colored Baptists fourth, with 12,650. The reason the Catholic congregations only number two-fifths as many as the Methodist Episcopal, is because their parishes are so much larger and more populous. In some cases a Catholic parish embraces from 12,000 to 16,000 communicants, all using the same edifice. It is a common thing in the cities for Catholic churches to have five and six different congregations every Sunday.

To recapitulate, the Roman Catholic Church is first in the

number of communicants and value of house property, and fifth in number of organizations and houses of worship; the Methodist Episcopal Church is first in the number of organizations and houses of worship, and second in the number of communicants and value of church property.

Let us now see how the five leading denominational families, or groups, stand. The Catholics, embracing seven branches, come first as to communicants, with 6,258,000; the Methodists, embracing seventeen branches, come second, with 4,589,000; the Baptists, thirteen branches, are third, with 3,743,000; the Presbyterians, twelve branches, are fourth, with 1,278,000; and the Lutherans, sixteen branches, are fifth, with 1,231,000. It will be observed that the combined Methodist branches have about 1,600,000 fewer communicants than the combined Catholic branches. As to value of church property, the Methodist family is first, the figures being $132,000,000. The Catholic family is second, $118,000,000; the Presbyterian third, $95,000,000; the Episcopalians fourth, $82,835,000; the Baptists fifth, $82,680,000. As to organizations, or congregations, the Methodists are first, with 51,500; the Baptists second, with 43,000; the Presbyterians third, with 13,500; the Catholics fourth, with 10,270; and the Lutherans fifth, with 8,595.

Thus, among denominational families, the Catholics are first in the number of communicants, second in value of church property, and fourth in number of organizations and houses of worship. The Methodists are first in the number of organizations and houses of worship, and value of church property. These figures are for the five leading denominations, and the five chief denominational families. The grand totals for all denominations, Christian and non-Christian, are as follows: Ministers, 111,000; organizations, 165,250; houses of worship, 142,600; value of church property, $680,000,-000; communicants, 20,643,000. According to these figures, nearly one person in every three of our entire population is a member or communicant of one or another of the 143 denominations. This cannot, I should say, be regarded as an unfavorable showing for the churches. It indicates a religious population of 57,720,000. That is, the communicants, with all adherents added, constitute 57,720,-000, leaving about 5,000,000 to compose the nonreligious and antireligious classes, including freethinkers and infidels.

Of the 165,250 organizations, all are Christian but 1,855, or a little more than one percent, and all are Protestant, except 12,131, or a little over seven percent. That is, Christian organizations form nearly ninety-nine percent of the total, and Protestant organizations about ninety-three percent. Of the 20,643,000 members all are Christian except 347,623, and all are Protestant except 6,605,494. That is, Christian members form ninety-seven and one-quarter percent of the total, and Protestant members sixty-eight percent. The Catholic percentage is about thirty and one-half and the Jewish and miscellaneous only one and a half.

I call your attention to the fact that of the 153,122 Protestant organizations all but 747 are evangelical, and of the 14,037,417 Protestant members all but 128,568 are evangelical. That is, counting the Universalists with the evangelical class, where I think they really belong, ninety-five percent of Protestant organizations are evangelical; and over ninety-nine percent of Protestant communicants belong to evangelical denominations.

In the last ten years the net increase in our population was a little less than twenty-five percent. A comparison of the returns of churches representing 16,500,000 members, shows that in the same period their net increase was about thirty-five percent, or ten percent greater than the increase of the population. The largest percentage of gain was sixty-eight, which belongs to the Lutheran family; the next was fifty-seven percent by the Methodist Episcopal Church, South; the third, forty-eight percent, by the Protestant Episcopal Church; the fourth, thirty-nine percent, by the Presbyterian family; the fifth, thirty-seven percent, by the Regular Baptists, North, South, and Colored; the sixth, thirty-three percent, by the Congregationalists, and the seventh, thirty percent, by the Methodist Episcopal Church.

We must, of course, remember that all the houses of worship have been built by voluntary contributions. They are valued at $680,000,000, and furnish sitting accommodations for 43,500,000 persons. They have been provided by private gifts, but are offered to the public for free use. The government has not given a dollar to provide them, nor does it appropriate a dollar for their support.

27. The Social Gospel as a Unitive Force

In the last several decades of the nineteenth century, there emerged what came to be known as the social gospel, a movement led largely by social and theological liberals to relate the insights of faith to the solution of the pressing social and economic problems of the time. One of the early leaders was Josiah Strong (1847–1916), who as general secretary of the Evangelical Alliance engineered three conferences (1887, 1889, and 1893) in which the cause of social Christianity was advanced. Another early leader of the social gospel was Graham Taylor (1851–1938). At the 1889 conference of the Evangelical Alliance, he spoke on the theme "Arousing and Training the Activity of the Laity." Then a professor at Hartford Seminary, Taylor later became professor of social economics at Chicago Theological Seminary and founder of the Chicago Commons, a settlement house. In the early twentieth century, the social gospel movement found such cooperative agencies as the Federal Council of Churches good vehicles for its viewpoint; the social gospel and the unitive Christian movements often made common cause. Even after the social gospel declined somewhat after World War I, its insistence that men of faith should be concerned with social problems was accepted by others, and its emphasis on the role of the laity was to be reaffirmed by those of many different positions—often in much the same words that Taylor used in 1889, reprinted here. On the social gospel, see C. Howard Hopkins, The Rise of the Social Gospel in American Protestantism (New Haven, 1940), Henry F. May, Protestant Churches and Industrial America (New York, 1949), and Robert T. Handy (ed.), The Social Gospel in America, 1870–1920: Gladden, Ely, Rauschenbusch (New York, 1966).

source: National Needs and Remedies: The Discussions of the General Christian Conference Held in Boston, . . . under the Auspices and Direction of the Evangelical Alliance for the United States (New York, 1890), pp. 264–274.

The divinest voice to be heard in Christendom, articulated by mightiest deeds of our modern Christianity, proclaims everywhere the priesthood of the people. It is the call of the Priest-King for the kingdom of priests promised him in the day of his power. Judged by the volunteering, it is the muster-day of his army. He has the dew of his youth. As foreseen in the military vision of the Psalmist-Seer, the march of the priestly people has begun. "In holy attire," the vestment of the common priesthood, "they offer themselves willingly." Not singly, but in whole battalions, they join forces, and march forward in phalanx movement, with an enthusiasm, holier and wiser, and therefore braver and stronger, than the crusaders ever knew.

Was ever such recruiting known as has gathered the youth of Christendom into one vast Sunday school army, since, only one hundred years ago, that little band of young men in Gloucester joined hands and volunteered to save and sustain Robert Raikes' "ragged school," when there was no money to hire the paid teachers to conduct it?

To the flower of what army would we compare the hundreds of thousands of young men in the Christian associations of our land, and in the auxiliary bodies which they lead? What grander tactics are there than theirs, by which they already control the physical culture of the young manhood of the nation; by which they are building this year two millions of dollars into structures that are sanctuary, school, armory and drill-room, fortress, life-saving-station and home parlor all in one; by which they man, equip, and fortify for Christ every strategic point, on whole systems of railways, not by sufferance, but by the urgency of the railway managers; by which their budget this year calls for and secures the investment of four million dollars of the business capital of this country.

Grander than earth's proudest legions is the "great multitude of women" who publish the Word in home and school, mission-bands and Temperance Union, and the thousand forms of woman's work for woman and for the world, through the church.

Fair as the moon, clear as the sun, terrible as an army with banners are the 600,000 youth who are looking forth from the Christian Endeavor societies of our churches, as an enlisted, sworn, disciplined force ready for active service on the field. With them and their allied young Christians of other names, new loyalty, unity, type of membership and ministry have been added to the church. Although this is the day of an aroused activity in the membership, it has come none too soon.

It takes a whole kingdom to save a whole world. It takes all the people to make a whole kingdom.

Fast and far is the world outgrowing our churches, with their class memberships and with ministries constituted of the smallest fraction of their class. We know the world seems smaller as it is drawn nearer together; but it is more complex. There is more of it all the while to win, save, master, in less space and time. It gains upon the church in the density and complexity of its life, faster even than the church's territory gains upon its area. Yet there are as surely diversified capacities in regenerated human nature as there are in fallen humanity. But they are dormant. How shall we awake them? Our greatest resources are undeveloped. How shall we arouse them? Talents of the first order lie folded in the napkin, dead and buried, lost to life because unused. How shall we resurrect them? Much of the energy, alive, aroused, and spending itself with glorious abandon, is misdirected and "spent." How shall we apply this precious power? Our leaders are trying to do the work of a thousand people instead of putting a thousand people to work. In the very existence of every church there should appear the freest offer of the gospel's divine power to every weak heart and struggling life, to every feeblest word and work for the good of fellowmen, to every right cause battling for life and supremacy. How shall the church become the kingdom it was meant and made to be on earth? The providence of God answers us both through the world's need of the church, and the Spirit's movements among the people to apply the Word to work its power to life. To arouse the whole membership to minister, then, these three suggestions seem to be prompted by God through our times:

I. Proclaim to the church *the priesthood of its people.* The ideal of the church in both Testaments is "a kingdom of priests." The bottommost fact underlying the existence, power and promise of the Messianic kingdom in the One Hundred and Tenth Psalm is that of a whole people offering themselves willingly in priestly ministry. Through the Apostle Peter, God proclaims the New Testament church to be what, through Moses, he declared the church of the old covenant to have been, "an elect race, a royal priesthood, a holy nation, a people for God's own possession." "Laity" is not a New Testament word. Even the idea of such a class in the membership in antithesis to an exclusive ministry, is not to be found in the records of the church of the New Testament. "They that were scattered abroad went everywhere preaching." It knew no secularized membership, who relinquished, or, much less, were denied the right, duty and privilege of the freest exercise of the Christian's priestly prerogative. The ministering membership was its only recognized constituency. For at least two hundred years few were found to challenge what a great church Father took for granted, when in his appeal for priestly work, he asked, "Are not we laics priests?" Had they not all wrought as such, it is difficult to see how the early church could have won its mighty conquests.

Every evangelical polity recognizes the priesthood of its people. This does not deny the existence of the ministry as we know it, and know it to be essential to the church, but it pledges our Lord the Messianic promise of more help than that of any class in the church, however able or representative that may be.

In every great spiritual advancement and aggressive movement of the church, a new activity of the membership has been, not only an attendant result, but an impelling power.

The names of Luther, Zinzendorf, Wesley, and every leader in the great succession do not stand alone in history. They are the rallying points about which the men and women of their times were marshaled by the Lord of Hosts.

The increasingly significant name and place given the lay-representation in the ecclesiastical courts of almost all our denominations is the deserved recognition of their essential service by the whole church and her Lord. In all the splendid pageant of the Roman Catholic Centenary at Baltimore the most significant expression of the occasion found utterance through the meetings of Catholic laymen.

The rise of the church membership from a secularized laity to its primitive priesthood is at once the greatest movement and highest glory of our modern Christianity. It is clearly the movement of God in the life of our times. It heralds the day of Christ's power.

The proclamation of the priesthood of the people is a twofold arousement to activity. It not only is the divine call upon every one to work, but is the assurance that there is work for every one. A whole world of work is implied by the call for a whole people of priests. Many are kept out of Christian work by the narrowness of the prevailing idea of what it is. They think of it only as taking public part in religious meetings, or as making personal appeals to individuals, or as doing the work of the minister "in little." But the whole is greater than any of its parts. The gospel is "the gospel of the kingdom." "He made us to be a kingdom and priests."

The work of the church is as large when defined by life's need of it as in the letter of its written charter. All that men need it to be the Son of Man meant it to be. No more arousing call to activity is to be made upon people or ministry than to bring them into personal contact with the great world's need of the applied gospel. To hear the throbbing of the common heart is a new call to the holy office, a new ordination to service. "To every man his work" is given. One need not choose or refuse another's work. Because one could not if he would, or should not if he could, do the minister's work, is no reason why he should not do his own work. What that is will soon appear when we explore and survey the place for it in the hearts and homes, the lives and work of our fellow-men. It will leave no doubt that there is work enough for every one to have something to do; it shows that there are as many kinds of work as there are workers to do it. Over against every aspiration and aptitude of the Christian heart, lie the provinces for its work in the great field, which is the world. The love for little children called into being, amidst the tenement population of lower New York, the "college settlement" of graduates from some of our New England women's colleges. There, while pursuing their various avocations, these Christian young women live for the sake of Christ's little ones and the incidental good they can do for them by being among them; and the child-life of their neighborhood is said fairly to bask in the sunshine of their presence. In the distinctions of sex and the call they make for differing agencies, many find their Christian calling to the "Boys' Club," the kindergarten, and all the manifold phases of woman's work for woman. The differences of race make requisition upon differing spiritual temperaments and talents. The economic and social conditions which mold by their environing forms the lives and characters of men, are summoning to the help of the poor and the helpless some of the best brain and heart to be found in English and American universities. Even the moral and spiritual segregations of men and women into the classifications of vice and crime, generate in the Christian heart that enthusiasm for humanity which blossoms with love for the unlovely, whose fruitage is redeemed lives, and saved communities. Such an outlay of demand and supply as is presented in the Convention of Christian Workers for the United States and Canada by reports of the preoccupying and preventive, reformatory and restorative, remedial and constructive Christian agencies annually represented there, makes an irresistible appeal to everything in the heart of the whole church or of any one of its members.

Larger ideas of what the church is, what church membership means, what there is for the Christian to do in this world, must prevail, if the vast latent power of the so-called laity is to be developed, or the ranks of the regular ministry are to be supplied. There can be no better source of the depleted ministerial supply than to bring the young men of our colleges into direct personal contact and cooperation with the most practical forms of city evangelistic work. There, down upon the hard pan of our civilization, is to be seen the possible reach of Christian agencies, the essential scope for ministry, the vital relation between the living church and all else that lives, and the heroic type of personal service, which are needed today to attract and "call" young men from the fascinations of worldly pursuits to the chivalry of the Christian ministry. The score or more of undergraduates who were thus sent into the city fields last summer by the committee of Christian Workers to spend their vacation in toil for their fallen fellow-men, bore thence not only their divine commission to ministry, but a distinct call to that very heroic type of ministry. No diviner definition of the church and its mission is to be found in the Word, than that to be read in the spiritual wants of fellow-men as they may be discovered by such a cooperative canvass and visitation of the community as the Evangelical Alliance institutes among the churches. The voice of highest hope in all the wilderness of the world's want is that which everywhere proclaims "The kingdom of priests is at hand. Prepare ye the way of the Lord."

II. To arouse lay activity, offer to train the membership for ministry.

The lack of training, with the consciousness of incompetence it begets, is perhaps the most insurmountable obstacle which the membership encounter in responding to the call to engage in Christian work. Their willingness to work is gradually overcome by their fear that they cannot do the work at all, or the certainty that they cannot do it well. They therefore become unwilling to attempt what the most capable of them often come to believe they have no ability or aptitude to do. The spiritual energy of those aroused to the working point, is generally left either to scatter and be spent without any definite knowledge of what to do or how to do it, or to find its own way to efficiency at great waste of time, power and enthusiasm.

This obstacle to the worker is the chief hindrance of Christian work. The lack of trained helpers is the despair of every successful leader, the paralysis of the most effective methods. The demand for trained specialists, inexorable in every subdivision of human labor, is nowhere more imperative than in Christian work. More workers are not as much needed as better and more kinds of workers.

The offer to train creates the demand to be trained, or brings it to an expression. Every adequate provision for training to Christian service has demonstrated the deep desire prevalent among our church membership to fit themselves for active cooperation in church work. The School for Christian Workers at Springfield even so soon after its establishment can accommodate but one fifth of the applicants for its training in parish, Sunday School and YMCA work.

When the Hartford Theological Seminary offered popular courses of study in all its departments of instruction to the public this fall, nearly five hundred of the Christian men and women of the city thronged its classrooms to form their afternoon and evening weekly classes. To the summer schools our Christian people are flocking by thousands to learn how to study the Word and use it to work with.

But where the provision for training is not offered, the demand for it will surely create the supply. The will to be trained, equal to the will to work, shall find its way. At first it may need to be so strong as to work its own way through any apprenticeship to some mastership in Christian service. Training is the work to which Christians are now called to devote themselves. Should not the mastery of some one of the useful arts of the Kingdom be thought to be a necessary part of every Christian's education and calling? Should parents and educators call the education they provide for the young, "liberal," without some provision of special training for distinctively Christian usefulness? Can an education be Christian without this? Has any one a Christian's occupation who has no fitting for any of his Master's work? The new generation of young church members begin to act as if they thought "No," and as if they had a will to work which would find its way to be trained for it. At the demand of Sunday School workers a whole new literature and normal-training system have sprung into being, and are gradually taking on more effective forms. Even where there is neither provision for training nor any conscious demand for it, the determination to provide for the felt need of it upon the part of any who recognize it to be the need of the church and the world, may secure the means to train the workers, and the workers to take the means. Dr. Chalmers thus fairly willed the "Workers' weekly meetings" of the Free Church of Scotland into existence. The will of the church can have its way.

As to method, existing agencies afford ample instrumentalities. Why should not every Bible class be a workers' training class? Why should it not be a society organized to do a definite work of its own in the church and community? Would not the truth with which the scholars are taught to do something, be more to them and do more for them? The normal class should also be a working class in our churches as it is in our great normal schools. Work and word go together. Learning and life are vital to each other.

Every Christian Association and Endeavor Society should not only have a training class for workers but it should be a great workers' training class itself. Beside the self-culture for service, and the associated training agencies, indicated, great institutions for training Christian workers are taking their place among the providential provision for the needs of our times. The School for Christian Workers, already mentioned, led the way for a great following. The Lay Evangelistic Training School established by Mr. Moody in Chicago, the Missionary Training School in this city of Boston, and many humbler institutions are arising throughout Christendom. They have come to stay and grow, and multiply, for they not only meet the exigencies of the present, but are building for the future. Among them all none is more significant and far-reaching in its aims than the proposed "Christian Industrial School," of Springfield, Massachusetts, whose preliminary announcement has just been issued. With its five schools in one—schools for general preparation, for teaching the trades, for preparing manual training and kindergarten teachers, and for trained mechanic missionaries, it appeals at once to the most practical needs and the most powerful tendencies of the times. Of the skilled labor of their apprentices every branch of the church's work stands in pressing want. For their Christian artisans with a purpose to do Christian work for their fellow-workers at the bench, at the case and at the forge, the foundry, shop and factory will speedily prove to be, in its founder's words, "as important fields of Christian usefulness as a Sunday School, a YMCA building or a mission chapel." The whole world is the open field for the self-supporting mechanic missionaries, manual training schools and kindergarten teachers, and volunteer or paid workers whom these institutions are calling, training and consecrating to the world-work of the kingdom.

III. An aroused and trained activity in the membership necessitates the more thorough and practical training of the ministry for leadership. A ministering people, and a church which is a kingdom, demand a theological seminary which shall be a Christian university. It must teach the work as well as the word, method as well as theory. It must be in a city large enough to provide it with all that a hospital clinic is to the medical school, where students can be sent forth from their class rooms to do something with the truth they learn. It must recognize the diversity of Christian work over against the diversity of personal talent and capacity. No longer should it pursue that forcing process which is abandoned almost everywhere else, whereby it attempts to turn out all its graduates as candidates for only one function of ministry, viz., preaching, with heads like those of a paper of pins, all of one size with just the same things in them, and standing in one and the same order. Why should not a theological seminary broaden its regular course of pastoral training by giving a wide selection of optional studies, wherein men of differing aptitudes might, after they had laid a general basis of theological culture, choose that specialty to which they are adapted, and bring out what is in them for the Lord's use? Indeed, why should they not go farther in this direction and offer special courses to Christian specialists, who would devote their specific aptitudes and talents to branches of Christian service other than the pastoral office? Are not thoroughly trained Christian journalists, physicians, teachers and missionaries as needful to the coming of the kingdom as pulpit preachers? If the church calls women to occupy two thirds of the positions of usefulness on her mission fields, should their sex deprive them of the training and equipment to be acquired in her theological schools?

The changed relative position of ministry and laity calls upon our theological seminaries to train the ministers to be the leaders of the church's work. Of the exercise of the long-neglected "Episcopal" function of supervisionary leadership upon the part of her ministry, the modern church stands in greatest need. To be the leaders they are called and ordained, and should be trained to be, the ministry need only to lead. If they fail in this it is not because they are denied the opportunity, but because they are not trained in leadership. Scant time and small space are granted in the usual theological curriculum for the study, much less for the observation, of the church's greatest agencies for her work, such as missionary methods, the Sunday School, city evangelization, the Endeavor and Association work. While almost the whole effort is directed toward the preparation of the sermon, it is forgotten that the pulpit is not the only fulcrum of the gospel's power. The parish and its outlying fields contain many another. Trained mind is no less a scepter, and trained personality is more and more the medium for the transmission of power, but training in leadership must supplement both, if the minister is to sway that God-given power for the King. Fewer and fewer churches, fewer and fewer ministers may fulfill their whole function by preaching alone. Of his hosts our Master is Lord. He is marshaling them to be led in his work and word.

The changed relative position occupied by the church in the community also imposes new conditions, both upon lay activity and its ministerial leadership. Adjustment to these social tendencies and forces which challenge the supremacy of the Christian church in modern society, is necessary both to the winning of the soul and the coming of the kingdom. The leaders of her laity need to be taught no less of theology perhaps, but a great deal more of sociology. They need to know not only more about God, but a great deal more about their fellow-men. It is not enough to know the individual man, for he is to be known more and more through our knowledge of the type of man, and the hereditary and environing conditions of which he is so largely a product. It is no longer enough that a minister mans his own parish, for of the reformatory movements and popular causes his church is a divinely appointed leader. The leadership of the very reforms and charities which were born of her, the church will surely and swiftly forfeit, unless her leaders be trained to lead them.

The science of Christian society in which her people and their leaders need to be trained is only that of her own promised kingdom. For that kingdom of the Son of Man the whole earth is space, the weary heart of man has place, every nation will make room, when his people offer themselves willingly in the day of his power.

In the vast auditorium building in Chicago, one after another of its features seems great enough to be the purpose of the whole magnificent structure. The massiveness and proportions of the architecture, the interior decoration, the stage which is the focus of ten thousand seats, the singer, actor, orator who may sway thence the mighty throng, the "cloud of witnesses" encircling the whole horizon—each in turn gives precedence to the other. Yet all of them together but magnify the greatness of our country, of whose power the whole great building is a symbolic product, and to promote whose civilization and destiny it is built.

So the Christian church is being reared in every land, in all the grand proportions and with all the spiritual adornments befitting the temple in which God promises to dwell with men. But it exists not for itself, its art or cultus, its creed or worship, its ministry or membership. It is all for the King. It is his palace and the throne-room of his universal sway. When its cap-stone is brought forth with shoutings of "Grace, Grace unto it," and He shall present unto himself a glorious church, may we have some part in that chorus of men and angels, and some name and place in the holy Catholic church when it becomes the kingdom of our Lord and of his Christ.

28. The Lutheran Search for Unity

THE COMPLEX divisions of the Lutheran tradition in the United States have already been mentioned (see Document 6). The road toward consolidation within that denominational family has been a long and hard one, but it has been marked by significant achievement. Conrad Bergendoff (1895–   ), for many years president of Augustana College and Theological Seminary, in 1947 described the long journey toward Lutheran union in a passage from which this selection has been drawn. With the development of the ecumenical movement after the famous World Missionary Conference at Edinburgh in 1910, Lutherans felt even greater need to move toward greater internal unity. Not only have a number of unions of Lutheran churches occurred, but there has also been the formation of cooperative agencies, such as the National Lutheran Council.

In the early 1960's there were two further significant events of Lutheran unity. In 1961–1963 the American Lutheran Church (of German background) merged with several smaller churches of Danish and Norwegian antecedents to form the American Lutheran Church, and in 1962 the Lutheran Church in America brought together the former United Lutheran Church in America, the Augustana Lutheran Church (of Swedish background), and several smaller bodies of Finnish and Danish origins. Thus with the Lutheran Church—Missouri Synod, there were three major Lutheran churches of over two and a half million members each where once there had been more than twenty.

SOURCE: E. C. Fendt (ed.), *What Lutherans Are Thinking: A Symposium on Lutheran Faith and Life* (Columbus, 1947), pp. 372–379. Reprinted by permission of Augsburg Publishing House.

Before American Lutherans could speak unitedly to and with other churches, either in America or Europe, on the subject of ecumenicity, it was necessary that they learn to understand each other. Probably some of the reluctance of Lutherans to participate in unity movements was due to an unquiet mind concerning relationships within the household of the Lutheran faith. The inclusion of this paragraph in the General Council's Committee statement of 1913, wherein the Council gave its reply to the Faith and Order invitation, seems significant: "The General Council believes that it is its first duty, and the first duty of every particular Church, to seek to gain a unity in the true faith among those of its own household, that is, among all Lutherans throughout the world, and promises solemnly to set itself to the great work of bringing the many ecclesiastical divisions of Lutheranism throughout the world into fuller consciousness of the unity of the one and same faith in which they stand, and, on the basis of that same pure faith, into the unity of fellowship with each other."[1]

Two hundred and seventy-five years of Lutheran history in America lay back of that statement. In all those years there had never been a united Lutheranism, and the prospect in 1913 was not clear. The Swedish Lutherans on the Delaware had maintained themselves from 1638 to the days of Muhlenberg a century later. There had been some negotiations for a close cooperation between the Swedish and the German churches in Pennsylvania, Delaware, and New Jersey,[2] but to no avail, and the Swedish congregations were gradually absorbed by the Anglican Church. The German colonists organized the Ministerium of Pennsylvania (1748) and embarked on a program of expansion and inward development which affected all the subsequent synods in the East. Meanwhile great migrations of European Lutherans were colonizing the Mississippi Valley, but these colonies had little in common. Coming from diverse Lutheran countries in Europe, they knew little or nothing of other Lutherans than those in their homeland. There the Lutheran church had practically no intercourse with Lutherans in other countries. Bearing an isolationist tradition, these colonists proceeded to restrict still further the dimensions of their faith by cutting the ties which bound them to the larger Lutheranism of their homeland. Partly, this was due to sharp doctrinal differences with the parent church as in the case of the Missouri Synod (1847) and the Iowa Synod (1854). The Norwegian settlements perpetuated and intensified their different traditions in Eielsen's (1846) and the Norwegian Synod (1853); the Swedish congregations found most of their needs fulfilled in the Augustana Synod (1860), which during its first decade included a Norwegian group. The Danes, the Finns, even the Icelandic group, considered size no element in the concept of the church and followed the example of the more numerous European Lutheran bodies in creating their own autonomous synods. W. H. Greever[3] has tellingly contrasted

1. *Minutes*, Toledo, 1913, p. 227.
2. Acrelius, I. *A History of New Sweden*, trans. by W. M. Reynolds, Hist. Society of Penn., 1847, pp. 245f.
3. *Lutheran World Almanac*, 1934–1937, pp. 92–93.

the apparent purpose of Midwest Lutherans of the nineteenth century with the motto of Muhlenberg a century earlier. While the latter proclaimed as his motto, *Ecclesia plantanda est*, the unexpressed motto of the former groups seemed to be, "The church must be transplanted." The result was a garden with all the varieties of Europe plus indigenous types which developed under the conditions of the New World environment.

Yet something of the attractive force of Christian unity brought scattered parts of the church together in more or less enduring union. The first comprehensive organization of Lutherans in America took the name of "The General Synod" (1820). It was essentially a federation of autonomous synods and from the start was subject to withdrawals. But for the first time a vision appeared of a united Lutheranism in the New World. Theological dissension and suspicion of encroachments on congregational independence limited the effectiveness of the synod, but in the field of theological education, home missions and charities, permanent results were achieved. The revival of Lutheran self-consciousness reached American Lutheranism both directly from European movements and, indirectly, through the spirit and the purpose of the newer emigrants into the West. The ferment of a conservative, orthodox theology, combined with a spirit of independent Lutheranism over against unionistic movements in American Protestantism, finally split the General Synod. In 1867 the General Council became the spokesman of that large part of the Lutheran Church in America which was intent on conserving the verities of the sixteenth-century Reformation in the new American environment. It could not gain, however, the adherence of those Lutherans who saw in the Missouri Synod a bulwark against unionism, on the one hand, and the rise of a centrally organized church, on the other. These included some Norwegians, but were mainly German in origin, and in 1872 they founded the third general group of Lutherans with the designation of "Synodical Conference." This body has maintained itself up to the present. The General Synod and the General Council merged in 1917 with the Synod of the South which consisted of district synods in the South who withdrew during the Civil War from the General Synod to form the United Lutheran Church. Two thirds of American Lutheranism had thus found congenial relationships in these two organizations.

The greater part of the remaining third is at present seeking more effective unity in the American Lutheran Conference. The composition of this rather loose federation is interesting. The Norwegians in the Norwegian Synod had joined the Synodical Conference in 1872, but most of them withdrew in 1883, only to have their own ranks split in 1887 by the separation of the Anti-Missourian party. This party in 1890 joined with the Norwegian Augustana Synod and the Danish-Norwegian Conference (both organized 1870) to form the United Norwegian Lutheran Church of America. But the union did not include the Norwegian Synod nor the Hauge Synod, which had absorbed most of the Eielsen Synod; these remained independent until their merger in 1917 with the United Church, which now was renamed the Norwegian Lutheran Church of America.[4] But even this union was incomplete, for the Norwegian Free Church, which had withdrawn in 1896 from the United Church of 1890, declined to join the united church of 1917. But the Free Church was willing to accept membership along with the Norwegian Lutheran Church of America in the American Lutheran Conference in 1930.

A third element in this Conference is the Augustana Synod, which had belonged to the General Council between 1870 and 1917. The American Lutheran Church, a fourth member, was a consolidation of the former Ohio and Iowa Synods who had been unable to find congenial relationship either with the General Council or the Synodical Conference and merged with the Buffalo Synod in 1930 into one body. The fifth member is the United Danish Church, which has its name from a union in 1886 of former members of the Danish-Norwegian Conference and a party protesting against the doctrinal stand and practices of the Danish Lutheran Church (organized in 1872).

All of these bodies had developed within the century before the organization of the American Lutheran Conference in 1930. They represented the newer Lutheran immigration of the nineteenth century—Norwegian, Swedish, German, Danish—which had not been willing to join either with the older American Lutherans of the East nor the newer orthodoxy as developed and interpreted by the Missouri Synod. They were affected by, and they themselves affected the other great groups. In the Conference they found much in common though it is not at all clear that this position is more than a temporary and transitional one.

4. Since 1945 the Evangelical Lutheran Church in America.

This hasty review of the changing relationships of the many Lutheran groups in America suggests that, though history and geography may have isolated them in various ways, they have not been happy in isolation. Each in its own manner has tried to express the underlying conviction that a unity of faith calls for an embodiment of such unity. Illustrative of the general attitude are statements which are part of the records of the major organizations. The Ministerium of Pennsylvania in 1818 resolved that "in its judgment, it would be well if the different Evangelical Lutheran synods in the United States were to stand, in some way or other, in true union with one another."[5] Almost half a century later, in 1866, the representatives of the synods who gathered to organize the General Council agreed to this preamble:

> We are fully persuaded that with our communion scattered over a vast and ever-widening territory, with the ceaseless tide of immigration to our shores, with the diversity of surrounding usages and of religious life, with our various nationalities and tongues, our crying need of faithful ministers, our imperfect provision for any and all of the urgent wants of the Church, there is danger that the genuinely Lutheran elements may become gradually alienated, that misunderstandings may arise, that the narrow and local may overcome the broad and general, that the unity of the Spirit in the bond of peace may be lost, and that our Church, which alone in the history of Protestantism has maintained a genuine catholicity and, unity, should drift into the sectarianism and separatism which characterize and curse our land.[6]

Those who did not unite with the Council but after half a dozen years formed another general body, the Synodical Conference, felt they must justify their action. Dr. W. Sihler, at the organization meeting of the new body, admitted "frankly that we are perfectly satisfied with the doctrinal basis officially adopted by that body (the General Council) and could enter into affiliation with the Council on that basis." But he and the other founders of the Synodical Conference claimed that the Council was unwilling to discipline synods in its membership whose actions were not in conformity with the professions of the Council. Furthermore, the

5. Jacobs, H. E., *A History of the Evangelical Lutheran Church in the United States*, 2d ed., p. 357.
6. *Proceedings of the Convention Held by Representatives from Various Evangelical Lutheran Synods*, Reading, Pa.: 1866, p. 9.

Missouri Synod wanted no "open" questions but definite answers to questions on the church, the ministry, church government, the Antichrist.[7]

It was from the General Council and General Synod that forces came which made these organizations means to greater ends. The General Council had resulted from the defects of the General Synod. Yet the latter had made significant contributions to the character of American Lutheranism. "The General Synod," in the judgment of H. E. Jacobs, "was a protest against the socinianizing tendency in New York and the schemes of a union with the Reformed in Pennsylvania and with the Episcopalians in North Carolina. It stood for the independent existence of the Lutheran Church in America, and the clear and unequivocal confession of a positive faith. It failed, as its founders in the several synods had failed, in specifically determining the contents of this faith."[8]

A decade after the formation of the Council steps were taken to bring closer together the Council, the Synod, and the Synod of the South. The three bodies worked together on a common liturgy, a common hymnbook, in deaconess and mission work. "In 1911 the doctrinal differences between the three General Bodies were removed by constitutional amendment in the General Synod, and the greatest confessional barrier in the way of Lutheran unity between them was eliminated."[9] The approaching quadricentennial observance of the Reformation proved a powerful stimulus as well as an excellent opportunity for the merger, which, in fact, was achieved in 1917. The president of the General Council in the last presidential report of the Council estimated that "the steady influence of the General Council during a half century toward a true and sound Lutheran Confession and Praxis, as thus now finally expressed in the common faith of all the bodies intending to unity, is perhaps the greatest achievement of the General Council as a body."[10]

The resulting United Lutheran Church was in a position to

7. "The Organization of the Synodical Conference," A.W. Meyer, in Ebenezer, ed. by W. H. T. Dau, St. Louis: 1922, pp. 321–332.
8. Jacobs, p. 362.
9. Minutes of the First Convention of the United Lutheran Church in America, 1918, pp. 38–39.
10. Minutes of the General Council, 1917, p. 23.

affect greatly the Council, which in 1918 grew out of the National Lutheran Commission for Soldiers' and Sailors' Welfare. The first officers of the National Lutheran Council were from the United Lutheran Church and the Norwegian Lutheran Church of America, which had consummated its union half a year before the United Lutheran Church. The new Council was a common agency of the cooperating synods in dealing with social and secular problems, especially such as arose out of the war. It won the adherence of most of the Lutheran synods in America, the largest group not cooperating being the Synodical Conference. The National Lutheran Council, even though its activities are restricted, represents the most comprehensive union of Lutherans in America, bridging the gap that separates the synods of the United Lutheran Church from those in the American Lutheran Conference. . . .

29. A Jew Speaks to Christians

SPURRED BY the deepening social concerns of religious peoples of various backgrounds, encounters between Jews and Christians increased in the twentieth century. One of the pioneers in the new period of Jewish-Christian relations was a Reform rabbi, Stephen S. Wise (1874–1949), who in 1906 completed a term of service in Portland, Oregon, to become the spiritual leader of the Free Synagogue in New York. A forceful, eloquent, outgoing leader, Wise was a close friend of John Haynes Holmes, a Unitarian minister who was also a prominent spokesman for the social interpretation of religion. The story of their friendship has been told by Carl Hermann Voss, Rabbi and Minister: The Friendship of Stephen S. Wise and John Haynes Holmes (Cleveland, 1964). In his autobiography, Wise described his encounter with Christian leaders and congregations.

SOURCE: Challenging Years: The Autobiography of Stephen Wise (New York, 1949), pp. 280–288. Copyright 1949 by G. P. Putnam's Sons. Reprinted by permission.

It was in Oregon that, with much and wide practice, I learned a difficult lesson—namely, how to speak to Christian congregations with entire candor about their faith as well as about my faith and my people. I learned the meaning of the Dantean phrase, to flatter by truth speaking. I came to feel rather early in my preaching that I would be unworthy of the privilege of standing in Christian pulpits if I failed to tell the truth as I saw it about Christian and Jew.

I had to tell what, of course, I knew, that Christianity was the daughter and Israel the mother, irrespective of the later repudiation of mother by daughter. I felt that it was incumbent upon me to say that Christianity was under unlimited indebtedness to Judaism—owing to Judaism the Bible Old and New, patriarchs, judges, kings, prophets, priests, apostles, psalms, ethical religion, the Sabbath, and prayer individual and congregate. I always felt that upon me lay the holy duty of urging the establishment of such fellowship between Jew and Christian as would be worthy of both faiths. Often I saw fit to remind Christian congregations of the truth about Jesus, that he was above all a Jew in faith and life and practices alike. Whenever I felt there was need, I made it clear that the Christian attitude toward the Jew had through the centuries been a rejection of the Prayer on the Cross, "Forgive them, Father, for they know not what they do." Nothing, it seemed to me, could be more Christless than such unforgiveness.

It must be told with equal candor that I have rarely, if ever, come upon sharp dissent from the summons of one Jew to Christians to be equal to Christian penitence. Christian churches from end to end of the land have patiently and forbearingly, even gladly, heard the word of a Jew dealing with the highest and holiest concern of Christendom. From time to time I have had rather queer moments, none queerer than having a blessed old lady in a Christian church mildly protest, "Why do you say that the psalms are Jewish? Surely you know that the psalms are Christian and have always been sung in our Christian churches."

Because of such moments I have made it almost a rule to recite the Twenty-third, or the Nineteenth, or the One Hundred and Twenty-first Psalm, and to quote a phrase in its matchless Hebrew original of one or another of these psalms. I have found that Christians are ready, even eager, to hear the truth concerning Judeo-Christian relations and to listen reveringly to the psalms Jesus knew and loved and doubtless uttered in his worship.

Christian churches and their members made me feel that I must speak frankly and forthrightly lest they imagine I was repudiating Judaism and accepting Christianity in its place. Nothing could have been less true. On the other hand, I willed to correct a most grievous error that was common among the masses of Christendom in America, the idea that there was no basic relation between the Jews and Jesus other than that they had crucified him, as Christians would put it!

Jesus was a Jew, Hebrew of Hebrews. Whatever I believe with respect to the imputed miracle of his birth, his mother, Mary, was a Jewish woman. He was reared and taught as a Jew. He worshiped in the synagogue. He spoke no language save Hebrew, the harsher Hebrew of the Galilean country in which he grew up and of the synagogue in which he preached.

Jesus did not teach or wish to teach a new religion. His own word reads, "I come not to abrogate but to fulfill the Law." When he was asked which was the greatest commandment of the Lord, he replied in the words of the Torah, the Pentateuchal Scroll of the Law, still a major utterance of Jewish worship, "Thou shalt love the Lord thy God with all thy heart, with all thy soul and with all thy strength." This commandment is inscribed to this day upon the traditional doorpost of the Jewish home and in the phylacteries of the Jew. When he was asked about yet another great commandment of the Lord, he quoted once more from the Hebrew Bible, his and mine, "Thou shalt love thy neighbor as thyself." Thus taught and lived Jesus the Jew. In every courteous withal self-respecting way I tried to bring this home to the multitude of Christians who throughout the years have heard me with the attention worthy of the august theme.

One thing more I felt it my duty to say frankly at all times and under all circumstances to Christians. Time and again I dealt with the story of the crucifixion, saying that a people who heard Jesus gratefully one Sunday was not likely to slay him the following Friday, that, if some Jews had a part in his death, it should not be forgotten that power when threatened neither resigns nor yields. Moreover, it would be absurd to imagine that Judea, the little dependency of mighty Rome, possessed and exercised the power of slaying. Moreover I have felt it to be my sacred duty, in addressing Christian groups and committees, to remind them that even if it could be proven, as of course it cannot be, that Jews and only Jews were responsible for the crucifixion, those who called themselves his followers dare not overlook or ignore Jesus' last appeal on behalf of his persecutors.

I ventured to urge upon Christian bodies yet another truth that was not implicit in the relations between Jew and Christian, namely, that in stressing Christian doctrine of immortality, the life and teachings of Jesus the Jew were neglected, even minimized, in contrast with the maximum importance laid upon the death of Jesus. It seemed to me more urgent to dwell on the life and teachings rather than solely or chiefly on the death of Jesus.

Only once in nearly half a century of dealing with the relation of Jesus to Israel did a question arise and, when it arose, caused a very severe storm. Just before Christmas, 1925, I preached on Sunday morning at Carnegie Hall on "Jesus, the Jew." What I said that morning I had said before and said later, again and again. It was neither novel nor startling in any sense, save to such Jews and Christians as hold every barrier to be sacred. Simply and clearly I laid down the following, as I thought, undebatable theses:

1. Jesus was man, not God;
2. Jesus was a Jew, not a Christian;

3. Jews have not repudiated Jesus, the Jew;
4. Christians have, for the most part, not adopted and followed Jesus, the Jew.

The New York newspapers carried full reports of my address on Monday morning. Two incidents happened on the day of publication that made no end of trouble, not so much for me as for the United Palestine Appeal, the fund-raising agency of which I served as chairman. Monday afternoon, the President of the Orthodox rabbis' society of the country issued a blast against me and my heresy and proceeded to excommunicate me. The same day a denominational Christian Ministers Association met in Philadelphia and hailed me as brother. I know not which was more hurtful —the acceptance of me as brother and welcoming me into the Christian fold or the violent diatribe of a fellow rabbi.

The liberal rabbis of the country, for the most part, rallied to my support. One exception was an inveterate foe of Zionism; the other, an associate in the U.P.A., bade me refrain from sensational sermons about Jesus and Christianity and devote myself instead to the teachings of the Hebrew prophets, though he knew that no man in the rabbinate had sought more than the writer, not only to preach about the prophets, but to relate their teachings to the problems of our time.

The matter did not end here. An Orthodox religious group sought to displace me from the chairmanship of the United Palestine Appeal. Nothing could have been finer and more loyal than the attitude of virtually all the Zionist leaders, including that brilliant, withal occasionally circuitous, leader of the Zionist movement, Louis Lipsky.

In the midst of the excitement, a letter came to me from Nathan Straus, the grand old man of American Jewry, uniquely beloved both for his munificent philanthropies and for his warmth of heart. This letter had a profound, and to me very helpful, effect on the controversy, which was then at its height:

December 25, 1925

Dear Dr. Wise:

I saw with the greatest sorrow in this morning's newspapers that you have offered your resignation as chairman of the United Palestine Appeal. I wish, as a Jew and a Zionist, who have given a great part of my life and large sums of money to Palestine and to all Jewish and nonsectarian causes, to protest against your action. I know that the United Palestine Appeal will never accept your resignation and I know that they should not.

Suppose you did say something with which some Jews did not agree! What of it? Is all your life of service for Jews and for America to be ignored by those people who take a newspaper headline and are prepared to destroy you and are ready to sacrifice your usefulness in connection with our great work for Palestine? I can hardly believe the newspaper reports that a lot of Rabbis, in good standing, should condemn a man like you, with your record and your position, without giving you a chance to explain what you meant. They should have known that no word would ever come out of your mouth that would not have the effect of making Jews still stronger Jews and better Americans. And that, if you said anything at all about Christianity, it would only be in order to remind Christians, as you and I always do, that the first thing for them to do is to be just to Jews. In order to show you how deeply I feel in the matter, I authorize you, as chairman of the United Palestine Appeal, to announce that, in addition to having created a trust fund of five hundred thousand dollars ($500,000), the income of which is being and shall in perpetuity be used for welfare purposes among all the people of Palestine without regard to race or creed, I herewith set aside an additional sum of one hundred and fifty thousand dollars ($150,000) of which amount one hundred thousand dollars ($100,-000) shall be devoted to the early erection of the Nathan Straus Welfare and Relief Center of Palestine for all its needy people and for the housing of the administration offices of the Hadassah, and fifty thousand dollars ($50,000) to be devoted to the general purposes of the United Palestine Appeal under your leadership.

Faithfully yours,
[signed] Nathan Straus

There came the night, about a fortnight later, when, at a hotel, a special and prolonged meeting of the Administrative Committee of the Zionist Organization of America was held. Hours of discussion took place on my proposal that, in view of my "Jesus, the Jew" sermon, I withdraw from the chairmanship of the United Palestine Appeal. The vote was overwhelmingly in favor of my retention of the office. I was called to the hotel and informed of the decision. I was too moved to speak and limited myself to the utterance of two Hebrew words of the Book of Jonah. I did not even translate them; it was not necessary. I said only, "*Ivri Anochi,*" "I am a Hebrew." The incident was ended, and kindling enthusiasm followed throughout the campaign, which yielded the largest amount that had been collected up to that time, more than five million dollars.

In 1909 I proposed to my dear friends John Haynes Holmes of the Unitarian Church and Frank Oliver Hall of the Universalist Church that we together arrange a series of union services, which services, despite grave and sometimes violent opposition, were held. The purpose of these union services was not alone to show that Jew and non-Jew could meet from time to time in the spirit of common worship of the universal Father. It was designed to do more than that—to bring about on the part of the three congregations represented in the union service united or common action on behalf of those social ideals to which every one of us was separately committed, and for the furtherance of which we together set out to win the enthusiasm of our several congregations. In other words, we did not worship together solely or even chiefly for the sake of common worship, but rather that in the spirit of such common worship we might be fused together in the prosecution of a common purpose. That purpose was service to and furtherance of those high causes that all of us alike felt, and feel, were the central and essential things in our common religious aspirations.

When we arranged for our common service, each of us was mindful of the necessities of the case, each of us was meticulously scrupulous to avoid giving offense to the congregations of the others. We were of one mind and of one spirit in being utterly vigilant that no word be uttered, no prayer be offered up, no hymn be chanted that did not include within itself the spirit of the three congregations worshiping together. I must confess that I have been in attendance at and participant in other union services when, as it seemed to me, ministers, believed to be and believing themselves to be liberal, have failed to choose out of their rich hymnody such chants as it would be possible for Jews to sing without confusion or embarrassment, have used stereotyped formulae with respect to the triune God in invoking the benediction, or in offering petition in the presence of congregations made up largely or partly of Jews.

But the more important circumstance to be borne in mind with reference to the union services of more than three decades ago is that when we worshiped together none of us did or would abate one jot or title of our respective positions, of our several loyalties. Into our common worship, held for a number of years, chiefly in the interest of our common social ideals, there entered only those elements to which all of us together might without reluctance assent. We knew, as we worshiped together, that we would leave the place of our common worship and return to our various church bodies, each of us not less but more deeply and ardently loyal to his own heritage, because for an hour we had found it possible to link our hands in common worship. Each of us had gathered the resolution to move his people to make earnestly rather than laggardly, passionately rather than inertly, for those great social ends of life that, after all, are the final and supreme test of the verity of religious profession and the sincerity of religious practice.

If Jews and Christians are to worship together from time to time, we who are Jews can enter into the spirit of Christian worship, and Christians for a time can enter into the spirit of Jewish worship. But let me make it clear that I hold it would be an incalculable loss to the spiritual life of man if we Jews were to abandon, assuming such abandonment to be possible, our own particular type and form of worship. For that worship rests upon and has grown out of two thousand years and more of tradition, and it is compact of historical associations, of ancient traditions, of precious memories. It would be a most lamentable impoverishment of our common spiritual life if either the simplicity of the liberal Christian service, such as that which obtains in the Community Church, were to be given up, or the beauties and splendors of the traditional Jewish liturgy were to be abandoned.

Thus Christians worshiping with Jews might find the Shema, the affirmation of the divine unity, quaint and interesting, and might even hold the Hebrew Kaddish or memorial prayer, to be beautiful and moving, but to the Jew, the Shema and the Kaddish are infinitely more. When I speak the words of the Shema, I do far more than recite the Jewish creed. There comes before me, as in a vision, the spectacle of Israel suffering, of Israel triumphant. The storied martyrdom of Israel rises before me as in a dream, my people's soul lives in me again, and I live again the memories of my people as I utter those deathless words of the Jew's spiritual and eternal affirmation of God's unity. For I behold a mighty procession of priests and prophets and seers and apostles and martyrs marching on and on, pilgrims of the invisible, sustained by that unfaltering trust which moved the Jew throughout the ages to live by and for the truth of the Divine unity.

I can join in the Pater Noster or the Lord's Prayer, but the recital thereof stirs no memories in me. As I hear it or recite it, I frankly confess that I seek to reconstruct it, as it may be reconstructed, into that Hebrew tongue whence the form and spirit of it were in part derived by him who first uttered it. As I join in the Lord's Prayer, I think always and inevitably of its Hebrew original, and I think back to the time when Jesus first learned it from his Jewish mother, for in the century associated with Jesus brief prayers containing the spiritual yearnings of the people had, under certain circumstances, been prescribed for Jews. But in truth it is almost impossible for me to put into the Lord's Prayer, however rich I find it, all that it means to the devout Christian to whom it bears memories and traditions as does the Shema to me.

No one can be more bent than I am upon achieving perfect understanding and fellowship between Jew and Christian. But if in order to have the understanding of Christendom I must cease to be a Jew, or I must do that which will make for the minimizing of my Jewishness, then I must do without such understanding—as my fathers have had to do without it for hundreds of years, yea for more than a millennium. I crave the understanding and the reverence of the Christian world, but for myself as a Jew and not for me as a chameleon. I covet understanding of the Jew, not seeking to utter in accents that are not his own the Pater Noster but affirming simply and earnestly and everlastingly as did the holy mothers and glorious fathers of Israel—Hear, oh Israel, the Eternal is our God, the Eternal is one.

30. Social Idealism and Interfaith Cooperation

As THE social interpretation of religion gained in importance among many religious groups in America despite its controversial nature, it provided avenues for interfaith cooperation. In 1929 the National Conference of Christians and Jews was founded. It became active on national and local levels in striving to overcome prejudice and promoting the national good. Under its auspices was issued in the early years of World War II a booklet which called attention to some remarkable parallelisms in the professed social ideas of Catholics, Protestants, and Jews. The ferment of the social gospel and social action movements within the major religious traditions is revealed in these selections.

SOURCE: Benson Y. Landis (ed.), *Religion and the Good Society: An Introduction to the Social Teachings of Judaism, Catholicism and Protestantism* (New York, [1942]), pp. 39–41, 43–50, 52–54, 59–61.

A Comparison of Social Ideals

This section contains an arrangement of many social teachings of the religious bodies of the United States for the purpose of indicating the extent of the harmony that obtains. These quotations reveal "parallelisms" in the declared ideals of Judaism and Christianity. They demonstrate that on confronting specific social situations, the religious leaders are able frequently to come to the same judgments and conclusions. No claim of complete agreement is here made, but a careful reading of the words of Catholics, Protestants and Jews that follow will easily reveal a considerable area of common thought and social values. It is also recognized, of course, that there are other social issues on which the religious bodies disagree.

THE BASIS OF THE SOCIAL ORDER

Archbishops and Bishops of the Administrative Board of the National Catholic Welfare Conference: "Our economic life . . . must be reorganized not on the disintegrating principles of individualism but on the constructive principle of social and moral unity among the members of human society. In conformity with Christian principles, economic power must be subordinated to human welfare, both individual and social; social incoherence and class conflict must be replaced by corporate unity and organic function; ruthless competition must give way to just and reasonable state regulations; sordid selfishness must be superseded by justice and charity. Then only can there be a true and rational social order; then only can we eliminate the twin evils of insufficiency and insecurity and establish the divine plan of a brotherhood of man under the fatherhood of God." (1940)

Federal Council of the Churches of Christ in America: "Practical application of the Christian principle of social well-being to the acquisition and use of wealth, subordination of speculation and the profit motive to the creative and cooperative spirit." (1932)

General Conference, Methodist Episcopal Church: "We repudiate the entire concept of class war. The fact that class consciousness exists is a challenge to remove it, not to accentuate it. Class consciousness has no place in the democratic community; the very idea of brotherhood assumes cooperation in the interests of all rather than war in the interests of a class. We declare ourselves for democracy." (1936)

Pope Leo XIII in the Encyclical on the Condition of Labor: "The great mistake that is made in the matter now under consideration is to possess oneself of the idea that class is naturally hostile to class; that rich and poor are intended by nature to live at war with one another. So irrational and so false is this view that the exact contrary is the truth. Just as the symmetry of the human body is the result of the disposition of the members of the body, so in a state it is ordained by nature that these two classes should exist in harmony and agreement and should, as it were, fit into one another so as to maintain the equilibrium of the body politic." (1891)

Central Conference of American Rabbis:[1] "The duty of social-mindedness. It is the tragic record of humankind that many of those who find comfort in the existing order often fail to apply themselves seriously to the consideration of the ills that plague society. It is part of the great social message of the prophets of our faith that salvation can be achieved only through the salvation of society as a whole . . . Instead of questioning God's goodness because of the evils in individual and communal life, we should

---

1. The organization of Rabbis in Reform Judaism.

address our God-given intelligence to the extermination of those circumstances which allow slums, vice, feeble-mindedness, poverty, degeneracy and the like to continue, with only palliative efforts for their improvement." (1928) . . .

SOCIAL RESPONSIBILITY OF OWNERSHIP

National Council of Congregational Churches of the United States: "Translating the ideal of Jesus into industry and economic relationships means: A frank abandonment of all efforts to secure something for nothing, and recognition that all ownership is a social trust involving Christian administration for the good of all and that the unlimited exercise of the right of private ownership is socially undesirable." (1925)

Rabbinical Assembly of America:[2] "When Judaism teaches the divine creation of the world, it points explicitly and implicitly to the attitude that God intended the world's resources to be used in the interest of all mankind. This attitude is affirmed again and again throughout Jewish tradition. The natural resources of the world are a divine gift to mankind. Each generation inherits vast stores of wealth which all society has slowly accumulated. No single individual contributes to the sum of the world's goods more than an infinitesimal share. From all these considerations it follows that the wealth of the world should be used socially. Nor has any individual the right to own without social responsibility what all have created and what all must use. Such concentration of wealth is an abuse of the right to private property. It is the equivalent of an unjustifiable expropriation of the great masses of mankind." (1934)

The Archbishops and Bishops of the Administrative Board of the National Catholic Welfare Conference: "Our present economic order rests upon the sanctity of private property. Private property, however, is not well distributed at present among the members of human society. . . . If the majority of our citizens possess insufficient private property to be independent of a wage income for even a short period of time, then there is grave danger to the entire social fabric. Social stability rests upon this basis of individual ownership of property. There should be more of it and

2. The organization of Rabbis in Conservative Judaism.

not less of it, if our existing economic system is to remain secure."
(1940)

The General Conference, The Methodist Church: "We stand
for the principle of the acquisition of property by Christian processes, and believe in stressing the principle of stewardship in its use;
in the practical application of the Christian principle of social well-
being to the acquisition and use of wealth and the subordination of
the profit motive to the creative and cooperative spirit." (1940)

Pope Pius XI in Reconstructing the Social Order: "The right to
own private property has been given to man by nature or rather by
the Creator Himself, not only in order that individuals may be able
to provide for their own needs and those of their families, but also
that by means of it, the goods which the Creator has destined for
the human race may truly serve this purpose.

"It follows from the two-fold character of ownership, which we
have termed individual and social, that men must take into account in this matter not only their own advantage but also the
common good." (1931) . . .

THE RIGHT OF ORGANIZATION

Central Conference of American Rabbis: "The same rights of
organization which rest with employers rest also with those whom
they employ. Modern life has permitted wealth to consolidate
itself through organization into corporations. Trade organizations
for mutual benefit within specific industries are quite common
among employers. Workers have the same inalienable right to
organize according to their own plan for their common good and to
bargain collectively with their employers through such honorable
means as they may choose." (1928)

*National Council of the Congregational Churches of the United
States:* "Translating the ideal of Jesus into industry and economic
relationships means: The right of labor to organize with representatives of its own choosing and, where able, to share in the
management of industrial relations." (1925)

Central Conference of American Rabbis: "The Conference
recognizes the right of labor to organize and to bargain collectively
through representatives of its own choosing as an instrument by
which to secure its rights at the hands of employers. It further
recognizes the right of labor to share more equitably in determining

the conditions of labor as well as in the reward. At the same time the Conference declares it to be the obligation of labor to perform faithfully and energetically the work for which it is justly paid, and that, as hours are reduced and wages increased in keeping with the modern standards of life and happiness, labor should not relax but intensify its efforts both as a return to the employer and out of regard for the public welfare." (1920)

Rabbinical Assembly of America: "We believe that the denial of the right of workers to organize and form group associations so that they may treat as economic equals with their employers is tantamount to a curtailment of human freedom. For that reason we favor the unionization of all who labor. We demand legislation to protect labor in its right to bargain collectively with its employers through representatives of its own choice without any pressure or influence to be exerted by the employers on the organization of the workmen for such purposes or on the choice of their representatives." (1934)

Pope Pius XII, in a letter to the Bishops of the United States: "Since association is one of man's natural requirements and since it is legitimate to promote by common effort decent livelihood, it is not possible without injustice to deny or limit either to the producer or the laboring and farming classes the free faculty of uniting in associations by means of which they may defend their proper rights and secure the betterment of the goods of soul and body, as well as the honest comforts of life." (1939)

Pope Pius XI, in Reconstructing the Social Order: "Just as citizens of the same municipality are wont to form associations with diverse aims, which various individuals are free to join or not, those who are engaged in the same trade or occupation will form free associations among themselves for purposes connected with their occupations." (1931)

The Archbishops and Bishops of the Administrative Board of the National Catholic Welfare Conference: "Labor can have no effective voice so long as it is unorganized. To protect its right, it must be free to bargain collectively through its own chosen representatives." (1940)

The Federal Council of the Churches of Christ in America: "RESOLVED that the Federal Council record its conviction that not only has labor a right to organize, but also that it is socially desirable that it do so because of the need of collective action in the maintenance of standards." (1940)

The Federal Council of the Churches of Christ in America: "The Churches should stand for: The right of employees and employers alike to organize for collective bargaining and social action; protection of both in the exercise of this right; the obligation of both to work for the public good. . . ." (1932)

General Conference of the Methodist Episcopal Church: "The immediate application in every industry of the principle of collective bargaining is not only essential to the protection of the modern industrial worker, but it is the first step toward that cooperative control of both the process and the proceeds of industry which will be the ultimate expression of Christianity in industrial relationships." (1912)

Social Service Commission of the Northern Baptist Convention: "Individual workmen cannot hope to bargain on equal terms with a corporation; so collective bargaining becomes necessary in order that industry may become stabilized." (1921)

General Convention, Protestant Episcopal Church: "The right of employees to organize and to bargain collectively is necessary to maintain an economic balance between labor and capital; but the same principle which should compel the employer to respect this right should also constrain the organized employees to respect the liberty of their unorganized—or otherwise organized—fellow-workers." (1934)

General Convention, Protestant Episcopal Church: "Labor has the right equally with capital to organize effectively, and corresponding responsibility for the exercise of the power so attained in accordance with the moral law. Negotiations through collective bargaining must take the place of strikes." (1922)

CONCILIATION, MEDIATION, ARBITRATION

National Council of Congregational Churches of the United States: "Translating the ideal of Jesus into industry and economic relationships means: Adequate provision for impartial investigation and publicity, conciliation and arbitration in industrial disputes." (1925)

Central Conference of American Rabbis: "In conformity with the principle of the welfare of society as fundamental, we record our adherence to the principle of the arbitration of industrial disputes rather than resort to open conflict. In any break in industrial relations the moral responsibility for the evils that ensue rests with that group which refuses to enter into the orderly processes of arbitration and mediation." (1928)

General Assembly of the Presbyterian Church in the U.S.A.: "The employment of the methods of investigation, conference, conciliation and arbitration in all industrial disputes." (1910)

Pastoral Letter of the American Hierarchy: "A dispute that cannot be adjusted by direct negotiation between the parties concerned should always be submitted to arbitration." (1919)

Minimum and Living Wage

Pope Pius XI, in the Encyclical Letter, "Quadregesimo Anno": "In the first place the wage paid to the workingman must be sufficient for the support of himself and his family. . . . Labor, indeed, . . . is not a mere chattel, since the human dignity of the workingman must be recognized in it, and consequently it can not be bought and sold like any piece of merchandise. . . ." (1931)

National Council of Congregational Churches of the United States: "Translating the ideal of Jesus into industry and economic relationships means: That the first charge upon industry should be a minimum comfort wage and that all labor should give an honest day's work for an honest day's pay." (1925)

Central Conference of American Rabbis: "In the moral stewardship of the earth, society must guarantee each of its members the chance to labor and to earn a living wage. Such a wage must be considered the first charge upon any industry. Those industries which do not pay their workers a living wage or which try to establish themselves economically by beating down the standards of living of their employes cannot be tolerated by any just social order. The definition of a living wage includes more than the immediate needs of the worker and his family on a generally accepted standard. It implies also sufficient to enable him to make full provision against sickness and old age." (1928)

The Archbishops and Bishops of the Administrative Board of the National Catholic Welfare Conference: "Industry, therefore, should provide not merely a living wage for the moment but also a saving wage for the future against sickness, old age, death and unemployment. Individual industries alone, however, cannot in each single case achieve this objective without invoking the principle of social insurance. Some form of government subsidy granted by the entire citizenship through legislative provision seems to be a necessary part of such a program." (1940)

The Federal Council of the Churches of Christ in America: "The right of all to the opportunity for self-maintenance; a wider and fairer distribution of wealth; a living wage, as a minimum, and above this a just share for the worker in the product of industry and agriculture." (1932)

Catholic Bishops' Program of Reconstruction: "The employer has a right to get a reasonable living out of his business, but he has no right to interest on his investment until his employees have obtained at least living wages. This is the human and Christian, in contrast to the purely commercial and pagan, ethics of industry." (1919) . . .

ECONOMIC DEMOCRACY

Central Conference of American Rabbis: "In the production and distribution of the material goods of life, the dictatorship of any class, capital or labor, employer or employe, is alike autocracy. The solution of the ills which beset our social order are to be found not in any class conscious struggle but in the triumph of sound humanitarian principles which regard mankind as ONE." (1928)

Rabbinical Assembly of America: "We hold that only a cooperative economy, only one which has for its objective the enrichment of all rather than profit for a few—only such an economy can be moral, can elevate man and can function successfully." (1934)

The Archbishops and Bishops of the Administrative Board of the National Catholic Welfare Conference: "The true remedy will be found, according to the mind of Pope Pius XI, in accomplishing two reforms in our social order. In the first place there must be reestablished some form of guild or vocational groups which will bind men together in society according to their respective occupations, thus creating a moral unity. Secondly, there must be a reform of morals and a profound renewal of the Christian spirit which must precede the social reconstruction." (1940)

Pope Pius XI Encyclical on "Reconstructing the Social Order": "An honest discussion of differences based upon the desire of social justice . . . can be and must be an approach towards the mutual cooperation of vocational groups. . . .

"Nature induces those who practice the same trade or profession, economic or otherwise, (to) combine into vocational groups. . . .

"In these associations . . . the common interest . . . of the whole (vocational) group must predominate; and among these the most important is the directing of the activities of the group (industry or profession) to the common good (of society). . . .

"The aim of social legislation (i.e., social-governmental policy) must, therefore, be the reestablishment of vocational groups (i.e., whole industries and professions organized); the government's function thereafter is that of 'directing, watching, stimulating and restraining as circumstances suggest or necessity demands.'"

"Let employers and employed join in their plans and efforts to overcome all difficulties and obstacles and let them be aided . . . by the wise measures of public authority." (1931)

The Federal Council of the Churches of Christ in America: "Industrial democracy is a goal comparable to that of political democracy. Both are relative terms. There is more than one way of making progress toward their realization. In one stage of development, cooperation through collective agreements between the representatives of management and of workers, counseled by technical experts, may be the most advantageous. Even in this elementary form of industrial relations, the right of workers to organize and to be represented by counsel or agents of their own free choice must be recognized as fundamental. In another stage, participation of workers in management may be possible and desirable; in another, workers might provide their own capital and assume full responsibility; in still another, the government might assume and exercise the powers of ownership, control, and management for the common good." (1932) . . .

INTERNATIONAL ECONOMIC COOPERATION

The Committees on Ethics and Economics, the Catholic Association for International Peace: "A full social organization of the economic and social organism, which is a world organism, and a supplementary and supervisory international governmental order, must somehow come into existence if two things are to be done: Make the international interdependence itself efficient in producing all the goods that the changing variety of the world's resources, equipment and technique can give; distribute these goods so that the good of all universally will be obtained. Social justice demands both. And the emphasis lies upon a social organization that will include every human element within the thing organized so that all will share in determining production, prices and distribution of the income." (1934)

National Council of Congregational Churches of the United States: "Translating the ideal of Jesus into international relations means: The removal of every unjust barrier of trade, color, creed and race and the practice of equal justice for all nations.

"The administration of the property and privileges within each country so that they will be of the greatest benefit not only to that nation but to all the world. . . .

Racism

The Ecumenical Conference on Church, Community and State, Oxford: "The Christians see distinctions of race as part of God's purpose to enrich mankind with a diversity of gifts. Against racial pride or race antagonism the Church must set its face implacably as rebellion against God. Especially, in its own life and worship there can be no place for barriers because of race or color. Similarly the Christian accepts national communities as part of God's purpose to enrich and diversify human life. Every man is called of God to serve his fellows in the community to which he belongs. But national egotism tending to the suppression of other nationalities or of minorities is, no less than individual egotism, a sin against the Creator of all peoples and races. The deification of nation, race or class, or of political or cultural ideas, is idolatry, and can only lead to increasing division and disaster.

"It is a first responsibility of the Church to demonstrate within its own fellowship the reality of community as God intends it. It is commissioned to call all men into the Church, into a divine society that transcends all national and racial limitations and divisions. In the services of worship, in its more informal fellowship, in its organization, and in the hospitality of the Christian home, there can be no place for exclusion, or segregation because of race or color. 'There is neither Jew nor Greek, bond nor free, for ye are all one in Christ.' To allow the Church's lines of action to be determined by racial discrimination denies the Gospel whose proclamation is its task and commission." (1937)

Pope Pius XI: "Catholic life means activity compounded of charity, of virtue and of God's law, which, permeating such life, makes it the life of God. There is no other way of thinking in the Catholic sense, and such a way of thinking is neither racist nor nationalist nor separatist. . . . We do not wish to separate anything in the human family. We regard racism and exaggerated nationalism as barriers raised between man and man, between people and people, between nation and nation. . . ." (From an address delivered in 1938)

The Federal Council of the Churches of Christ in America: "The assumption of inherent racial superiority by dominant groups around the world is neither supported by science nor justified by ethics. The effort to adjust race relations upon that basis and by the use of force is a denial of the Christian principles of the inherent superiority of ethical values and the supreme worth of personality. As it applies to the relations of white and Negro people in America it is a philosophy that leads only to suffering and despair.

"Christians must seek as never before to remove suspicions, fears, misunderstandings, and prejudices between racial groups and to foster mutual understanding, tolerance, respect for personality, and the spirit of cooperation. We must replace attitudes and customs based upon past fears and hatreds by those based upon mutual interest and present services." (1924)

31. Cooperation among Conservatives

In MOST forms of religion in America, the social and ecumenical spirit was associated with broadly liberal views. Within the Protestant denominiations, the fundamentalists of the 1920's and 1930's and the neo-fundamentalists or "conservative evangelicals" of the 1950's and 1960's were usually suspicious of social and ecumenical Christian movements as embodied in Federal, National, and World Councils of Churches. Recognizing the need for cooperative agencies of their own, some of the smaller, conservative denominations, with the support of like-minded leaders from major denominations, organized the National Association of Evangelicals in 1942. At the founding meeting, William Ward Ayer, pastor of the Calvary Baptist Church of New York, addressed the conference on the theme "Evangelical Christianity Endangered by Its Fragmentized Condition." Seeking to overcome some of the problems of a pluralized Protestantism through voluntary association rather than through organizational unity, he was sharply critical of the Federal Council of Churches as being related to modernism and Marxism. On the N.A.E. see James DeForest Murch, Cooperation without Compromise: A History of the National Association of Evangelicals (Grand Rapids, 1956).

SOURCE: Evangelical Action: A Report of the Organization of the National Association of Evangelicals for United Action (Boston, 1942), pp. 41–46.

Perilous times confront the Christian Church. Difficulties loom in the path ahead. Evangelical religion has suffered much in totalitarian countries, and it takes no great prophetic vision to see that in our own nation tendencies are developing which in due time will work considerable hardship upon unorganized Christianity.

We have great faith in our God's ability to deliver and lead His people, and it implies no lack of trust in God to clearly note the exigencies of the hour. It is my responsibility to awaken your minds to the dangers inherent in evangelical Protestantism's divided and fragmentized condition.

I. Our Fragmentized Condition Is Dangerous to a Genuine Evangelical Testimony to the World

Organizational unity is neither desirable nor necessary. Unanimity in religious things is possible only in church totalitarianism. The boast of evangelical Christianity is its liberty of thought, freedom of expression, and the right to differ, especially on nonessentials. But, if there cannot be unanimity, there must be unity, even in division. We must find a common meeting place for common purposes. There must be a hub in which the spokes of our several organizations can meet in order to make for firmness of purpose and service, and for solidarity in testimony.

There is certainly a common doctrinal ground upon which we all stand, and we occupy common spheres of activity, giving testimony to a glorious Christ in a lost world.

II. There Are Dangers to Our Organizational Existence because of Modern Attitudes of Government

Ours is a day of regimentation. Everyone is being counted; everyone labeled; everybody signed up. Soon everybody will be classified. As America advances further into some form of "statism," let us not be deceived into believing that religion will escape. Governmental regimentation and classification in religion has ever been deadly to its free expression and growth. It has always tended to make the Church the inferior handmaiden of the state. It has circumscribed testimony, strangled evangelistic effort, and has set the religious life of nations into such rigid forms as to hinder its mobility.

Increasingly our government is demanding official representation for all national organizations and groups. Some have felt that we are not far from having a Minister of Religion in the President's cabinet. Our government is becoming increasingly paternalistic and feels that it should direct the activities of all phases of our national life. It is coming to recognize only three great divisions in religion —Catholic, Jew, Protestant. It demands that there shall be official representatives of these three groups to function with government in its program. The Federal Council of the Churches of Christ in America steps forth and claims to be the official representative of all Protestant churches. The government, therefore, gladly does business with the Federal Council as representing Protestantism.

However, the Federal Council, though well organized, strong and competent in certain fields of religious activity, does not represent the great body of evangelical Christians in faith and doctrine. It claims to be the spokesman of twenty-two national churches, which is only forty percent of the total available. We feel sure that in doctrine and in many other matters it does not represent more than ten percent of this forty percent of the total denominational group. I would not deny the Federal Council its proper existence, but I feel that it does not represent me in many of its programs and pronouncements.

In the field of radio, the Federal Council of Churches and affiliated liberals control the free radio time assigned to Protestants upon two of the great networks, and is endeavoring to control the religious time upon local stations. Almost without exception they sponsor non-Gospel programs on the time allotted to them. There is not an outstanding evangelical speaker broadcasting under the direction of the Federal Council who, without fear or favor, preaches Christ and Him crucified. In a recent conference on radio broadcasting, held under the auspices of the Ohio State University, it was recommended that religious programs should be addressed to a cross-section of the public, to Protestants, Catholics, Jews, and nonbelievers, and not to members of any one faith. It was recommended that religious programs should not appeal for contributions, either directly or indirectly, for the support of the radio program itself, nor should it charge for sermons, pamphlets, or religious objects distributed through religious programs to be used by the sponsor as a means of raising funds.

Now there is some virtue in these attitudes, but the result of the execution of such a program will be the complete elimination of Protestant evangelical broadcasting. Under the present set-up, free time is given to the liberals alone. Gospel broadcasters must pay for their time. Access to free time on the radio chains is not possible, and there is a strong effort being made to hinder us from buying time to preach the Gospel.

Unfortunately, considerable radio racketeering is indulged in by evangelical preachers. They have raised large sums of money by means of radio broadcasts, handled it loosely, and given no accounting to anyone in financial matters. These men in their selfishness and carelessness are jeopardizing the whole evangelical radio program. The government is "catching up" with them and, I suspect, will not long permit them to operate and profit personally through radio broadcasts.

We should have in America a strong organization of evangelical broadcasters which will provide a "front" to deal with the government and properly present the fundamental broadcasters' case, in times of emergency. This organization will furnish also a clearing house for Gospel broadcasts and eliminate racketeers who are injuring all of us. Some of our so-called fundamentalists have gone to Washington, claiming that they officially represented fundamentalism, and have demanded certain privileges. I have been told upon good authority that these men have made the Federal Communications Commission angry, and they have said that they will not recognize factionism. However, they will recognize and must recognize accredited authority. We must awaken to the fact that we are rapidly approaching some form of totalitarianism in America and that rugged individualism in all forms and all places, at least for the duration, is out. We must surrender some of our independence for a solid interdependence and, trusting in God, we must stand against growing paganism in our land.

All dissociated groups are in danger. Politicians are careful, however, not to antagonize strongly united groups.

III. There Are Dangers to Our Country and to the Kingdom of God in Our Unrelated Divisions

In evangelism lies the hope of a godly America. We cannot keep our liberties without godliness.

> Ill fares the land to hastening ills a prey,
> Where wealth accumulates, and men decay.

Modernism destroys foundations and provides a culture for the growth of the germs of all forms of evil. It destroys faith in the Bible, in Christ, in righteousness, in revivalism, and has given us the God-forgetting paganistic civilization which is so disastrous to every good thing in our land. Today, this same modernism would silence every voice raised in behalf of Christian patriotism, for many modernists have a greater interest in the outworking of some form of Marxism than in the salvation that comes through our Lord and Savior, Jesus Christ. The inroads of wild socialistic theories through the power of organized minorities in government are creating a cancerous condition in America. Not only is there surreptitious entrenching of radicals in high places in our governmental life, but a tendency is manifest even on the part of high officials to smear any who call attention to these cancerous adhesions to our body politic.

It is not boasting to declare that evangelical Christianity has the America of our fathers to save. While our army and navy fight the enemy without, we have the enemy at home to battle, and he is in some ways more dangerous than the enemy abroad. We unhesitatingly declare that evangelicals have the "keys of the kingdom." Millions of evangelical Christians, if they had a common voice and a common meeting place, would exercise under God an influence that would save American democracy.

The old slogan, "United we stand; divided we fall," is certainly applicable to the dangers of the fragmentized condition of evangelical Christianity in America.

32. The Spread of the Ecumenical Spirit

IN THE 1950's the burgeoning ecumenical movement, which drew strength from currents of theological renewal that stressed the primacy of faith and the centrality of the Bible, led many to rejoice in the growing sense of Christian unity. Some hoped that the ecumenical spirit would soon overcome some of the worst features of divided Christianity. One of the clearest statements of this perspective was offered by H. Richard Niebuhr (1894–1962), professor of Christian ethics at Yale. As a contribution to an overall study of theological education, he wrote a preliminary volume in which the following passage appeared. As a realist, he was aware how deep-rooted the fragmentation of the Christian movement was, yet he believed that the ecumenical movement was overcoming its worst effects. The passage was widely quoted when it appeared, though by the stormy 1960's new controversies and shifting theological moods made it seem overoptimistic.

SOURCE: H. Richard Niebuhr, in collaboration with Daniel Day Williams and James M. Gustafson, *The Purpose of the Church and Its Ministry* (New York, 1956), pp. 16–17, 23–27. Copyright © 1956 by Harper & Row, Publishers, Inc. Reprinted by permission.

Thus implicitly and explicitly the denominations in their concern for the education of ministers, and the schools entrusted with the task, make it evident that they think of themselves increasingly as branches or members of a single community, as orders and institutions with special duties or assignments to be carried out in partnership with other branches of one society. The idea of *Una Sancta*, of One Holy Church, is very pervasive despite relatively rare expression. There are exceptions; denominations and even more frequently small parties in them, contend for the sole validity of a particular form of creed, organization or liturgy. Rivalries and contentions also exist. Sometimes these are reminiscent of the tensions to be found in the relations of states and provinces to nation as a whole, sometimes to the more acerbic dissensions among the branches of the armed forces, all equally pledged to the defense of the country; sometimes they seem very similar to the tensions found among Roman Catholic religious orders; sometimes they seem like economic competition. In the permissive atmosphere of freedom apparently wild and individualistic doctrines flourish; new founders and new religions with new schools appear; false or true prophets rise in protest against established and bureaucratized organizations of religious life; zealous groups maintain that all others are out of step except their select company. But to the sympathetic observer the increasing unity of American Protestantism is more striking than its apparent diversity. He notes that the primary context of Protestant theological education in the United States and Canada is the Christian community in its wholeness. The contention for this orientation of thought and life continues indeed to go on in many a school and poses for it its deepest problems; but the movement toward participation in the universal Church is the dominant one. . . .

The American and Canadian Church scene that we have sketched indicates how much institution and community belong together, yet how distinct they are. In part the realization of the Church community in the New World waits on the development of institutions able to give it form and wholeness; in part the institutionalization in denominations expresses the variety and unity characteristic of the community on this part of the planet.

To describe the Church as a community of memory and hope, sharing in the common memory not only of Jesus Christ but also of the mighty deeds of God known by Israel, expecting the coming into full view of the kingdom on earth and/or in heaven; to describe it further as the community of worship, united by its direction toward one God, who is Father, Son and Holy Spirit yet worshiped more as Father or as Son or as Holy Spirit in this or that part of the community; to describe it as a community of thought in which debate and conflict can take place because there is a fundamental frame of agreement and because there are common issues of great import—to do all this and the much more that needs to be done would be to essay the work of a large part of theology. It must be sufficient here to note that the schools which serve *in* the Church and serve the Church cannot abstract community from institution nor institution from community; nor can any churchman. One or the other of these polar characteristics of the social reality may be emphasized, but it cannot be defined without some reference to the other pole or served without some concern for its counterpart.

We must deal more briefly with certain other polarities in the

Church's existence. Among these are the complementary yet anti-thetical characteristics of unity and plurality, of locality and universality, of protestant and catholic. The Church is one, yet also many. It is a pluralism moving toward unity and a unity diversifying and specifying itself. It is, in the inescapable New Testament figure, a body with many members none of which is the whole in miniature but in each of which the whole is symbolized. Every national church, every denomination, every local church, every temporal church order, can call itself Church by virtue of its participation in the whole; yet every one is only a member needing all the others in order to be truly itself and in order to participate in the whole. Without the members there is no body; without the body no members. Schools cannot prepare men to work simply in the whole Church but must equip them for particular service; yet they cannot do so unless they keep them mindful of the whole and loyal to it.

The Church is local and it is universal. Where two or three are gathered in the name of Christ there he is present, but all to which he points and all that he incarnates is present also. Among other things the universal Church is present, for Jesus Christ cannot be there without bringing with him the whole company of his brothers, who have heard the Word of God and kept it, who were not created without the Word. He is never present without the company of the apostles and prophets, the patriarchs and singers who speak of him; nor without the least of his brothers of whom he speaks. The localized Church implies the universal, but the universal no less implies the local; without localization, without becoming concrete in a specific occasion, it does not exist. The school which educates men for service in this Church cannot but focus their attention on the parish and the meeting; it cannot make them aware of the significance of parish or Sunday morning service unless it turns from the localized occasion to the universal community represented and adumbrated in the occasion.

The Church is protestant and catholic. This is not only to say that there is much historic Protestantism in those institutions called Catholic churches, and much historic Catholicism in the institutions called Protestant. It is also to say that the principle of protest against every tendency to confuse the symbol with what it symbolizes and the subject with the object, is a constituent element in the being of the community, even apart from the institutional organizations. The Church as the people of God, whether under the Old or the New Covenants, is always the party of protest against religion in the religious human world. It protests against every effort to bring the Infinite into the finite, the Transcendent into the immanent, the Eternal into the temporal. The only finite symbol of God it tolerates is the symbol of emptiness—the empty Holy of Holies, the empty tomb. But protest has no meaning apart from what is protested against. The Church cannot be protestant without being catholic. The principle of catholicity—as the principle of incarnation rather than the principle of universality—is as much an ingredient of churchliness as is the principle of protest. Unless the Infinite is represented in finite form, unless the Word becomes flesh over and over again, though only as oral preaching, unless the risen Christ manifests himself in the visible forms of individual saintliness and communal authority there is no human relation to the Infinite and Transcendent. Negative and positive movements—the one in rejection of all that is little because God is great, the other in affirmation of the apparently insignificant because God is its creator, redeemer and inspirer; the one away from the world that is not God, the other toward the world of which he is Lord—must both be represented where the Church exists.

The final polarity to be considered in this adumbration of the form and nature of the Church is that of Church and world. This is like the first polarity of subject and object insofar as it is not a polarity in the Church but one in which it participates as itself a kind of pole. The Church lives and defines itself in action vis-à-vis the world. World, however, is not object of Church as God is. World, rather, is companion of the Church, a community something like itself with which it lives before God. The world is sometimes enemy, sometimes partner of Church, often antagonist, always one to be befriended; now it is the co-knower, now the one that does not know what Church knows, now the knower of what Church does not know. The world is the community of those before God who feel rejected by God and reject him; again it is the community of those who do not know God and seem not to be known by him; or, it is the community of those who knowing God do not worship him. In all cases it is the community to which the Church addresses itself with its gospel, to which it gives an account of what it has seen and heard in divine revelation, which it invites to come and see and hear. The world is the community to which

Christ comes and to which he sends his disciples. On the other hand, the world is the community of those who are occupied with temporal things. When, in its sense of rejection, it is preoccupied with these temporal matters it is the world of idolatry and becomes foe of the Church. When it is occupied with them as gifts of God—whether or not the consciousness of grace becomes explicit —it is the partner of the Church, doing what the Church, concerned with the nontemporal, cannot do; knowing what Church as such cannot know. Thus and in other ways the relations of Church and world are infinitely variable; but they are always dynamic and important. To train men for the ministry of the Church is to train them for ministry to the world and to introduce them to the conversation of Church and world, a conversation in which both humility and self-assurance have their proper place.

If our interpretation of the spirit of the Protestant theological schools is in any way correct then it is Church defined somewhat in the foregoing manner that constitutes the society in which they function and whose objectives they serve directly and indirectly, consciously or unconsciously. Different schools and different denominations doubtless represent different perspectives and emphases in their understanding of this Church; yet they participate in the common life insofar as they respect and gain profit from each other's contributions.

33. Quests for Justice and Peace

MARTIN LUTHER KING, JR. (1929–1968) *was directly influenced by the social gospel. He expressed his indebtedness to the most prominent leader of that movement, Walter Rauschenbusch (1861–1918). In his search for a relevant strategy in his struggle against racism, King was much informed by his study of Gandhian nonviolent techniques. He sprang into national prominence in 1956 as leader of the Negro community of Montgomery, Alabama, in its successful boycott against segregation in public buses. As the central figure in the Southern Christian Leadership Conference, he labored effectively to secure a larger measure of justice and fair treatment for American blacks. About a year before his assassination in 1968, he spoke out against American involvement in the Vietnam war, moving into the forefront of a cause then unpopular in many quarters. What follows is the first part of an address, "Conscience and the Vietnam War," given late in 1967 through the Canadian Broadcasting Corporation in a series of Massey Lectures. The struggle to end the war in Vietnam soon gathered support (and also opposition) across the spectrum of American religious pluralism, as prominent leaders from the major religious groups demonstrated together, and were sometimes jailed together. Many came to feel that unity in a social cause was more important than institutional unity.*

SOURCE: Martin Luther King, Jr., *The Trumpet of Conscience* (New York, 1968), pp. 21–25. Copyright © 1967 by Martin Luther King, Jr. Reprinted by permission of Harper & Row, Publishers, Inc., and Joan Davis.

It is many months now since I found myself obliged by conscience to end my silence and to take a public stand against my country's war in Vietnam. The considerations which led me to that painful decision have not disappeared; indeed, they have been magnified by the course of events since then. The war itself is intensified; the impact on my country is even more destructive.

I cannot speak about the great themes of violence and nonviolence, of social change and of hope for the future, without reflecting on the tremendous violence of Vietnam.

Since the spring of 1967, when I first made public my opposition to my government's policy, many persons have questioned me about the wisdom of my decision. "Why you?" they have said. "Peace and civil rights don't mix. Aren't you hurting the cause of your people?" And when I hear such questions, I have been greatly saddened, for they mean that the inquirers have never really known me, my commitment, or my calling. Indeed, that question suggests that they do not know the world in which they live.

In explaining my position, I have tried to make it clear that I remain perplexed—as I think everyone must be perplexed—by the complexities and ambiguities of Vietnam. I would not wish to underrate the need for a collective solution to this tragic war. I would wish neither to present North Vietnam or the National Liberation Front as paragons of virtue, nor to overlook the role they can play in the successful resolution of the problem. While they both may have justifiable reasons to be suspicious of the good faith of the United States, life and history give eloquent testimony to the fact that conflicts are never resolved without trustful give-and-take on both sides.

Since I am a preacher by calling, I suppose it is not surprising that I had several reasons for bringing Vietnam into the field of my moral vision. There is at the outset a very obvious and almost facile connection between the war in Vietnam and the struggle I and others have been waging in America. A few years ago there was a shining moment in that struggle. It seemed as if there was a real promise of hope for the poor, both black and white, through the poverty program. There were experiments, hopes, new beginnings. Then came the buildup in Vietnam, and I watched the program broken and eviscerated as if it were some idle political plaything of a society gone mad on war, and I knew that America would never invest the necessary funds or energies in rehabilitation of its poor so long as adventures like Vietnam continued to draw men and skills and money like some demoniacal destructive suction tube. And so I was increasingly compelled to see the war not only as a moral outrage but also as an enemy of the poor, and to attack it as such.

Perhaps a more tragic recognition of reality took place when it became clear to me that the war was doing far more than devastating the hopes of the poor at home. It was sending their sons and their brothers and their husbands to fight and to die and in extraordinarily higher proportions relative to the rest of the population. We were taking the black young men who had been crippled by our society and sending them eight thousand miles away to guarantee liberties in Southeast Asia which they had not found in southwest Georgia and East Harlem. And so we have been repeatedly faced with the cruel irony of watching Negro and white boys on TV screens as they kill and die together for a nation that has been unable to seat them together in the same schools. We watch them in brutal solidarity burning the huts of a poor village, but we realize that they would never live on the same block in Detroit. I could not be silent in the face of such cruel manipulation of the poor.

My third reason moves to an even deeper level of awareness, but it grows out of my experience in the ghettos of the North over the last three years—especially the last three summers. As I have walked among the desperate, rejected, angry young men, I have told them that Molotov cocktails and rifles would not solve their problems. I have tried to offer them my deepest compassion, while maintaining my conviction that social change comes most meaningfully through nonviolent action. But, they asked, and rightly so, what about Vietnam? They asked if our own nation wasn't using massive doses of violence to solve its problems, to bring about the changes it wanted. Their questions hit home, and I knew that I could never again raise my voice against the violence of the oppressed in the ghettos without having first spoken clearly to the greatest purveyor of violence in the world today: my own government. For the sake of those boys, for the sake of this government, for the sake of the hundreds of thousands trembling under our violence, I cannot be silent.

For those who ask the question "Aren't you a civil rights leader?"—and thereby mean to exclude me from the movement for peace—I answer by saying that I have worked too long and hard now against segregated public accommodations to end up segregating my moral concern. Justice is indivisible. It must also be said that it would be rather absurd to work passionately and unrelentingly for integrated schools and not be concerned about the survival of a world in which to be integrated. I must say further that something in the very nature of our organizational structure in the Southern Christian Leadership Conference led me to this decision. In 1957, when a group of us formed that organization, we chose as our motto: "To save the soul of America." Now it should be incandescently clear that no one who has any concern for the integrity and life of America today can ignore the present war.

As if the weight of such a commitment were not enough, another burden of responsibility was placed upon me in 1964: I cannot forget that the Nobel Prize for Peace was also a commission—a commission to work harder than I had ever worked before for "the brotherhood of man." This is a calling which takes me beyond national allegiances, but even if it were not present, I would yet have to live with the meaning of my commitment to the ministry of Jesus Christ. To me the relationship of this ministry to the making of peace is so obvious that I sometimes marvel at those who ask me why I am speaking against the war. We are called to speak for the weak, for the voiceless, for the victims of our nation, and for those it calls enemy, for no document from human hands can make these humans any less our brothers.

And as I ponder the madness of Vietnam and search within myself for ways to understand and respond in compassion, my mind goes constantly to the people of that peninsula. I speak now not of the soldiers of each side, not of the junta in Saigon, but simply of the people who have been living under the curse of war for almost three continuous decades now. I think of them, too, because it is clear to me that there will be no meaningful solution until some attempt is made to know them and to hear their broken cries.